CW01022237

DEAD WOMAN PICKNEY

THE EMANCIPATION PROCLAMATION IN JAMAICA

On the 9th July, 1838, the Governor, [Sir Lionel Smith] issued his Proclamation, for Abolishing Slavery, as follows; -

Praedial Apprentices – In a few days more you will become free labourers; the Legislature having relinquished the remaining two years of your apprenticeship.

The first day of August next is the happy day when you will become free, under the same Laws as other freemen, whether white, black or coloured.

I your Governor give you joy of this great blessing.

Remember that in freedom you will have to depend on your own exertion for your livelihood, and to maintain and bring up your families. You will work for such wages as you can agree upon with your employers.

It is in their interest to treat you fairly.

It is in your interest to be civil, respectful, and industrious.

Where you can agree and continue happy with your old masters, I strongly recommend you remain on those properties on which you have been born, and where your parents are buried.

But you must not mistake, in supposing that your present houses, gardens, and provision grounds, are your own property.

They belong to the proprietors of the estates, and you will have to pay rent for them in money or labour according as you and your employers can agree together.

Idle people who will not take employment, but go wondering about the country, will be taken as vagrants, and punished in the same manner as they are in England.

The Ministers of Religion have been kind friends to you – listen to them – they will keep you out of troubles and difficulties.

Recollect what is expected of you by the people of England who have paid such a large price for your liberty.

They not only expect that you will behave yourselves, as the Queen's good subjects, by obeying the laws, as I am happy to say you always have done as apprentices, but that the prosperity of the Island will be increased by your willing labour, greatly beyond what it ever was in Slavery. Be honest towards all men – Be kind to your wives and children – spare your wives from heavy field work as much as you can –make them attend to their duties at home, in bringing up your children, and in taking care of your stock – above all make your children attend Divine Service, and School.

If you follow this advice, you will, under God's blessing, be happy and prosperous.

—*from* W. A. Feurtado (1890) *The Jubilee Reign of Her Most Gracious Majesty Queen Victoria in Jamaica. Being A Complete Account of the Principal and Important Events Which Occurred in Jamaica During the Fifty Years Reign of Her Most Gracious Majesty Queen Victoria, From the Year 1837, To The Year 1887, and Also A Full and Complete Account Of The Jubilee Rejoicings In Jamaica in 1887.* Kingston, Jamaica: Cottage Grove, Upper Elletson Road, pp, 8-9.

JAMAICA

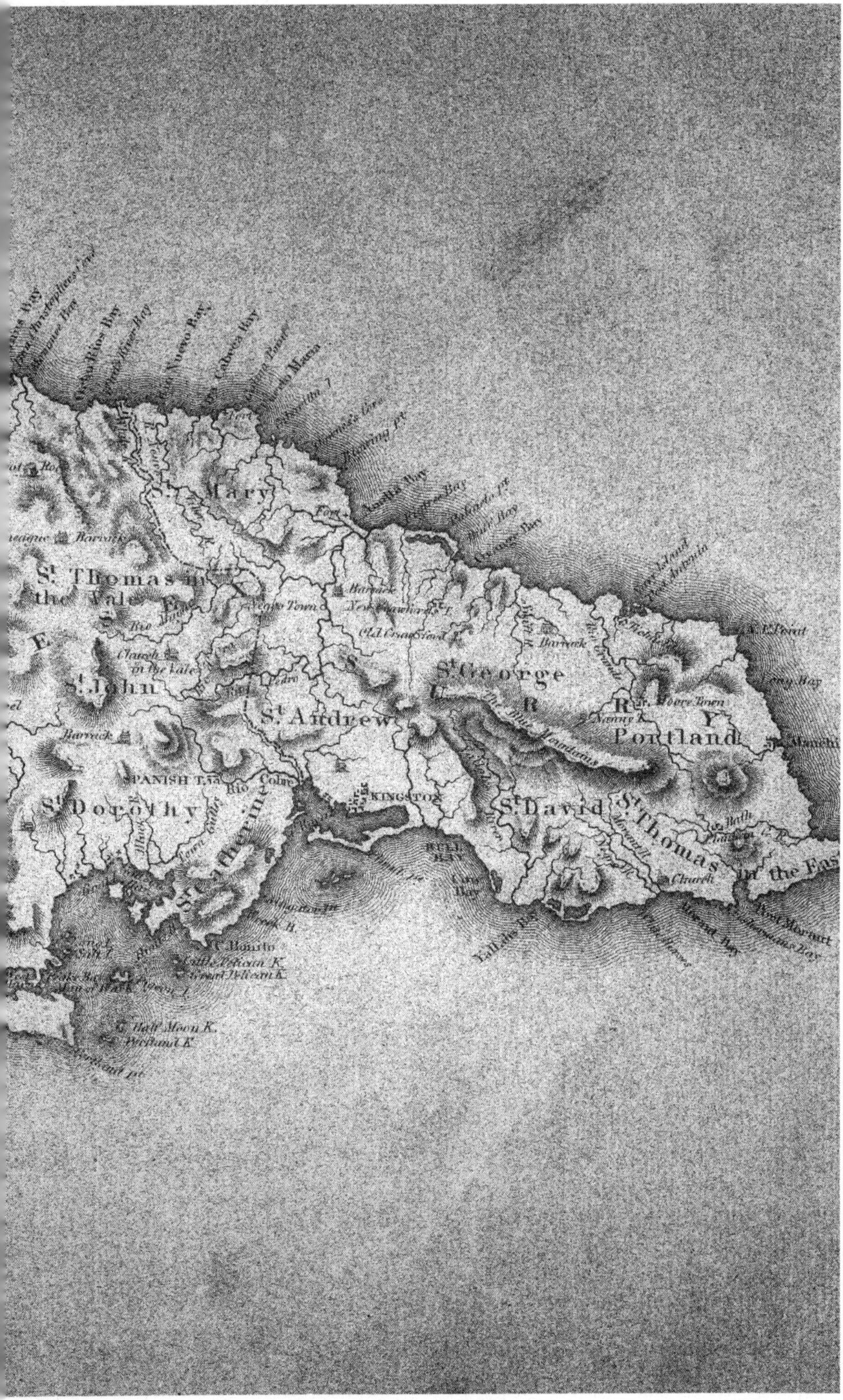

Mary
St. Thomas in the Vale
Church in the Vale
St. John
Barrack
SPANISH T.
St. Dorothy
St. Andrew
KINGSTON
BULL BAY
St. George
Portland
Long Bay
N.E. Point
St. David
St. Thomas in the Eas
Church

Life Writing Series

Wilfrid Laurier University Press's Life Writing series celebrates life writing as both genre and critical practice. As a home for innovative scholarship in theory and critical practice, the series embraces a range of theoretical and methodological approaches, from literary criticism and theory to autoethnography and beyond, and encourages intersectional approaches attentive to the complex interrelationships between gender, class, race, ethnicity, sexuality, ability, and more. In its commitment to life writing as genre, the series incorporates a range of life writing practices and welcomes creative scholarship and hybrid forms. The Life Writing series recognizes the diversity of languages, and the effects of such languages on life writing practices within the Canadian context, including the languages of migration and translation. As such, the series invites contributions from voices and communities who have been under- or misrepresented in scholarly work.

SERIES EDITORS:
Marlene Kadar, York University
Sonja Boon, Memorial University

DEAD

WOMAN

PICKNEY

A MEMOIR OF CHILDHOOD IN JAMAICA

— Second Edition —

YVONNE SHORTER BROWN

FOREWORD BY SONJA BOON

WILFRID LAURIER
UNIVERSITY PRESS

Wilfrid Laurier University Press acknowledges the support of the Canada Council for the Arts for our publishing program. We acknowledge the financial support of the Government of Canada through the Canada Book Fund for our publishing activities. Funding provided by the Government of Ontario and the Ontario Arts Council. This work was supported by the Research Support Fund.

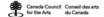

Library and Archives Canada Cataloguing in Publication

Title: Dead woman pickney : a memoir of childhood in Jamaica / Yvonne Shorter Brown ; foreword by Sonja Boon.
Names: Brown, Yvonne Shorter. author. | Boon, Sonja, writer of foreword.
Series: Life writing series.
Description: Second edition. | Series statement: Life writing series | Includes biblio-graphical references.
Identifiers: Canadiana (print) 20210231645 | Canadiana (ebook) 20210231688
   ISBN 9781771125475 (softcover) | ISBN 9781771125482 (EPUB) | ISBN 9781771125499 (PDF)
Subjects: LCSH: Brown, Yvonne Shorter—Childhood and youth. | LCSH: Brown, Yvonne Shorter—Family. | LCSH: Racially mixed children—Jamaica—Biography. LCSH: Maternal deprivation—Jamaica. | LCSH: College teachers—British Columbia—Biography. | LCSH: Jamaica—Race relations. | LCSH: Jamaica—Social conditions. LCSH: Jamaica—Biography. | CSH: Jamaican Canadians—Biography.
Classification: LCC F1886 .B76 2022 | DDC 972.92/05092—dc23

Cover and interior design by Lime Design.
Front cover image is of Yvonne Shorter Brown at Mico College, Kingston, Jamaica. Image courtesy of the author.

Text © 2022 by Yvonne Shorter Brown
Foreword © 2022 by Sonja Boon

This book is printed on FSC® certified paper. It contains recycled materials and other controlled sources, is processed chlorine free, and is manufactured using biogas energy.

Printed in Canada

Every reasonable effort has been made to acquire permission for copyright material used in this text, and to acknowledge all such indebtedness accurately. Any errors and omissions called to the publisher's attention will be corrected in future printings.

No part of this publication may be reproduced, stored in a retrieval system, or transmitted, in any form or by any means, without the prior written consent of the publisher or a licence from the Canadian Copyright Licensing Agency (Access Copyright). For an Access Copyright licence, visit http://www.accesscopyright.ca or call toll free to 1-800-893-5777.

Wilfrid Laurier University Press is located on the Haldimand Tract, part of the traditional territories of the Haudenosaunee, Anishinaabe, and Neutral peoples. This land is part of the Dish with One Spoon Treaty between the Haudenosaunee and Anishnaabe peoples and symbolizes the agreement to share, to protect our resources, and not to engage in conflict. We are grateful to the Indigenous peoples who continue to care for and remain interconnected with this land. Through the work we publish in partnership with our authors, we seek to honour our local and larger community relationships, and to engage with the diversity of collective knowledge integral to responsible scholarly and cultural exchange.

CONTENTS

Foreword to the Second Edition

———

I'M WRITING THIS FOREWORD from my ad-hoc pandemic basement office. As a working space, the basement leaves much to be desired, but one thing it does have is books. Over the past year and a half, I've created a nest for myself, cocooning with literary and theoretical writings that make my heart sing. These include such classics as Dionne Brand's *A Map to the Door of No Return: Notes to Belonging* (2001) and M. NourbeSe Philip's powerful *Zong!*, two works that have fundamentally and profoundly shaped my understanding of and engagement with the transatlantic slave trade and its afterlives. But they also include more recent works, from El Jones' *Live from the Afrikan Resistance!* (2014), Christina Sharpe's *In the Wake: On Blackness and Being* (2016), Kaie Kellough's *Magnetic Equator* (2019), and David Chariandy's *I've Been Meaning to Tell You: A Letter to my Daughter* (2018), to books I've picked up during the pandemic itself, among them Chantal Gibson's *How She Read* (2019), Desmond Cole's *The Skin We're In: A Year of Black Resistance* (2020), Junie Désil's *eat salt | gaze at the ocean* (2020), Karina Vernon's *The Black Prairie Archives: An Anthology* (2020), Tessa McWatt's *Shame on Me: An Anatomy of Race and Belonging* (2020), Saidiya Hartman's *Wayward Lives, Beautiful Experiments* (2020), Afua Cooper and Wilfried Raussert's *Black Matters* (2020), and, as of this week, Rinaldo Walcott's *The Long Emancipation* (2021).

As I look over my shelves (and, it must be admitted, my piles), I note that all of these writers—poets, activists, scholars, and theorists—have one thing in common: they centre the complexities of Black being in a world that has never honoured Black living and Black thriving. And in this way, they engage in what Christina Sharpe, in her powerful *In the Wake: On Blackness and Being* has referred to as "wake work"; that is, to what it might mean "to imagine new ways to live in the wake of slavery, in slavery's afterlives, to survive (and more) the afterlife of property" (18).

Interrogating slavery's wake—and engaging in wake work—are precisely what Yvonne Shorter Brown sets out to do in *Dead Woman Pickney*. The question she asks is not only "What does it mean to be a motherless child?"—quite literally the "dead woman pickney" of the book's title—but how does one *come to be* a motherless child? That question takes us much deeper, and also, well beyond Shorter Brown's personal life story. In the process, the everyday details of Shorter Brown's troubled childhood come to be understood in the context of social, cultural, and political processes that shaped not only her own life history, but that of Jamaican society as a whole. As she writes:

> After reading much of the history and sociology of the making of Creole society in Jamaica I weep for the brutal history into which we were born—that of a racist slave society in which families sorted their children and kin by their physiognomy: clear skin and black skin, "good" hair and "bad" hair, straight noses and flat noses, and all the tricky combinations of interracial mixing that were such ammunition for racist abuse. (150)

Calls for racial justice and reparations have echoed for centuries, since even before the abolition of slavery. They have grown ever more urgent over the ten years between the first and second editions of *Dead Woman Pickney*.

A tangled chronology plays itself out in my mind, episodes of violence interwoven with a flourishing of Black political, creative, activist, and critical resistance. I see the shooting of Trayvon Martin, in Florida in 2012, and the emergence of Black Lives Matter in 2013. I see the Caribbean Community (CARICOM) establishing a

Reparations Commission, and one year later, read Ta-Nehisi Coates's "The Case for Reparations." Here, Coates details a long history of racist policies and practices that followed in the wake of slavery and have affected every aspect of Black lives in the United States. In the two months following the publication of Coates' essay, two Black American men—Michael Brown and Eric Garner—were killed during incidents of police violence.

A global reparations conference took place in 2015. That same year, Sir Hilary Beckles, then Chair of CARICOM's Reparations Commission, wrote a public letter to then British Prime Minister David Cameron. Observing the long shadow of slavery on the social, cultural, economic, and psychological life of Jamaica and Jamaicans, he called for reparations, writing: "You owe it to us as you return here to communicate a commitment to reparatory justice that will enable your nation to play its part in cleaning up this monumental mess of the empire." Cameron, however, was not swayed. Instead, while announcing substantive British financial support for a new prison in Jamaica, Cameron stated, "I do hope that, as friends who have gone through so much together since those darkest of times, we can move on from this painful legacy and continue to build for the future." A year later, in 2016, Philando Castile was shot and killed by police during a traffic stop in Saint Paul, Minnesota.

It can be easy to say that these killings took place in the USA, that reparations are a matter for other countries in other climes, and that *Dead Woman Pickney* takes place in Jamaica. We might want to argue that these things did not—and do not—happen in Canada. We might say, then, that these are not, therefore, our stories. After all, we are Canada the Good, the end point of the Underground Railroad. Don't we—through multiculturalism—not only acknowledge, but also celebrate and honour racial and ethnic difference?

And yet, as Desmond Cole (2020) and Robyn Maynard (2017) point out, Canada is not nearly as warm and welcoming as we might like to think. The over-surveillance of Black bodies goes back centuries, and as Cole observes, "Passive-aggressive racism is central to Canada's national mythology and identity. White supremacy warns Black people against setting our own standards and pursuing dreams that stray too far from the global atmosphere of anti-blackness" (64). The narratives gathered in Karina Vernon's *The Black Prairies Archive* bear this out. Even as they reveal beautiful, resilient, and complex lives, they also reveal the profound challenge of Black living in a white supremacist world.

In *Dead Woman Pickney*, Yvonne Shorter Brown shares Jamaican histories, yes, but these histories are also our histories. Salt cod from Atlantic ports fed enslaved Africans in the Caribbean. Molasses, meanwhile, shaped the Newfoundland palate. Salt from Caribbean islands—extracted and gathered through enslaved labour (Prince 1831) —sustained the fishing and export of cod to European markets. Nor can we forget other episodes in Canadian history: the torture and hanging of Marie-Joseph Angélique, the Shelburne race riots, the election of Mifflin Gibbs as the first Black town councillor in Victoria, the founding of the community of Amber Valley in Alberta, the activism of Viola Desmond, and the demolition of Africville, among others. Black history *is* Canadian history.

Tangles of racist violence and Black resistance have marked the last ten years in Canada. Black Lives Matter Canada, the first iteration of the BLM movement outside of the United States, was founded in 2014. That same year, Nova Scotia activist, academic and spoken word poet El Jones published *Live from the Afrikan Resistance!*, speaking and writing to politics, history, and community in an African Nova Scotian context. For Jones, spoken word is a site of both resistance and reclamation. As she writes: "Our ancestors were spoken word artists converting the language of the oppressor into tools of liberation with every word they reclaimed" (vii).

But that resistance is complicated. In "The Skin I'm In," a 2015 cover story for *Toronto Life* magazine, Desmond Cole detailed his long experience of being racially profiled by police and the effect that this has had on his life, writing,

After years of being stopped by police, I've started to internalize their scrutiny. I've doubted myself, wondered if I've actually done something to provoke them. Once you're accused enough times, you begin to assume your own guilt, to stand in for your oppressor. It's exhausting to have to justify your freedoms in a supposedly free society. I don't talk about race for attention or personal gain. I would much rather write about sports or theatre or music than carding and incarceration. But I talk about race to survive. If I diminish the role my skin colour plays in my life, and in the lives of all racialized people, I can't change anything.

In 2016, Somali-Canadian Abdirahman Abdi was killed by Ottawa police. Pierre Coriolan, a Haitian-born man, was killed by Montreal police in 2017. Another Black man, Nicholas Gibbs, was killed the following year. Machuar Madut, meanwhile, a member of Winnipeg's South Sudanese community, was killed by Winnipeg police in 2019. In 2020, Eternity Martis published *They Said This Would Be Fun: Race, Campus Life, and Growing Up*, a searing indictment of her undergraduate experience at Western University.

My mind plays through this chronology pausing at some points and at others, rushing ahead. There is pain here. Silence. Erasure. Too many of these stories replay the histories of violence and capture of the transatlantic slave trade. But they also point to the creative and critical responses of Black writers, thinkers, and activists; they point to determined resistance and refusal. "(forgive) the repetitious a long-winded account," writes Junie Désil, "we tell stories twice / sometimes more   different angles / so you *feel* the story" (36). Emancipation, Rinaldo Walcott reminds us, is not the same as freedom: "The phrase *the long emancipation* does not simply suggest that Black people are still enslaved, but rather it insists that Black people continually are prohibited and interdicted from authorizing what exactly freedom might look like and mean for them collectively" (2021, 105).

We are inheritors of these tangled histories. While the transatlantic slave trade was abolished over 150 years ago, we continue to live in its wake. Just as that wake buffeted – and continues to buffet—Yvonne Shorter Brown's life, so too does it continue to buffet our own. As visual artist and scholar, Camille Turner observed in a 2019 interview, "We didn't create this history. None of us did. We weren't here, but it is what shaped us. By not dealing with it, we can never move on from here. We can't really move into a future where things are equitable. So I think it's really important to acknowledge these stories."

In *Dead Woman Pickney*, Yvonne Shorter Brown interrogates the complexities of racialized belonging in the afterlives of slavery. One thing that stands out in *Dead Woman Pickney* is the way that she teases out the complexities of race, racialization, and racism. While "race" marks itself on the body—through skin colour, facial features, and hair—it also intersects with class and gender. This nexus of race, class, and gender shapes every aspect of Brown's life. The afterlives of slavery pervade not only formal educational and social systems, but also everyday interactions, from intimate relations between lovers, relationships between elders and children, children's friendships, and hierarchies at work. While Brown takes time to foreground the formal colonial curriculum and the expectations it placed on individuals, what stands out in even higher relief are the ways that the afterlives of slavery permeate personal and intimate relationships, informing questions of love, morality, worth, virtue, responsibility, and identity. Brown's memoir demonstrates that colonial histories are never "over," but weave themselves into our presents in complicated, knotty ways. If Brown leaves us with any clear message, it is that untangling all of this is ultimately impossible. There is no easy answer, no clear or direct path towards resolution or recovery.

When Brown first published her memoir in 2010, she had not yet learned the full story of her mother's life and eventual death. This question, though seemingly central to her work, remained unanswered. As Erika Jeffers writes, "it seems as if both Brown and the reader end this book not knowing, specifically, what a mother is"

(Jeffers 2012, 526). And yet, that *not* knowing is perhaps, the point. Indeed, the lack of resolution is a poignant *revelation*, an homage to the many silences that characterize this work; that is, the way that silence shapes not just intimate, but social, cultural, and political relations. In this new edition, Brown offers us the story of her mother's life and death as a coda to her own journey. The facts she reveals layer themselves through the story of Brown's own life, in this way offering a poignant resolution of sorts. And yet, as a reader, I am still reminded that, in the end, Brown remains the "dead woman pickney" of her title, a woman who will remain, eternally, a motherless child.

"We did not put ourselves in this current cultural climate, but we *are* responsible for getting each other out," writes Eternity Martis, echoing Camille Turner. She continues:

> I have complete faith that we can: we are glowing with rage, the kind that can shatter glass ceilings and scorch the earth. We are emotional with grief, with tear that can flood oceans and put out blazing fires. We are soft with compassion, yet powerful enough to dissolve borders. Our words are cutting, deep enough to slash through the pages of history and write it anew. (238)

We need to attend to the vitality and urgency of Black storytelling. We need *Dead Woman Pickney.* As Martis writes, "Speak up. Rage. Because the time for silence has passed" (238).

—SONJA BOON, ST. JOHN'S, JUNE 2021

References

"Artist Highlights N.L's Slave Trade Connection in Bonavista Exhibition" CBC Newfoundland and Labrador. 18 August 2019. https://www.cbc.ca/news/canada/newfoundland-labrador/camille-turner-nl-slave-ships-connection-1.5240589

Beckles, Hilary. "Open Letter to Prime Minister David Cameron."
The Gleaner 27 September 2015. https://jamaica-gleaner.com/article/
commentary/20150928/open-letter-prime-minister-david-cameron

Brand, Dionne. *A Map to the Door of No Return: Notes to Belonging*,
Vintage Canada, 2001.

Chariandy, David. *I've Been Meaning to Tell You: A Letter to My Daughter*,
Penguin Random House, 2018.

Coates, Ta-Nehisi. "The Case for Reparations." *The Atlantic*, June 2014.

Cole, Desmond. "The Skin I'm In." *Toronto Life*. 21 April 2015. https://
torontolife.com/life/skin-im-ive-interrogated-police-50-times-im-black/

———. *The Skin We're In: A Year of Black Resistance*, Penguin Random House, 2020.

Cooper, Afua and Wilfried Raussert, *Black Matters*, Roseway, 2020.

"David Cameron Rules Out Slavery Reparation During Jamaica Visit."
bbc.com 30 September 2015. https://www.bbc.com/news/uk-34401412

Désil, Junie. *eat salt | gaze at the ocean*. TalonBooks, 2020

Gibson, Chantal. *How She Read*. Caitlin Press, 2019.

Hartman, Saidiya. *Wayward Lives, Beautiful Experiments: Intimate Histories
of Social Upheaval*, Penguin Random House, 2020

Jeffers, Erika. "Dead Woman Pickney: A Memoir of Childhood in Jamaica."
Callaloo 35.2 (2012): 524-6.

Jones, El. *Live from the Afrikan Resistance!* Fernwood, 2014.

Kellough, Kaie. *Magnetic Equator*. McClelland and Stewart, 2019.

Martis, Eternity. *They Said This Would Be Fun: Race, Campus Life, and
Growing Up*. McClelland and Stewart, 2020.

Maynard, Robyn. *Policing Black Lives: State Violence in Canada from Slavery
to the Present*. Fernwood, 2017.

McWatt, Tessa. *Shame on Me: An Anatomy of Race and Belonging*, Penguin
Random House, 2020.

Philip, M. NourbeSe. *Zong!*. Wesleyan University Press, 2008/2011.

Prince, Mary. *The History of Mary Prince, A West-Indian Slave, Related by
Herself*, 1831.

Sharpe, Christina. *In the Wake: On Blackness and Being*. Duke University
Press, 2016.

Vernon, Karina, ed. *The Black Prairie Archive: An Anthology*. WLU Press, 2020.

Walcott, Rinaldo. *The Long Emancipation: Moving Toward Freedom*.
Duke University Press, 2021.

Acknowledgements
for the First Edition

————

THIS MEMOIR is excerpted from my doctoral dissertation. During the ten years it took me to conceive, research, write, and find a publisher, many people encouraged me by sharing their own stories and affirming the creative potential of historical trauma. It would be impossible to name everyone, but all share any success this endeavour enjoys. I would like to take this very exciting moment of publication to express my gratitude to those colleagues and friends whose supervision, suggestions, critical reviews, and know-how pushed the work forward to publication.

I want to thank the University of British Columbia for its generous program of professional development for its employees. I was able to complete my doctoral studies through release time and generous tuition fee waivers. Professor Jean Barman, my research supervisor, was most compassionate in validating my research proposal grounded in memory, history, and narrative. Without her support and encouragement this memoir would not have moved from dissertation to publication. I could not have had more helpful committee members than Dawn Currie, Gloria Onyeoziri, and Graeme Chalmers. My supervisor and colleague Jim Gaskell showed compassionate understanding when the emotional fallout from my research and writing affected my disposition at work.

I thank my Caribbean contemporaries who shared "lie and story" about growing up in the Caribbean. Special thanks go to Barbara Binns, Nadine Chambers, Marlene John, Noga Gayle, Oswald Lewis,

Stan Raymond, and Maxine Wishart for their time and patience. I am indebted for all the many favours they have rendered over the years of writing.

All writing needs to appeal to audiences. I value the feedback from critical readers, in various capacities as professors, friends, and acquaintances. They boosted my confidence and convinced me that there would be readers for my book. I trust that they are right. My appreciation goes to Benita Bunjun, George Elliott Clarke, Afua Cooper, Cecille Depass, Hyacinth Evans, Gary Fletcher, Hartej Gill, Euphrates Gobina, Lee Gunderson, Colin Hewitt, Paul Krause, Kara MacDonald, and Abdul Rasheed Na'Allah, and Bill New. Carol Duncan not only read my work but referred me to Wilfrid Laurier University Press and its Life Writing series.

Thanks to the hard-working and conscientious editorial and marketing teams at Wilfrid Laurier University Press. Lisa Quinn, the acquisitions editor, heard a unique voice and chose to include it among the excellent volumes in the Life Writing series. Stacey Belden's thorough copyediting has improved my grammar. Rob Kohlmeier's patience and care as managing editor are laudable. Leslie Macredie, website and marketing coordinator, is responsible for the extensive research and promotion of *Dead Woman Pickney*.

Acknowledgements
for the Second Edition

***

IT IS TIMELY that the publication of the second edition of *Dead Woman Pickney* coincides with the groundswell of support for the Black Lives Matter Movement for social and economic justice for Black people globally. As importantly, the book is published towards the ending of the United Nations, International Decade for People of African Descent (2015–24). Of note, also, is the mounting evidence to support longstanding charges of genocide against the representatives of the church and state who were committed to and supported actively the Canadian, colonial government's Indian Act, and who furthermore implemented the draconian, assimilationist policies associated with the Indian Residential School System, (from the late 1800s to the 1990s). This very cruel educational system has had such disastrous long term impacts on the First Nations people of Canada.

As a first-generation settler from Jamaica (in the West Indies) who was welcomed as a guest on the unceded traditional territory of the Coast Salish, Musqueam, and Squamish nations in what is called British Columbia, I was very much influenced by their anti-colonial struggles. I saw many parallels with the post-emancipation, anti-colonial struggles in Jamaica. I became interested in the implementation of the goals of the 1972 policy paper, "Indian Control of Indian Education," put out by the National Indian Brotherhood. As a participant observer and ally in various capacities—as a student, a teacher, a teacher educator, a student advisor, and school trustee—I owe a huge debt for my intellectual awakening to the repressed histories of colonization and empire-building that we shared.

As a rather historically ignorant immigrant to Canada, I did not know even the formal history of racialized chattel slavery that had made me who I am, until I worked side by side with First Nations colleagues and learned from their teachings, research, and generosity, that I carried within me vivid collective memories of parallel anti-colonial struggles. Although I cannot repay the debts I owe for allowing me to live and thrive on their unceded Coast Salish, Musqueam, and Squamish land, I can at least return a special thanks and formally pay tribute to the First Nations. The First Nations House of Learning located on the unceded Musqueam Territory (at the University of British Columbia) was a special place of unconditional welcome to all. The literal embrace and generosity of my First Nations colleagues and teachers were like the assurance of being in the nurturing arms of a mother. Special thanks to my professors and colleagues, some of whom may have left us, but their mark on my psychic liberation still remains: Verna Kirkness, Roland Chrisjohn, Jo-ann Archibald, Felicity Jules, Ethel Gardener, Alannah Young, Rosalyn Ing, Michael Marker, Sharilyn Calliou, Sonia Sterling, Rod McCormick, Lorna Williams, Madeleine McIvor, Nora Greenway, Lee Brown, and the many First Nations students of all ages that I taught in the public schools and the university.

I acknowledge that the shared embodied memories of immigrants from various colonies and empires have been of inestimable value to my creative non-fiction writing. In listening and making space for the expression of diverse voices in my counselling, teaching and community service, I learned parallel versions of my own story of loss, grief, and intergenerational traumas from the Doukhobor, Japanese, Chinese, Iranians, Nigerians, Eritreans, Somali, Ethiopians, South Africans, Bosnians, Rwandans, to name just a few, that are not recorded in the history textbooks and international education policies that I learned from.

I have been gratified by the critical response to the first edition of *Dead Woman Pickney* by critics, general readers, professors and students who have used my book as a text. I will attempt to name as many as I can, fully knowing that I will forget some. Please understand that this was due to memory lapse and that even if you are not named I thank you too. You know who you are.

The very first reviewers of *Dead Woman Pickney* were Damion Blake of the University of the West Indies and Virginia Tech for the Humanities and Social Sciences History Network and Judith Soares of the Women and Development Unit, University of the West Indies, for the *Caribbean Quarterly*. They gave me the assurances that I needed to soothe the vulnerability that I felt for revealing so much of my life story. So did formal responses from Professors Carol Duncan, Afua Cooper, Cecille DePass, and Jin-Sun Yoon.

Since the publication of the first edition of *Dead Woman Pickney* in 2010, Professor Henrice Altink in the Department of History at University of York, has been particularly instumental in guiding me through her extensive work on the history of African-Jamaican women from slavery to the present. She generously shared her extensive knowledge of the relevant holdings of the Jamaica Archive and the National Archive in the UK. Much of the new information contained in the historical grounding of the coda to the second edition are the result of her tutelage. Gratitude to Professor Altink for opening the gateways to archival research. Professor Emerita Bridget Brereton of the history department of the St. Augustine campus of the University of the West Indies and co-editor of UNESCO General History of the Caribbean was most gracious and generous in agreeing to meet with me in 2019 in Trinidad and Tobago, one of the sites of memory of African enslavement. Not only had she purchased and read the first edition; she had very probing historical questions. She went further to underscore the need to study the immediate post-emancipation period. I have taken her advice and encouragement. Professor Benita Bunjun of St Mary's University in Halifax, Nova Scotia has been most generous in giving me access to their library.

Professor Joy DeGruy's work on the post-traumatic slavery syndrome helped me to cope with and understand the legacy of intergenerational traumas that follow from unresolved pain that we carry from the enslavement experience. Two of Professor Saidiya Hartman's books fleshed out my methodology of going to sites of memory in the Caribbean Islands and to important trading ports in Great Britain—London, Bristol, Liverpool, and Glasgow—to memorialize the transatlantic trade in African people like my mother and her people. The titles of Saidiya Hartman's books are *Lose Your Mother: A Journey Along the Atlantic Slave Route* and *Scenes of Subjection: Terror, Slavery, and Self-making in Nineteenth Century America.* In spite of many data gaps in memory and the archives, Hartman's concept of "critical fabulation" gave me the confidence to write against the official silences of women's material reality and the obfuscations of family lore.

Towards the end of writing the coda to the second edition of *Dead Woman Pickney*, I read the Jamaican psychiatrist Dr. Frederick W. Hickling's work, *Psychohistroriography: A Post-colonial Psychoanalytic and Psychotherapeutic Model.* Serendipitously, I discovered that he had been the Chief Medical Officer at Bellevue Mental Hospital in Kingston, Jamaica in the 1980s where he implemented his model. This was the institution that my mother spent an estimated ten years, and where she died and was allegedly buried. I am grateful to Professor Hilary Robertson-Hicking and Professor Emeritus Frederick Hicking for agreeing to talk to me about my search. They were most gracious in inviting me to their home to share a meal with their friends and colleagues in 2018.

The real value of a writer's work comes from reader response. I received written comments on social media, telephone calls, invitations to book clubs, and was a guest presenter in classes that have used my book as a text. In this regard, Professor Duncan's inclusion of my book in her undergraduate and graduate courses consistently over the last ten years stimulated dialogues among three generations in her classes. It has been most gratifying when young people tell me that because of reading *Dead Woman Pickney* they have been able to understand where their parents are coming from or, that they have been able to ask their parents questions and have the kinds of conversations that they have never been able to have before. I thank those who included me on their book club lists and who gifted copies to friends and family in the United States, the United Kingdom and in the Caribbean. I thank the following readers for engaging me in heart-to-heart conversations of how parts of my story resonated with theirs or their work: paediatricians Anna Jarvis and Edith Lorrimer, Annie Bunting, Reverends Vincent Smith and Venice Gunltey, Hyacinth Evans, Karen Ford-Warner, Pansy Hamilton, Marjory Rainford, Pauline and Byron Sterrat, Vincent Conville, Leroy Wilson, Allan Brown, Effie Neilson, Carol Pinnock, Nadia Hohn, Olga Nash, Primrose Penneycook, Judy Grant, David-George Morgan, Erin Bull, Kathy Friedman, Jan Anderson, Junie Desil, Doreen Paul, Gilfred Morris, Robert and Heather Vernon, Lami Cooper Diallo, Lloyd Finlay, Reggie Smith, Lillian Allen, Audrey Johnson, Kevin Hewitt, Michelle La Flamme, Alice Jungclaus, Justice Aston Hall, Jenny Gordon, and Mary Bishop. I thank Itah Sadu of A Different Booklist in Toronto for hosting a very early book launch. Ann Marie Grant-Lazarus's genealogical searches were indispensable to my tracking and tracing my mother and her people. Her work is shown in the composition of the family charts.

Siobhan McMenemy, Senior Editor of Wilfrid Laurier University Press did not hesitate when I proposed to write a coda about finding mother to the first edition of *Dead Woman Pickney*. With her vote of confidence and encouragement, I had to do my best. Clare Hitchens, Sales and Marketing Coordinator, has done a superb job with the advanced, international promotion and marketing. I am bursting with joy about Lara Minja's design of the book cover. Her design is a visual interpretation my story. I hope readers will be pleased as much as I am. Murray Tong, Managing Editor, has had the most challenging job to bring together all the moving parts of the coda—"Finding Mother"—together into such a readable coherent whole with the first edition.

. I must say special thanks to my sister Jamaican and colleague, Associate Professor Emerita, Cecille DePass of the University of Calgary, who has been my rock over the last thirty years. She has been mother–confessor, cheerleader, and first critic and editor for all of my published writing. I greatly admire and support her co-founding and editing the online, open access journal, *Cultural and Pedagogical Inquiry* hosted by the University of Alberta. My partner Colin Hewitt has listened to my rants, shared my joy and observed my pain over the last ten years. He has been a great travelling companion in all my trips to the archives in Jamaica and England and to the British and Scottish trading ports which once participated in the transatlantic trade of enslaved African people. Hewitt's travelogues and photography have been good counterpoints to the sad turf that I probe. He has often caught me before I take the plunge into deep melancholy. For the gift of love and laughter that has sustained me I thank him.

Finally, I acknowledge all the market women (higglers) like my maternal great-grandmother, Dorothy Goodwin, and my grandmother Minnet Goodwin whose entrepreneurial skills, hard work, and vision were foundational to the development of the internal marketing system and the survival of countless families. They are among the unacknowledged mothers of the nation of Jamaica.

—AUGUST 2021

INTRODUCTION

— to the Second Edition —

❖❖❖❖ ❖❖❖❖ ❖❖❖❖ ❖❖❖❖ ❖❖❖❖ ❖❖❖❖❖

THE FIRST AND SECOND EDITIONS of *Dead Woman Pickney* are linked by a single theme: a daughter's search for her missing mother and her mother's people. By my mother's people I mean those African-descended peoples in the Americas and the Caribbean, whose ethnicities and cultural uniqueness, the European enslavers (with the legal authority and sanctions of church and state) designated as their rightfully owned Black property. For hundreds of years, slave traders and plantation capitalists made black skin the body badge of enslavement and other forms of servitude. In the first edition, in which I tell the story of my struggles to grow up and thrive without my mother, I failed to answer two central questions which were: 1) How did I become a dead woman pickney? and 2) Who was/is my mother and her people?

Several readers expressed disappointment that I did not find the answers. I also shared their disappointment. Most serendipitously, I think my mother was disappointed too, that I did not find her. In the Coda I will trace the paths along which I travelled to look for my mother and her people, over the ten years, following publication of the first edition in 2010. In addition to the Coda, I have added some family photographs and clippings, to satisfy the curiosity of some readers who expressed their disappointment of not seeing any photographs of my family. I have chosen images that I hope will enhance my mother's story. I have also added three family charts, essentially the family trees that explicate my mother's story.

The text of the first edition remains unchanged, except for a few minor factual corrections. In the Prologue, I meditated upon the history of displaced Black bodies in the British Empire and within Canada, a former settler colony of France and Britain, the country where I had lived, at the time of publishing (the first edition), as a naturalized citizen for nearly forty years. As an active practicing educator and participant in the implementation of the Canadian Multicultural Policy within a Bilingual Framework from the 1970s to the 1990s, I have noticed and continue to notice a consistent absence from the public discourse concerning the settlement and history of Canada, of stories regarding the African or Black presence in Canada; besides of course, the story of the Underground Railroad. I have described our absent presence as the ghosts in the Canadian multicultural machine.

In the five chapters that follow the Prologue, I tell my life-story from my earliest memory beginning around 1947 until I became a teacher in 1965. In the Epilogue, I took up the theme of the disturbing connections I made of the use and abuse of Black bodies as coerced labour in the mass production of agricultural commodities such as sugar, molasses and rum, to satisfy the greed of the British Empire. I named the primordial pain of not knowing my mother. I linked that pain with the historical tragedy that I discovered when I read several historical accounts of the Middle Passage and the unknown number of captive bodies that perished during the ocean voyages. The scale, duration, and cruelties of the international trade in human flesh challenged my imagination and triggered unfathomable grief. The trade lasted some three hundred years and included some thirty-five thousand slave voyages. In the last line of the Epilogue, I wrote: "I say a silent requiem for my mother, Lucy May Reid and all those who perished in the cross-Atlantic trade in African bodies." This was not to be the end of my story. The mysterious absence of my mother and her family from my life continued to haunt by my grieving spirit.

When I left Jamaica in 1969 to become a teacher in Canada, I travelled alone, leaving all my family and kin behind. I was seeking adventure and a new life. I thought I was leaving behind all the painful memories of my childhood. Little did I know that I was not totally and utterly alone and that my memories and a "Black" identity were part of the cultural luggage and embodiment that accompanied me. I had had unseen company all the way. That company was my mother and by extension my maternal grandmother. How do I explain this? I have come to believe that she has dwelt in my subconscious all these fifty-odd years in Canada. She has haunted me with chronic grief that forced me to wonder repeatedly how my life might have been different had she raised me. She would show up faceless in my night and daydreams. I would think long and hard about how I missed her at certain stages in growing up and in my adult life, as a one-time wife, a mother of three lovely children, worker, teacher, and scholar. I think of how I needed my mother at the time of my first menses; when I needed to be taught about dating and mating; to explain the pros and cons of marriage and motherhood. I wished to talk to her about her life as a young person and about her childhood and family and her personal ambitions and, I do not know what else.

The subconscious hauntings of autobiographical memories, in both Jamaica and Canada, and experiences as an Afro-Jamaica immigrant in Canada, that drove me to write the first edition of *Dead Woman Pickney*, are still at work as I compose the additions to the second edition. This time, I write a Coda, as one would for a drama of several acts, the purpose of which is to provide answers to unanswered questions left from the first edition—the denouement. The following quotation, which I take from my doctoral dissertation, *Bodies, Memories, and Empire: Real Life Stories about Growing Up in Jamaica, 1947-1965*, sums up the paradoxes and complexities that the reader may encounter as I tell the story of the encounter of three families—Goodwin, Reid, and Shorter. I will argue that my mother's life cycle was caught in the maelstrom of the post-emancipation period in Jamaica that began in 1838 with the terms of the Emancipation Proclamation (see frontispiece), which reads:

The paradox is that the past is never past. It leaves its memorials as skeletons, traces, and ruins on the landscapes that compel the curious to ask questions and to seek answers. The past writes itself in the human body, memory being the most obvious. Long after memory fades, genealogy and lineage, especially in a slave society such as Jamaica, ensures that we do not forget the events of chattel slavery and the illicit mixing of bloods. Historians and archaeologists recreate and reconstruct the big events such as the existence of the original peoples of the Americas and the Caribbean region. They chronicle the big stories of battles of conquest and trade by the Portuguese, Spanish, Dutch, French, and British.

The unwritten stories that only elders tell of, draw on their individual and collective memories, of the minutia of their lives and struggles, and of the effects of big events on their lives. When the elders die, they take their archival memories with them and we are left to imagine and reconstruct the stories they told us and to fill in the gaps from the symbolic archives and the natural and human landscapes. In so doing, we add our own understanding of their lives and how they intertwine with ours. We inherit our social blueprint of trauma, accommodation and resistance. The past lives in the present and plays tricks with our collective unconscious.

DEAD WOMAN PICKNEY

PROLOGUE

✤·✤·✤·✤ ✤·✤·✤·✤ ✤·✤·✤·✤ ✤·✤·✤·✤ ✤·✤·✤·✤ ✤·✤·✤·✤ ✤·✤·✤·✤

MY BODY SIGNIFIES MANY STORIES. My female body, which is to say my brain, my heart, my soul, my flesh, my physiognomy, and my spirit, all are marked by events of the past into which I was born. It is the past of the colony of Jamaica, New World slavery, plantation economy, and English missionary education, set within the culture of the British Empire as it flourished and faded. A long past, yet my body remembers. This was the realization I came to when I was brought, at last, to question how I came to be born in Jamaica and how, in particular, I came to have this body that, by no will or permission of mine, caused so many moments of disruption and discomfort in multicultural classrooms and workplaces.

Multicultural discourse—how calm and irreproachable the expression—was for me an inviting door, one through which I believed I might easily pass in the search for understanding. And so my inquiry began, on my own behalf first, and then on behalf of African and "black" students. It was a simple quest for knowledge with which to make informed curricular and pedagogical interventions. During the course of my reading and reflection, I discovered the racial, economic, and sexual collision of Africa, Europe, and the Americas that—incredibly—had made me one among millions of coloured, mulatto, quadroon, octoroon children, the fruit of "black" virgins, Ewe, Ashanti, Twi, Guinea, Yoruba, Hausa, and Ibo, deflowered by white men. The "deflorescence" I speak of was no ordinary sexual act of biological maturation. It was the deliberate racialized sexual assault whose purpose was domination. White men from Portugal, Holland, Spain, France, Denmark, and England ravished the African women as they, simultaneously, plundered the African landscape for its gold, diamonds, iron, salt, gums, cloves, coffee, copper, leopard skins, rhinoceros horns, and, especially, for its ivory—the white and the black (the harvesting of black bodies became known as black ivory in the slave trade).

The harvesting of black ivory depopulated the continent, destroying clans, tribes, kingdoms, and nation-states. The rape of the healthiest and most beautiful women was relentless. It started at the point of capture and sale; it continued in the *barracoons* that were spread along what became known as the Slave Coast of Africa as well as within the officers' quarters in the slave castles.* We can imagine the sexual assaults, by white men and black, within the confines of the slave ships that plied the triangular trade, especially along the Middle Passage, and, thereafter, in the great houses of the plantations. Sexual assaults continued as an integral part of the violence that controlled and enforced labour in the tobacco fields of Virginia and Kentucky; in the cane fields of Barbados, Jamaica, Cuba, Puerto Rico, and Haiti; and in the rice fields of the Carolinas. White rape of black took place over a period of more than 350 years. For 250 of those years, it accompanied the legal trade in African bodies, and then it continued for another century of legal African chattel slavery, in what the Europeans conceived of as the New World.

My physiognomy is the living record of this terrible lineage. My mother is the descendant line of Africa enslaved: taken from the Slave Coast, a place unknown in origin, but probably somewhere that would have been known to my paternal descent—English and Scottish colonizers—as the Guineas or Ghana. I cannot be sure because too much of this lineage is lost or hidden. This, at least, I have

---

* Barracoons are the open pens in which captive Africans were held in chains until the merchant slavers amassed enough to fill the slave ships plying the coast.

direct experience of because my father's family hid my maternal lineage from me. In the same way, the knowledge regimes of schooling have, for the most part, hidden the facts and truth of the history of brutality against Africans from those who, like myself, have good reason to learn them. I struggle daily to heal the scars of wilful ignorance and epistemic violence that silence the history of enslavement in this, the so-called, New World.

I was born as a by-product of those in the service of empire in the colony of Jamaica. I grew up hearing that Africa has no history; Africa has no culture; "black" people were made to serve the white man. I continue to hear derogatory assertions about Africa. Africa is the Dark Continent. Africa is the basket case of the world. Africa is the land of savages and backwardness.

But what did that mean to me? Jamaicans were, and fundamentally still are, categorized as black, white, and—my own kind—coloured. If I was not "white," I was certainly not "black." I did not believe that assertions about "black" Africa described me, even partially. Only when I moved to Canada did I "become" black—that is, I had "blackness," in the North American sense, bestowed upon me. Only through living and working in British Columbia, and observing and experiencing First Nations and Aboriginal peoples' struggle to reclaim their land, language, and culture from English and French colonial domination, was I compelled to acknowledge, explicitly, the parallel struggles of "black" people, whose very name, written in lowercase, reduced them to their skin colour. How more diminished can a people be? While the struggles of Africans on the continent are similar to those of the indigenous peoples of Canada, the African-descended peoples in the Americas—Canada, the United States, the Caribbean, and South America—have had to fight against the stigma of "blackness" brought about by 450 years of trans-Atlantic European trade in their enslaved bodies and some 500 years of chattel slavery and domestic bondage. The legacy of this historical, legal, psychological, social, and economic dehumanization is carried over into contemporary official documents. For instance, in reading

Canadian census reports up to the 1990s I discovered that all immigrants were identified with a country of origin except for people of African descent, whose category was "black." How disconcerting to encounter in documents on Canadian multiculturalism a string of descriptors such as Chinese, Asian, Scottish, Irish, First Nations, Aboriginal, and black? All of these descriptors are properly related to place except black, which is placeless. As if to add insult to symbolic injury, when one uses black as a noun and capitalized, one is corrected, which reinforces the historically imposed inferior status. For me, living among people who claimed rights and entitlements based on their place-based identities, these realizations were both painful and shameful to live and work with. These people constantly reminded me that as a group African-descended peoples are regarded as marginal citizens, locally and globally. Although the relatively recent appellation African Canadian was meant to replace black, black remains, for complicated political reasons, the adjective and the noun for peoples of the African continent and its diaspora.

Briefly, moving beyond the public celebration of the Underground Railway that brought thousands of enslaved Africans from the slave states of America to freedom in Canada—fragile though that freedom turned out to be—my investigation revealed a complicated history of struggle against enslavement, cheap, temporary domestic, and farm labour and a people who at one time were deemed "unsuitable" for immigration to Canada by immigration authorities. While "black" people have been in Canada since the 1600s and have contributed much—some having attained high positions in the Canadian nation—they still struggle against discrimination in education, jobs, law enforcement, and housing. They still have to fight to be accepted as Canadian citizens.

In order to write this memoir, I have sought out my repressed physical and cultural heritage. I have confronted some haunting memories of my life in Jamaica and come to an understanding of how the dynamics of colonization, race, skin colour, commodity production, and empire played out in my family, schooling, and in the very landscape of the places in which I lived. The basic tool of this research, then, is my autobiographical memory, from which I construct real life stories. But I have found myself obligated to go beyond the examination of a single (that is, my own), life history. For it remains a major aim to forward the understanding I have already mentioned and contribute to the body of texts supporting critical dialogue—dialogue that, through necessary curricular and pedagogical interventions, has given greater credence to critical multiculturalism and anti-racist education.

The urge to write this memoir was motivated by my sense of how important it is to interrogate and inform educators about what it means to be an enslaved and colonized "other," teaching and learning in the multicultural and multiracial classes in Western educational systems. As an educator, born and educated in Jamaica between 1943 and 1965, and having lived and worked in Canada for forty years, I have become aware of, and affected and disturbed by, the phenomena that I have observed: the complex ways in which bodies in classrooms carry the memories of empire (especially of the English, French, and Spanish), in their physiognomy, speech, schooling, and social standing. I have remarked on how these bodies and memories are treated. Multiculturalist discourse notwithstanding, some bodies seem welcomed and invited to enjoy a right of place, while other bodies, conversely, seem out of place and the source of great discomfort.

Let us compare the high social standing accorded to white students speaking with the accents of England, Australia, New Zealand, or the United States with the relatively low standing accorded to, or even accepted by, some black and brown students from the Caribbean, India, and Africa. Culturally, linguistically, and directly through the curricula of their schooling, people from these former colonies share a common colonial and British imperial heritage. Yet white is the colour of the colonizer; black, brown, yellow, and red are the colours of the colonized. This distinction is the embodiment of the status differential, which, even without further reinforcement, represents an unspoken rebuff—one that leads some students to resist and act out the rejection they feel, while it makes others feel alienated from the education system. Many leave school or universities altogether and thereby decrease their life chances.

As both student and teacher, I have experienced and observed how destructive tensions arise when the hegemonic knowledge of the colonizer clashes with the repressed knowledge of the colonized, especially if articulated by those who, like myself, live within embodied memories. I have been especially struck by the ways in which knowledge about the colonized other is subjugated or erased in academic disciplines. Official curricular choices leave teachers unprepared to deal with traumatic stories of slavery, colonization, and political domination, whether historical or contemporary.

The omission and erasure of topics dealing with the presence of Africa and Africans in Western historical study are particularly pervasive. It has become fashionable as a pedagogical strategy for teachers and instructors to ask children and adult students to tell their own stories. However, of what use is it to the student to bring forward these stories and experiences when there is no epistemic base upon which to validate and honour them within a critical and ethical framework? Worse yet, what does it mean for some students to be perennial strangers in classrooms where they will learn next to nothing of their ancestral histories and heritage?

Under these circumstances, I confront my painful memories of childhood and write my life history to learn of the circumstances of my birth; to delve into the history of the society into which I was born and raised; to find out the story of my mother and her people; and to understand the erasure of Africa and its peoples from the official curricula of most schools and universities in the West. The crucial question is: How did I become a dead woman pickney?

— Chapter One —

Early Childhood Memories, 1947–50

❖❖❖❖ ❖❖❖❖ ❖❖❖❖ ❖❖❖❖ ❖❖❖❖ ❖❖❖❖ ❖❖❖❖

ONE DAY, A FATEFUL DAY, sometime in the fourth year of my troubled infancy, as I was just recovering from the asthma that nearly took my life, something particularly terrible happened to My Aunt Joyce and me.* The morning started out like any other. As usual, Harold's dutiful wife arose at the crack of dawn, usually after the second cock-crow, went to the outside kitchen, and lit the coal pot to make the hearty breakfast and lunch of boiled bananas, sweet potatoes, salt fish, and callaloo. The night before, she would have remembered to put the dried salted codfish to soak in a bowl of water, ridding it of the excess salt that had enabled its journey from far-off Newfoundland. Then she would come to my room, rip the cover off me, and shake my shoulders to rouse me from my deep sleep. "Yvonne! Yvonne! Get up, up!" I would groan and say: "Me wa' fe sleep, me tyad." "You too young fe tyad. Put on yuh clothes and go outside to tek in de fresh morning air."

---

* Note that the author capitalizes "My Aunt Joyce" to signify the special importance that she held in her life at this early stage. Later in her memoir, she refers to her aunt simply as Aunt Joyce.

She repeated this ritual for as long as it took to get me fully awake and out of bed. I would dress and stumble through the door, frowning and grumbling, leaving her and Harold behind in the bedroom. The morning air was cold and damp. I would get goose bumps and shiver until my teeth clattered, whimpering like a puppy dog. When she determined that I had had enough morning air, she would order me to wash my face, clean my teeth with fine salt, and gargle my throat.

A cup of hot bitter cerasee tea waited for me at the table. "Drink yuh cerasee tea. It good fe clean out yu blood." I had to drink this bitter concoction—sweetened with "D sugar," the poorest quality but most nutritious grade—before I got my breakfast of slimy oats porridge. "Oats porridge good fe you. It mek you bones strong." All this was part of a health regime to help me shake the debilitating asthma that threatened to stunt my growth and take my life. But it was a breakfast of bitterness that made me vomit and slime that would make me salivate volumes, which I could not swallow to please her. It was a battle of wills to keep me alive. She tried beating me for not eating, but to no avail. "Yu going to sit dere til yu drink dat tea and dat porridge." So I would sit there until I fell asleep with my face on the tabletop.

Later when the sun was hot enough to take the chill out of the bath pan of water that she had set out, My Aunt Joyce gave me my daily bath and talked to me about learning to read and count. She had taught me to count to five using five fingers, two eyes, one nose, ten fingers, and ten toes. Later, she bought me an ABC book and marbles for counting. "One day I will have to send you to Sunday School. I going to make you a nice frilly frock." I loved the baths because she talked lovingly to me about growing healthy and strong. There was a small tree growing close by, and she would coo about my growing out of the asthma just as the tree grew. Neighbours gave her many compliments on how well she was raising me. She loved it; I was a gift, the child she could not bear herself.

I would come to understand that this ritual of waking early to cook and feed her husband and send him off to work was the pattern that I was expected to follow when I too became a good Christian wife. She would dish out hefty portions of cooked food in three stacking bowls of an enamel carrier in the following order: in the largest bottom bowl, she would place fingers of boiled bananas and cover them with the cooking water to keep them from hardening. In the second bowl, she would artistically arrange slices of boiled "modder edward" sweet potatoes and, in the third bowl, the cook-up of salt fish, coconut oil, onions, pepper, and callaloo. She would then slide each bowl carefully into the slender metal frame that strung the two-sided handles one on top of the other. Finally, she would put the lid on the topmost bowl, and lock the metal frame. She would also pour coffee into the Thermos flask that would keep it hot until lunchtime.

While My Aunt Joyce was cooking, her husband performed his ablutions. I was taught that this big, tall, handsome black man was my Uncle Harold. He would play with me sometimes. He was the first man I saw use a pen and ink. I remember hiding and using the pen and ink to write a whole page full of zigzag marks to "Fadda Christmus." Uncle Harold laughed, snorting hiccups, when my Aunt Joyce showed him what I had done. I "kinda" liked Uncle Harold.

That morning, I watched Uncle Harold dress through the half-open bedroom door. He put on his clean white merino (undershirt) and long underpants. Over the top, he donned a crisply starched and ironed white, long-sleeve cotton shirt that his industrious wife had made for the husband she did not and could not love. He was himself a reputable tailor. He had made the grey woollen trousers that completed his work ensemble. He stuffed the long shirttail inside his pants, then strung a leather belt through the loops, buckled the belt, and patted the buckle with his super-long skinny fingers. He stood with legs astride in front of the bureau mirror, bending slightly forward to see his face.

He reached for the jar of coconut oil, unscrewed the cap, stuck his right index finger in and scooped a little of the congealed oil into the palm of his left hand. He rubbed both palms together to liquefy the oil and then rubbed the grease furiously through his mop of unruly kinks. First, he combed out the tangles with the coarse-toothed end of the comb, and then, with the fine-toothed end, he raked them into place. He finished off by brushing back along the lines of his widow's peak to reveal his flat forehead. His wife said that a peaked hairline was a sure sign of a wicked man. She should know whereof she spoke; she had intimate knowledge of his cruelties. I saw many beatings in my short time with them as a child, and, as a consequence, I was afraid of Uncle Harold.

Harold had to be turned out just right to meet his white and brown customers who expected him to be dressed respectably and (at least to their faces) to speak with enough deference to obtain and keep their patronage. Uncle Harold stood up straight and turned his back to the mirror, while he twisted his neck to see that he looked just as good behind as in front.

He stepped off the veranda to where his Raleigh bicycle leaned against the trunk of the breadfruit tree. He pointed the bicycle towards the gate and kicked the stand upright, then pinched each tire between his thumb and index finger to see how soft it was. He removed the pump from the upright bar, pulled out the connection tube and attached the pump to the tire, then pumped up each until he could no longer squeeze the rubber. He would carefully replace the pump and wash his hands in the washbasin set out for his ablutions. Then he would fold his trouser legs to taper them for riding his bicycle. These were held in place with metal clips, so that Uncle Harold would not get the chain grease on them when he pedalled to work. He hiked up his shirtsleeves above his wrist and clipped each just above his biceps.

"Harold, yuh breakfast ready." Harold would answer, "Hm hm," and move to the table. He sat at the table by himself, while Joyce busied herself washing up in the kitchen. First, he cautiously sipped the hot bush tea to test its heat. If it was too hot, he alternately blew furiously to get rid of the steam and slurped it noisily. After a few big gulps, he was bound to belch loudly, as he rubbed his belly and adjusted his bottom on the chair. Then he took the fork and crushed up everything on his plate to a messy mush. He shovelled the mush into his mouth, chewing with his mouth open and lips smacking. This lusty way of eating caused many altercations between Harold and Joyce. It would start when Joyce would holler: "Harold, chew with your mout shut. You sound like a striking hog. Yuh mek me stomach sick." To which Harold would reply: "You red kin bitch! You tink yuh betta ah me." When really furious, he would throw a few plates out on the concrete veranda, shout some sexist and racist obscenities, and storm out. He would mount his bicycle and pedal furiously fast, as though he had wound-up springs in his knees.

On calmer mornings, after the usual busy rituals of making the fire and cooking a working man's breakfast, Aunt Joyce dutifully saw her burly husband off to his tailor shop, in May Pen city centre. When Harold was ready to leave, she would hand him his carrier of food and Thermos flask of coffee at the door. He would grab them and mumble: "See you laata." She swiftly gave him a "cut eye," to show her scorn, and walked into the kitchen to dish out her own working woman's breakfast.

She would join me sitting at the table, praying to the bitter cerasee tea and slimy oats porridge. I had been soundly whipped once for dumping the porridge in my lap and throwing the tea through the window. We would sit in silence, she absorbed in her own thoughts as I watched her timidly from the corner of my eyes. I knew when she was really in a foul mood because one of her eyes jumped and danced, and she packed the food into her mouth without chewing. Her cheeks would bulge and when she was forced to chew to get rid of some of the food, one of her cheeks would puff up like a balloon and

Uncle Harold and Aunt Joyce.

squeeze the dancing eye to a squint. Occasionally, she would come out of her reverie and shout and threaten me: "Eat up. If yuh don't eat now yuh nat getting anyting to eat for the rest of de day." She often kept her promise. When I refused to put the mug or spoon to my mouth, she said: "Yuh stubborn like a mule, yuh is de bebil pickney."

It was the custom that after Harold had mounted his bicycle and pushed off to work and she had bathed me and combed my hair, Joyce would start her day's routine. Tidying up the house was a matter of pride, which she would do herself because no maid could do it to her satisfaction. She would open all of the windows and make the Simmons bed that she and Harold had fought on the night before. Then she would dust the bureau and night table. Afterwards, she would move into the dining room where my own makeshift bed was. She made it up before she moved to fold the tablecloth, walk out to the veranda, and shake it clean of crumbs. The next big task was to dust the waggonette, with careful attention to the glasses and cups and saucers. The floor followed. First, she would sweep it with the fine bamboo floor broom, then she wiped, waxed, and shined it with a coconut brush. After this, it was time to buff the floor with an old felt hat. I watched her many mornings as she did the floors. The routines followed the same pattern. She would assemble the damp cloth, the chunk of beeswax, and the coconut floor brush and get down on her knees, cushioned by soft rags. First, she would wipe sections of the hardwood floor clean. Then she would rub wax over the face of the brush. Cupping the brush in the clasp of both palms and outstretched fingers, she would kneel down and push the brush back and forth, back and forth, pausing occasionally to wipe the sweat from her forehead and sing or hum one of her favourite hymns:

Guide me, O Thou great Jehovah
Pilgrim through this barren land
I am weak but Thou art mighty
Hold me with Thy powerful hands
Bread of heaven, bread of heaven
Feed me now and evermore
Feed me now and evermore.

She would simply hum the words for the verses that she did not know. I was to see and hear her drown her sorrows in the words and melody of this hymn many times, when later I lived with her again. When the floors were as shiny as glass, she would go once over them with an old felt hat and give the floor its final buff. She was now ready to bathe and get dressed and to start her day's work.

Even though she ran her dressmaking business from home, she, like her husband, had to dress appropriately to meet and greet her customers. This day, in particular, she dressed in a beautiful pink linen dress with cutwork embroidery in the same colour all over the bodice. She was famous among the high-class women for this work. She would style her "good hair" to look like her favourite film star. She would dip the fine end of the comb in a little water and twist, while she combed to get beautiful curls to form a "V" in the front. Just like Greta Garbo, I imagine now. I watched her carefully as she used a special black cloth tube to roll the hair and make an oval-shaped rope draped to the nape of her neck. She would hold the roll in place with several hairpins. I thought My Aunt Joyce was so pretty. Her ivory skin contrasted with Harold's ebony and my honey-coloured skin.

When she had dressed herself to her standard of elegance, she would get the washerwoman, who arrived at work when the sun was halfway to the top of the sky, to help her move her Singer treadle machine and her cutting table out to the veranda. When it did not rain, she liked to work on the cooler veranda. I liked to lie spread-eagled on the cold smooth concrete floor and roll around enjoying the cool on my skin.

On this sad day when the awful thing happened, I had been sitting contentedly at My Aunt Joyce's feet dressing my dolls with the scraps that fell from her cutting table. I became aware that something had alarmed My Aunt Joyce. She looked towards the gate, where a grey lorry with a bright red stripe drawn across the cab pulled up to a sudden screeching halt sending a cloud of dust up in the air. My aunt jumped up panic-stricken and exclaimed: "What have you come for, Cyril?" I looked around and saw a very brown figure walking towards the veranda. He was a brown-skinned man wearing cocoa-brown oxfords, cocoa-brown pants, a cocoa-brown shirt, topped off with a cocoa-brown felt hat. When he stepped upon the veranda and greeted my aunt in a not-so-friendly manner, I looked from him to my aunt and saw a striking resemblance that I was not to understand until much later.

He looked around and saw me under the sewing machine flap, walked over, and bent down, while he made kissing sounds and beckoned me to come to him, much as if he was calling his puppy dog. I played strange because I did not know this man. He grabbed me, took me up, and said: "I am your father. Call me daddy." I did as I was told. I did not know what father or daddy meant. I was scared of the brown man. My Aunt Joyce and the brown man started arguing, and I heard My Aunt Joyce say: "Leave de chile alone wid me. Yu cyant look after har."

She pulled him into the bedroom and closed the door, behind which they had a big row. I stood outside listening, worried for my poor Aunt Joyce. When at last the door opened, her skin was flushed as pink as her dress. Beads of tears ran down her cheeks. Her dancing eye began to dance really fast. In a frenzy, she reached for a grip (suitcase) and packed all of the beautiful frilly frocks she had made for me to wear to the May Pen Methodist Sunday School. The brand new kid leather white shoes that I was also to wear to the Sunday School were packed. I loved the smell of the new leather.

The brown man took me up in his arms, kissed me all over, and emptied his pockets of sweeties (candies). The cigarette box in his pocket poked me in my ribs as he heaved me up and down above his head and held me against his chest. His breath smelled of rum and tobacco. I did not like the brown man. He said: "Yu comin wid daddy." My Aunt Joyce bathed and dressed me in a pink organdy cotton dress with white polka dots. The dress had a tiny white collar and a big bow, tied at the back. I was delighted to have my hair plaited in an upsweep and tied with my big pink ribbons. When I was dressed, My Aunt Joyce took me to the brown man, handed me and my grip to him, and suddenly turned away with her head hung low, before turning back and kissing me goodbye on both of my cheeks. Her tears left my cheeks wet. At that moment of innocent parting, I felt half happy that I was going for a ride with the brown man who had given me sweeties. Aunt Joyce stood alone in the doorway, dejected and forlorn, as the brown man revved up the loud engine of the lorry. She did not wave. I was torn between this brown stranger, whom I did not like, and My Aunt Joyce, whom I was learning to love.

I do not remember any parting interchange between My Aunt Joyce and Cyril. The brown man held me in one arm and my grip in the other and walked me to the grey lorry. He settled me on the passenger seat and put my grip on the floor in front of me. Then he drove off, kicking up dust and roaring the engine so loud that the neighbours came out to see what the raucous was about. He was taking me from May Pen in the parish of Clarendon to Windsor Castle in the parish of St. Mary. I was happy to go for the drive, but little did I know the wretched life that awaited me. It was not until some time in 1955 that I was finally reunited with My Aunt Joyce. Many difficult years would pass before then.

I often wondered what account My Aunt Joyce gave her husband of my disappearance and why I was not even allowed to say goodbye to him. I cannot imagine her getting any sympathy. This is how I imagine the scenario. After wolfing down his dinner and belching shamelessly, Harold takes a bath in the bathhouse, in the bath pan of water that Joyce had the washerwoman put out for his morning ablutions. He gets dressed in his American-style drape pants and long dinner jacket, puts his round silver timepiece, suspended from a heavy silver chain attached to his right pant loop, into his left fob pocket. Making concealed fobs was his specialty. He often boasted about how well he could make a fob. While he dresses, Aunt Joyce hurls obscenities at him to let him know in no uncertain terms that she thinks he is nothing but a dog. Harold laughs his fiendish hiccup laugh, mocking her impotence, and underscoring his power. He returns to the business of enhancing his sartorial splendour by donning a bow tie. He struts out the door, snorting and grinning hiccups. My Aunt Joyce is meanwhile left alone to stew in her misery. Harold will later return home, predictably drunk, and will return My Aunt Joyce's verbal assaults with a lashing.

Years later, on one of my obligatory visits during summer holidays from Mico Teachers' College, and in a rare moment of woman-to-woman intimacy, Aunt Joyce told me what had happened that day when my father took me away. By now, she was no longer My Aunt Joyce; she was simply Aunt Joyce, for reasons that will become clear as the story unfolds. She related that when she protested to my father for wanting to take me from her, he replied: "People don't have dem pickney and give dem whey like chickens." As if that were not insult enough, he further told her: "If yuh want pickney, yuh have yuh big pussy, go have yuh own pickney." Almost as though she found her recollection unbelievable, she raised her right hand and called on God as her witness. She flushed and sobbed probably as much as she had on the day my father took me away.

She did not have to call on God as a witness for me to believe her. What she did not know, and what I could not tell her, was that I had despised the man who was my father so much for his lack of human decency and integrity that I had disowned him when I was fourteen years old. I had vowed never to see or speak to him from the day he gave Harry Black licence to work me like a slave in his grocery shop and in his household. It would have been futile to tell Aunt Joyce all of this because, to my complete puzzlement, she had an everlasting love and loyalty to her brother, despite his ways. Her revelation to me only confirmed that I had done the right thing, the admonishment of the Old Testament commandment notwithstanding. Yet if I had told Aunt Joyce of my resolve, she would have abruptly changed her emotions and given me chapter and verse from the Bible why I would be damned in hell for doing such a thing, doubtless from the very same section that I would have used equally to justify my own position:

1 Children obey your parents in the Lord, for this is right.
2 Honour thy father and mother; (which is the first commandment with promise;

3 That it may be well with thee, and thou mayest live long on earth.
4 And, ye fathers provoke not your children to wrath: but bring them up in the nurture and admonition of the Lord.
   (Ephesians 6:1–4, Authorized Version)

How might I be well? In relation to a father who truly provoked me to anger, I was the one who had to decide what this promise meant. The Bible is silent on the matter, as were all the adults who stressed unquestioned obedience to parents. It was as if parents could abuse their children with impunity for there were no scriptural consequences for them.

I am not certain for what Aunt Joyce cried. Was she crying for what we had both lost between us or for her inability to have children? I dared not ask. I was overwhelmed by her recollection of this part of what had happened behind the closed bedroom door that day. The separation was traumatic for both of us. From the way she flushed as she sobbed, I can only imagine that she was reliving the ultimate humiliation of a childless wife in a society that placed so much store on the fertile woman and the virile man. Her husband very much played the virile man. Folk would say he was married to a "mule," as he would often call her. His scorn for her childlessness was supported by Old Testament stories of God cursing women by making their wombs infertile. I have no doubt now that she wept for the loss of the daughter she almost raised. And in spite of some terrible episodes involving Aunt Joyce and me later in our lives, I have wept many times during my life for the surrogate mother I almost had.

Her loving care was the closest I would come to knowing the loving care of a mother. There was not another social mother in my life. I do not know how long I stayed with her, but these early years of my life were deeply significant. I was a motherless child when she rescued me, nursed me to health, and showered her young maternal love on me. I remember my first Christmas. She dressed me up and carried me in her arms to the Grand Market on the night before Christmas. At the market, a mask of a horse's head scared me, and she cajoled me into going up and touching his long face. But when the person talked from behind the mask, I remember screaming so loudly that people gathered round to see what had happened to "de likkle girl." To appease me, she had carried me again in her arms to Mr. Black's shop and bought me red, pink, and green sweeties. When she took me home, she told me of a man called "Faader Chrismus," who would come through the ceiling to put gifts in the big red flannel stockings that she placed at the foot of my bed. She insisted that I had to go to sleep like a good little girl before he would come down. I tried to stay awake to see this "Faader Chrismus," but could not, and the next morning I woke up, excited to find a doll in my stocking, but very disappointed that I never saw "Faader Chrismus." My Aunt Joyce had dreams and ambitions for me. She was my first teacher. She began to educate me in good manners, for which she received much praise from friends and customers. She introduced me to reading, counting, and writing early. God bless her soul.

The incidents in my life that followed this fateful day attest to the sometimes-tragic consequences of my father's deeds. He was an arrogant brown man whose brain was pickled in alcohol and tobacco smoke. He was also one of the thousands of sons born to near-white wives and white fathers of the British planter class, reared in the attitudes and techniques that were used to intimidate and abuse black men, women of all shades, and their children. Sadly, from the day when my father took me away from My Aunt Joyce, I became only her niece—Cyril's daughter by the black wench. Yes, "the black wench" was the way both Aunt Joyce and her favourite brother referred to my mother. I have never heard that word from anyone else in Jamaica. I met the word again when I began to read fiction written about slavery in the southern United States.

By my father's actions, I had no contact with My Aunt Joyce for about eight years. During this time, all bonds of affection were severed, and she became plain Aunt Joyce. Years later when Aunt Joyce and I were reunited (I was about twelve, just before my first period at thirteen years old), the estrangement was obvious and irreparable.

She now had a surrogate son whom her philandering husband Harold had sired by an Indian woman. In the Jamaican classification of colour and physiognomy, this child could pass as hers. She led me to believe the same, until one of her maids told me the story. The truth was also to emerge several times during Harold and Joyce's disgraceful "tracing" matches, which I heard when I lived with them again between 1954 and 1959. The object of these loud and nasty public quarrels was to exchange dirty references to their racial, class, and gender attributes. With arithmetic precision, each tried to cancel the other out with the nastiest put-down. The tracing match usually became physical when one of them delivered a blow to fix the insult. When I first tried to part the fight, Uncle Harold would put me between them and push us both against the wall. Soon enough, I learned to scream for help from the neighbours rather than intervene.

Our relationship was tainted in ways that I am only now, as I write, beginning to understand. For one thing, I now think I held a grudge against Aunt Joyce for not coming to find and rescue me from my father's brutality. For another, I was confused by her repeated negative references to my mother. Her bad temper and propensity to hit and curse terrified me. At the same time, I loved her and even sometimes liked her. I have come to see her as a proud "white" woman who had married out of her race and class. She and her husband were locked in the deadly embrace of race, class, and gender inequalities. They lived out the curse of a racialized superiority–inferiority binary. Aunt Joyce resisted the sexist subjugation that was her lot. She was like a football, kicked by the blackguard and cad in a game whose rules she did not really know. History had dealt with her cruelly—she was paying for the "sins of the fathers."

As my father and I walked towards the truck, I noticed the red stripe and "PWD" written in big red letters on both sides. I later learned that PWD stood for Public Works Department. Cyril John Shorter (as he called himself, as if to assure himself of his importance) supervised road building in the parishes of St. Catherine and St. Mary.

From what I came to know, I guess that it must have been on one of the road-building projects in St. Mary that he met Eutedra Williams, the woman to whose home he was to take me. One of the many jobs that she did was to break stones at a spot on the roadside in front of her property. With a big iron stone hammer, she would break up big rocks that the stone carriers had brought to the roadside for the stonebreakers to break. She would have been seated on rags, wearing culottes that her cousin Miss Boris sent her from America and a man's shirt. She wore her broad straw hat to shield her face from the broiling sun. When the stone heap reached a certain height, Cyril John Shorter would drive up with two sidemen, and they would unload the wooden cubic-yard boxes that had no bottom and no lid. With one man on each side of the box, they would sling the box by the protruding handles upon the heap and shake it down until it was filled to the top. Once this was done, they would shovel more stone into the box in order to fill it up and level it off. They would repeat this measuring manoeuvre at another spot on the stone heap until all of the stone was parcelled out into discrete piles of cubic yards. Cyril John Shorter then counted the number of piles and wrote up the bill in order to have Eutedra paid.

After the sidemen had shovelled the stones onto the lorry, Cyril John Shorter would drive the truck to the next road-repair or road-building site where the stones would be dumped, then spread along the road or heaped into potholes. Marl would be trucked in from a nearby quarry and spread over the stones. Men would pour big ladles of hot asphalt that they had boiled in big drums right there at the roadside. Another man driving a big two-wheel roller would spread the tar over the top. When the asphalt dried, the road was smooth and very black. Children enjoyed running to school on the new road, the sound of their bare feet a pitter-patter accompaniment to the choral recitation of their times tables. Another pleasure of the road was to sink wiggling toes into its surface once the hot sun had softened the asphalt.

The journey from May Pen to Windsor Castle took all day. I fell asleep and awoke several times, while the smell of motor oil, gasoline, and the heat in the cabin made me nauseous. The brown man stopped at a house and put me to sleep, while he made soup. He woke me and fed me. I began to cry, and he told me very sternly to stop the crying—all the while his eyes were swivelling very rapidly from side to side, which frightened me. This was my first experience of the monster that was called my father. I was to see those eyes of his move from side to side in rapid fire when he was about to give me one of the many senseless floggings that have permanently scarred my body and my psyche.

The place where we stopped must have been the Rio Magno Public Works Office, located in St. Catherine, and out of which Cyril John Shorter worked for many years. He must have parked the lorry there because we boarded the Sunshine Bus at sundown and travelled until nightfall. When the bus stopped to let us off, we walked along a trail cutting through a field of high whistling sugar canes. A full moon seemed to follow us as we walked along. Sometimes the brown man would hoist me up on his shoulders, and I could see the shimmering leaves and blossoms of the sugar canes rippling like waves in the wind. Judging by the cool wind that caused their leaves to whistle, I think it must have been November or December. That is when the sugar canes, which are harvested in the new year, are already high and when the northeast trade winds blow.

The trail led down into a gully and then up to a knoll from which we could hear voices and see a flickering light. We entered the yard, and a boy and a girl ran to greet me. "Sister Yvonne! Sister Yvonne!" They were playing under a tree with the light from the "kitchen-bitch" (a home-made kerosene torch made from condensed milk tin cans, fitted with a handle and stuffed with a cloth wick). The brown man introduced me to his eldest child, my brother Trevor, and to Sonia, my sister and his eldest daughter. They knew me, but

I had no knowledge or memory of them. He then took me into the thatched hut and introduced me to Miss Eutedra Williams whom I should call Aunt Eu. "Eu" was short for Eutedra. I now wonder if she had been expecting my father to bring home yet another of his motherless children. It would have been just like him to bring me home unannounced and to assume no questions would be asked.

Miss Eu's thatch hut and its furnishings were extraordinary. The hut was of the best construction. It housed her four-poster bed, over which the white mosquito net was twisted, wrapped, and hung from the rafter. Opposite the foot of the bed stood the mahogany bureau with the big round mirror and a nice washstand with a marble top. Her pretty enamelled face basin, painted with a bunch of pink roses and green stems, rested in the centre. A tablet of green Palmolive or Pears bathing soap, imported straight from England, the Mother Country, poised majestically on the matching soap dish. To the right of the basin, a matching big-belly enamelled "water goblet" stood with handle akimbo. Its wide lip, which bore a permanently broad smile, stood ready to stick its water tongue forth with just a tip of the hand. There was a matching chamber pot and slop pail. Eutedra must have bought the toilet set from a Syrian trader on one of her trips to Port Maria, the capital of the parish of St. Mary, or to Kingston, the island's capital. Such a washstand and toilet set were normally only to be seen in rich white people's houses, accompanied by housemaids who would wash and maintain them and keep the water goblet filled at all times. The housemaid would empty the waste water from the basin, empty the slop pail and chamber pot, wash, disinfect, and replace them, and have them ready for the missus. In Eutedra's house, there were no housemaids, so these chores were bestowed upon Sonia and me, which was hardly a surprise.

The hut had no windows, but it had a front and back door made of bamboo wattle and daub that hung on bamboo frames. The frames lasted only as long as the duck ants and other termites would allow. Miss Eu had need of a new house because when it rained hard, as it often does in the parish of St. Mary, the thatch roof leaked like a sieve. There were not enough buckets, wash pans, pots, kerosene tins, or pudding pans to catch the water. There were times when the trenches around the hut deposited streams of water into, rather than away from, the hut. After heavy rainfalls, the smell of mildewed thatch and clothes was sometimes suffocating.

Miss Eu earned income from a variety of sources. Her medium-sized farm was the most diversified in the area. In fact, I think it was unique. First, she had acres of sugar cane. For this crop, she hired cane cutters to harvest the canes and carry them to her own mill, which was strategically located on the farm. Hired women and men continuously fed stalks of cane into the mill, operated by a yoked steer that took turns with a skittish mule and a stubborn jackass to move giant rollers round and round, squeezing out every drop of cane juice. The cane juice flowed into a big trough, from where it was siphoned into enormous copper cauldrons that were permanently mounted on an equally enormous stone and concrete fireplace. During crop time between January and April, men worked around the clock stoking the fire, which boiled down the cane juice into sugar crystals and molasses. The expert boiler and quasi-chemist would use lime, heat, and the dexterity of king-sized paddles to determine when the crystals were ripe enough to be poured into bamboo joints to make "head sugar" or into large kerosene tins to make "wet sugar." Quailed banana leaves were spread over each container of wet sugar and tied around with strips of banana bark, so that the leaf covers looked like green hats trimmed with brown ribbons. Eutedra distributed her own sugar products to the higglers, who retailed them in quart measures, ounces, or bamboo joints in the markets of Port Maria and Oracabessa. They collected farthings, three farthing, gill-and-quatty, penny ha'penny, and three pence. Moneyed people paid in crowns, half-crowns, and in five and ten shillings. The rich paid in pounds and guineas.

Eutedra Williams was (and still is) the most remarkable "superwoman" I have known. Even fifty years later, I have not met her equal. At first, I was her shadow as she did her daily tour of duty on her farm. She even played with me and talked baby talk to me. She made me a few multicoloured dresses because she was also a casual dressmaker. My father made us call her Miss Eu—she was one of his many paramours. I do not know how long she tolerated him and his three children in her two-room hut. My father really only came "home" in order to sleep with her. His other reason for coming "home" was to mete out punishment to my brother, sister, and myself when Miss Eu complained that we did not labour to her satisfaction. This she did often when she wanted to break up with Cee (as she called him when things were sweet between them). You see, Cyril had a habit of not bringing "home" any house money on payday. Being the businesswoman that she was, Miss Eu exacted our labour in direct proportion to how much my father owed her for our keep.

We had to wake at daybreak in order to make several trips down a slippery hill to the spring, from which we would fetch buckets and kerosene tins of water, enough to fill two twenty-gallon oil drums. My brother would then have to milk two cows and carry the milk cans to the gate for collection on their way to Bybrook Milk Condensery in Bog Walk. Meanwhile, my sister made up the wood fire in order to cook a heavy breakfast of yams, potatoes, and codfish or sardines. As time passed, I adapted to the harsh life on Eutedra's farm, grew, and became strong. We ate well. We drank the extra cow's milk from Eutedra's heifers. My father sometimes brought home cans of Libby's Bully Beef to supplement the chicken and pork from Eutedra's farm.

There was also salted codfish, herring, shad, and mackerel bought from Miss Mary Lyon's shop. This assortment of dried and pickled salt fish was imported from Newfoundland, Canada, and came to the shop by truck from Kingston in great big wooden barrels. There was an abundance of ground provisions: dasheen, coco, yams, sweet potatoes, breadfruit, green bananas, plantains, tomatoes, limes, oranges, and callaloos.

For a while, I was Miss Eu's pet. I followed her around as she did her daily work routine, and she usually took me with her when she went visiting her friends. One day Miss Eu was going to visit her dear friend Miss Edna. I followed much like a pup follows its owner. Miss Edna had just had a baby. As we entered the gate, we startled the chickens who were scratching for food along the pathway leading from the road to the little well-kept hut. These chickens spread their wings as if they were about to fly but were held back by their own weight. They squawked in protest at us for breaking their concentrated scratching.

Miss Edna did not have a husband and lived alone. She came to greet her friend by herself. Her head was wrapped in a lily-white cloth, and she wore a printed indigo blue smock with red and yellow flowers. Miss Edna greeted her friend Eutedra and welcomed her in. She said: "Praise de lawd Jesus me deliva de byaby ahright. Me hab a bunununus byaby bwoy." Just then, I pushed myself from behind Miss Eu's frock tail and darted forward to see the new baby laying sound asleep in the middle of the big Simmons bed. I believe it was the first time I had seen a young baby. I exclaimed out loud: "Him look like parson." Both women broke out in gales of uncontrolled laughter. Miss Eu gave me a maternalistic pat on the shoulder, hissed through her teeth, and said: "De pickney too ripe." Miss Edna, recovering from her astonishment, added to Miss Eu's comment by saying: "Out of the mouth of babes!" The women proceeded with their womanly conversation while I sat subdued in a corner like an obedient puppy dog. Did I make it obvious that the paternity of this child could not be concealed, even from a child as young as I was?

In time, I came to hear rumours about the fornication of upright ministers of religion of all denominations. Usually, the physiognomy of the illegitimate offspring carried the genetic traces that revealed the sexual transgressions. The clues might have been in the skin colour, the eyes, the nose, and especially the hair. It might also have been in the twitch of the nose, the gait, and the sound of the voice. The illegitimate offspring had an uncomfortable habit of being living, walking evidence of sexual immorality, against which these same ministers railed from the pulpit. In one district in which I lived later, several children in school bore the surnames of their mothers and not their fathers. Yet these children were the mirror images of a certain parson who was known for his total ministry to his largely female congregation. It was legal from slavery days for children to take on the surnames of their mothers, which were really the surnames of their slave owners. After emancipation, the law permitted children to be registered with their fathers' surnames only if the fathers consented, in writing, to have their names given to the children that they sired out of Christian wedlock. Dishonourable men could deny paternity with impunity—only the stark resemblances revealed the truth of the denials. A child discovers much about the realities of life by observing adult deceit and hypocrisy.

In seeking out the historical bases for this sociological reality of "illigitimacy" and its psychological consequences, I found the historians Brian Moore's and Michele Johnson's book entitled *Neither Led nor Driven: Contesting British Cultural Imperialism in Jamaica, 1865–1920* (2004, 96–136) to be immensely informative. In their chapter "Sex, Marriage and Family: Attitudes and Policies," they give comprehensive coverage, including the attitudes and roles of the various denominations and powerful clergy in stifling change and thereby allowing the practice to continue without men taking responsibility for their paternity.

I must have arrived at Windsor Castle in late 1947. I began school some time in 1948 at the age of five. For days before the opening of school, there was much talk between my father, Miss Eu, and the casual farmhands about the threat of school that went something like this: "School soon open" (this was a warning that the carefree days would be over soon). "Oonu free papa soon bun" (your free paper will soon burn—an expression that was a carry-over from slavery days, when official papers were issued to black or brown persons who bought their freedom certifying their free status; a white person could simply burn the "free paper," as the folk called these certificates, and the person would revert to the status of slave). "Yuh gwan wid you mishavin, teacha a go fix yuh" (this was a reminder to children of the beatings that the teachers would mete out for misbehaving).

I overheard my father and Miss Eu discussing my age paper (birth certificate). My father insisted that she should send me to school without the age paper because the teacher would accept me because of who he was. In preparation, my father purchased some fabric and had my brother and sister suited out. I remember my brother's embarrassment that my father had had short pants made with braces that crossed in the back. These were not the khakis that most children wore. I still remember how odd my brother looked among his friends. I remember less about what I or my sister wore, although I do remember her getting into fist fights defending herself when the big boys pulled her long thick plaits of hair or when they mocked our name, Shorter. One of her eyes was noticeably smaller, and she was said to have a "cast eye." The boys would tease her and call her "cock-eye Sonia." Invariably, she would pounce on one of the offenders, grab his ears, and scratch with her fingernails until he surrendered, screaming. In these tussles, her bodice would rip from the skirt of her tunic, or frock, as girls' dresses were called. She would have to pull up her skirt and walk around holding it up until she got home, if no one had a safety pin to lend her to pin it up.

Going to school was an escape from the all-day drudgery of farm work into a misery of another kind. On the morning that I was to start school, I was awakened some time after the second cock-crow and sent with my brother and sister to fetch water to fill up the two large oil drums, before leaving to walk some three miles to school. I had to run much of the time in order to keep up with the older children. By the time I got to school, the shortness of breath caused by my asthma would have returned. It was usual for me to arrive at school out of breath, hot, sweaty, and tired. Miss Montcrieffe, my first teacher at the Carron Hall Infant School, would put me to sleep for the morning.

I remember Miss Montcrieffe as a dark-skinned, tall, and gentle woman. She did not instill fear in us. She was a gifted artist. The scenes from the storybooks from which she would read us stories covered the blackboard. She would tell us a selection of stories repeatedly until we knew them by heart—so much so that we would recite along with her or come in on the refrains with the actions. We loved these recitations. I huffed and puffed and blew the house of the three little pigs down so many times. My favourite Bible story was "Jonah in the Belly of the Whale." I felt happy, triumphant even, at the part of the story when Jonah escapes from the belly of the monster, of which I knew not. My favourite fairy tale was "Hansel and Gretel and the Wicked Stepmother." We learned to count with our fingers and acted out songs such as "Three crows sat upon a wall / And one crow accidentally fall / Two crows sat upon the wall," and so on. The nature walks were enchanting. By Jamaican standards, Carron Hall was cold and rainy, so sometimes we could not go out on nature walks. But when we did, the landscape was so green and lush with wild flowers, dandelions, broom weeds, daisies, chirping birds, crawling ants' nests, and lizards. Miss Montcrieffe showed us different kinds of trees, shrubs, and grasses as well as the different leaves, branches, and roots. I can still remember her telling us about tap roots, main roots, and adventitious roots among the vegetation. We watched some of the young boys who lived at the dairy take some cows to pasture, while others milked the cows and fed the calves. On our way back from the nature walks, we would dig up clumps of clay and take them back to our classroom. After lunch and our naps, we would create clay animals and scenes both from fairy tales and from our nature walks. I loved this activity for the kneading and shaping, but I just could not get my cow to look like a cow.

I have remembered the nature walks and the infant-school program with such vividness that I sought out and found my infant-school principal, who was in her late eighties, to ask her about the philosophy behind the infant-school program and, in particular, the nature walks. I quote from her letter:

> The Nature Walks and conversations triggered by observing the wonders of plant and animal world opened a child's curiosity to take in knowledge and added to perception of his surroundings, adding pleasure to his reading about things in books. That child, mastering reading at an early age was way above the mind bogged down with the mechanics of putting thoughts into writing and intelligent speech. I may not be putting this into the language of a University graduate but I am sure you will agree that your Nature Walks enriched your vocabulary. Shy children opened up to talk about things they collected. They knew that the grass family had roots that differed from the roots of a pea or bean, which they saw growing roots in a glass jar at the school window. They watched its growth and watched the leaves unfold each day. Letter sounds were taught at 4 years. "B"—bark of a tree; "R"—root; "P"—peas; "F"—fly; etc., rough, smooth etc. It was actually learning made easy, reading skills acquired without conscious effort, and, fun, not drudgery. If children with disabilities missed learning skills in infant school, they lost out at "Big School." (Personal correspondence, January 2003)

Miss Rose was another infant-school teacher whom I remember fondly. She must have been a middle-aged woman. I recall thinking that when we surrounded her, she looked like the mother hen in the "Mother Hen and Percy the Chick" stories that she read to us. She was a Christian and a holy lady who taught us to pray by kneeling and bowing our heads. She taught us to sing hymns and to learn Bible stories. Joseph's multi-coloured coat that she drew on the blackboard was so pretty that I wished that I had one like it. My best memory of Miss Rose was of her teaching us the hymn "All Things Bright and Beautiful." She taught us all of the stanzas of this hymn with the aid of beautiful scenes that she drew on the blackboard. I carry with me the memory of one particular scene that she drew of the purple-headed mountains with the rivers running by and a sunset in the garden that brightens up the sky. This has been my favourite hymn since that time—so much so that I chose it as one of the hymns to be sung at my son's wedding, some fifty years later. As I sang with the congregation, I remembered Miss Rose and Carron Hall.

In remembering Carron Hall, I go beyond the immediate school environs to include scenes from the cane fields that spread over several hundred acres—fields that together grew millions of sugar canes on either side of the main and parochial roads. On our way to and from school, we would watch and participate in the life cycle and work regime of the sugar cane. During the planting season, large numbers of bare-chested black men, with beads of sweat rolling down their backs, would dig cane holes with pitchforks and machetes. Women with baskets of cane tops on their heads, would walk along the rows, dropping cane tops beside the holes as they went. Another team of men would come along, sink the tops in the holes, and cover them up with earth. They would use their bare heels to fix the cane tops firmly in the holes. Rainwater would collect in the furrows along the cane rows. When the sugar cane grew to a height of several feet, it was weeded by women with their hoes, dressed in long skirts and straw hats. By Christmas time, the canes were very tall and in bloom. The leafy cane tops, bearing silky white and light purple arrows, swayed in the gentle northeast trade winds to make a soothing whistling sound. Mrs. Elliott described the fields as dancing. On moonlit nights, this atmosphere was a great backdrop for children to listen to duppy (ghost) stories.

When the sugar cane was ripe, men with sharp machetes and bills cut the canes—the music and rhythm of machetes zinging in the air and the men whistling or singing work songs. During harvesting, children delighted in volunteering to help men and women cane carriers transport bundles of sugar cane to the roadside. They were loaded in carts and trucks and taken to Gray's Inn, the large sugar factory close to the coast in St. Mary. After carrying six bundles of sugar cane, we would get to choose the biggest and juiciest candy stripe cane to eat on our way home. Little girls' cotton dresses would dry stiff with cane juice and dirt, our legs and arms would sustain small snips from the sharp edges of the cane leaves.

I cannot leave the landscape of Carron Hall and its environs without writing about the people of Hazard. The memory of the people of this place has haunted me all my life. I have returned so many times in my imagination and my nightmares to scenes of abject poverty etched in my mind. Who were these people? Where did they come from? In my readings of Jamaican history, I have tried to find the answer to the condition of the people of Hazard. Now I find I write about the people and this place in order to understand their hold on me.

My encounter with Hazard begins with what happened when my sister Sonia brought our father's Bible to her school, a King James Version. The Bible was a very expensive edition, bound with leather, and had pages as thin as rice paper. The lettering was ornate, especially the red and gold calligraphy at the beginning of each book. Placed throughout were portraits of Saul, David, Jesus, and other notable characters. Finger grooves helped the reader locate passages. At the back of the volume, family births and deaths were recorded. I can only imagine now that such a Bible brought her much attention and envy. As I grew older and felt the need to show off in school, I was to do similar things.

On our way home from school that day, Sonia stopped suddenly and exclaimed that the Bible was missing from her bag. We all ran back breathlessly to search. We had to recover it for, as sure as the sun sets, our father would miss the Bible and give us a "murderation." She and Trevor speculated who might have stolen it—this person must surely live in Hazard.

The three of us had to get to this place beyond the school, which lay in the opposite direction from home, before nightfall. We also had to give ourselves enough time to go from house to house to ask if they had seen the Bible. My sister had hoped that someone would confess and give it up or at least provide us with a hint of who had stolen it. For my part, I had begun to get the nervous stomach-ache that would come when I anticipated my father's wrath and his floggings. As I ran to keep up with Trevor and Sonia, I could feel my heart thumping against my chest and heard it pounding in my throat. The wheezing of my asthma started up again. I began to cry like a little puppy in distress.

As we got into Hazard, the sights of the people both scared and transfixed me. It was the first and last time that I beheld such a scene in Jamaica, and it has stayed and haunted me until now. I remember clusters of thatched-roof huts with bamboo wattle and mud-daubed sides in various degrees of decay. Small preschool children ran around naked in front of the yards. As they ran about rather lazily, the little boys' penises and distended testicles flopped about. These jet-black skinny children had big heads covered with red hair and protruding navels, which looked very strange. From a string around their necks hung a pendant cashew nut, and a dot of indigo blue was stamped on each of their foreheads. A few mothers sat under a shade tree nursing naked babies, while old women fanned fires under big iron pots set on three rocks. They must have been cooking their dinner.

One father who sat in the doorway of a hut smoking a pipe got up to find out what we wanted. His eyes were bloodshot and his teeth were yellow. My brother told him that we were looking for our father's Bible, which had been stolen from school that day. He mumbled an answer that I could not understand and glared at us angrily so that we knew we had insulted him. We knew also that we must leave Hazard or risk a beating. We never recovered the Bible, and our tyrannical father, devoid of Christian charity, beat us within an inch of our lives for having lost his precious book. This experience was one among many of my sister's various adventures—episodes that my brother and I usually paid for with a hiding. We saw her as our common enemy, an inveterate liar who dragged us into situations that were bound to antagonize the tyrant. My father himself called her the "stiff-necked wench."

I later had a chance to visit Hazard again under different circumstances. Eutedra's brother owned a cane piece there—a relatively small plot of land cultivated in sugar cane that is to be sold to the large sugar factory—and I went with her to visit him. Her brother lived at the foot of a mountain from which cascaded a waterfall. As the volumes of water rolled off the mountaintop, they sprayed big clouds of mist that came to settle in a big, beautiful, blue lagoon. A stream ran out of the lagoon and fed an amazingly deep blue hole, into which people dipped their calabashes for drinking water. The blue shimmering lagoon pulled me forward like a magnet. The place was spooky. My head began to spin. I must have been about to fall in, because someone pulled me roughly by the scruff of my neck and asked, "You wah fe drowned pickney?"

Over fifty years later, when I visited Mrs. Elliott, my infant-school principal, I asked her about the people of Hazard. Our conversation went as follows: "Mrs. Elliott, who were the people of Hazard?" "Oh! Those people were beyond the reach of the church. They cut themselves off, smoked pangola grass, and beat their drums all night." She elaborated: "They kept us awake with their drums. We knew when it was daybreak because the drums were quiet. Very few of their children came to the infant school. When they came they spoke a language that we could not understand." She told a story of holding a little girl in her arms all day, until her older brother came to get her. He had to translate that she was saying she was alone and lonely for her brother and parents. I asked: "What is pangola grass?" and she responded: "Pangola grass was a grass imported from the United States to feed dairy cattle and horses because it made the cows give good milk. Pangola likes the clay soils of Carron Hall and parts of Manchester." "So what did it have to do with the people of Hazard?" I probed. She answered: "They smoked the dry grass and hallucinated. When those people got high it took them days to come down."

I was aware that some poor black people shunned the church and smoked ganja, but I had never heard of pangola grass before. I knew of Guinea grass, which was grown in special pastures to feed the plantation cattle in pens attached to the big plantations. When Mrs. Elliott explained about the pangola grass, I suddenly recalled that there was a verdant, green pasture directly opposite the cluster of huts. Big fat brown cows roamed and grazed in the pastures in satiated bliss. Ticks sucked their blood, while black birds perched on their broad backs and, in turn, fed on the fat ticks.

I infer that the monetary worth of these people was no longer calculable in the plantation ledgers of old, alongside the steers, mules, ploughs, and wheelbarrows. Speculating that Carron Hall and Hazard must have been plantations, I referred to the survey of plantations in Jamaica during the eighteenth and nineteenth centuries drawn up by Barry Higman (1988). Its maps and plans suggest evidence of cattle pens and pastures, with many sugar-cane pieces around, and the waterfall would have offered a source of energy for a waterwheel as well as a supply of fresh water for people and cattle.

Small farmers grew ground provisions in yams, potatoes, and taro as well as other vegetables. The African workforce lived in kraals called Negro houses, which were located on the edge of the plantation. Confirmation that Hazard was indeed a plantation was found in the 1941–42 West Indies Year Book including also the Bermudas,

The Bahamas, British Guiana, and British Honduras (1941–47). In this book I found that Alfred and William Champagne owned the Hazard estate, which was listed each year until 1946–47, when it no longer appeared as an entry.

In a conversation with Evadne Sherrief, a schoolmate of my brother and sister in Carron Hall, I confirmed that the Champagne brothers still owned the cattle pasture at the time I had been at school in the area. According to Higman, it was common for the cultivation of pastures to continue after estate owners ceased to produce sugar. The cattle were then raised for beef and milk. The dismantling of the plantation's sugarcane crop explains, at least in part, the poverty of this area. Other factors could have included declining sugar prices, natural disasters, and the need to mechanize sugar-cane-growing operations. In the same parish, there was a move by the big banana export companies away from the production of sugar and towards the cultivation of bananas.

Who were these people who were beyond the reach of the big Presbyterian Church that dominated the area? I speculate that they were direct descendants of the Ibo people brought from the Guinea coast to work on the sugar plantations. They had become part of the human refuse that was created following the dismantling of the sugar estates that dominated the large tract of land encompassing Carron Hall, Donnington, Hazard, and Montreal—throwaway people, left in Negro huts to rot, their children malnourished and infected with yaws and chigga, their minds numbed by pangola grass, and their souls eased at least by the frantic beat of their ancestral drums. The drums must have preserved their spiritual language, spoken their joys, their sorrows, and their rage. The drumbeat must have spoken to them, and for them, calling out to their deities and their kin in the faraway Iboland, their motherland, and their home.

The people of Hazard must have been struggling against all odds to preserve their African identity and pride in an alien land. Their way of life had resisted the call of church bells, pipe organs, and triumphal hymns that hailed the greatness of European civilization.

While the missionaries of the Presbyterian Church rang bells, played the pipe organ, and sang hymns with their African converts, the so-called Biblical sons of Ham beat their drums to remind them of Africa and their forced exile. These were the holdouts. They had refused communion with those who had enslaved them.

I have tried to find out more about Carron Hall and, in particular, about the role of the Presbyterian mission after "emancipation" when the plantations and estates were abandoned. I am trying to understand the whole area with respect to the cane pieces and the sugar estates to which they supplied cane. The sugar-cane pieces and cattle stand out. John Stewart, writing in 1823, advised prospective planters that the four great desiderata in setting up a sugar plantation are: (1) goodness of soil, (2) easiness of access, (3) convenience of distance to the shipping place, and (4) a stream of water running through the premises. He advised that if there was not a naturally occurring stream running through the property, one should be created from a nearby source, to send down a supply. If such cannot be obtained, a well or a pond should be sunk to draw or be collected from. This passage helps me to sketch out more clearly my memory of a reservoir in Carron Hall as well as the Hazard falls and the lagoon below. I wonder if that deep blue hole into which the water of the lagoon ran was man-made or if it resulted from the natural erosion of the limestone of the area. Certainly, there were many concealed sinkholes into which cattle sometimes fell.

What do the details of the ruins of the landscape of Hazard and Carron Hall invite me to remember? The works by Higman on plantation and slave economy in Jamaica, as well as his extensive study on the Mont Pellier Plantation in Jamaica, are particularly instructive in trying to piece together the memories imprinted on this landscape when I attended Carron Hall Infant School. Several things come to mind. First, the number of cane pieces that were being worked and through which I passed to school is indicative of the small cane farmers who had to grow their cane and sell it to the Gray's Inn Factory to earn their livelihood. After emancipation and the wholesale desertion of unprofitable sugar estates, small farmers took up the job of raising the sugar cane to sell to the factories that continued to process the sugar-cane cane into unrefined sugar, molasses, and rum.

Second, judging from the number of cattle that I remember roaming close to the area, after the abandonment of the large sugar estates, the motive power of cattle was no longer needed. Some estate owners abandoned the planting of sugar cane and either sold the land or let it lie fallow. Other owners switched from raising draft animals to raising dairy and beef cattle for local consumption by those who could afford to buy the milk and beef. It was obvious that the people of Hazard could not afford to buy such products, so they seemed to have been in a state of malnutrition. Some of the cane pieces were converted into pasture of guinea and pangola grass in order to support larger herds of cattle.

As Higman points out, in the heyday of sugar production, cattle pens and sugar-cane plantations had a symbiotic relationship. The cattle pens reared the steers and oxen for the motive power that ran the mills and the drays and carts that transported the cane. When the plantations no longer needed the motive power of cattle, and cattle rearing needed relatively less labour, the cane labourers were rendered redundant. The dairy where young boys were being trained, which I saw during my nature walks with the infant school, seems to have been established by the Presbyterian Church, to train some young black boys to work with cattle. In our correspondence, Mrs. Elliot mentions that milk cans were collected to be taken to the Bybrook Milk Condensery for the manufacture of sweetened condensed milk. Like a curse, poor mothers fed this sweetened condensed milk to their children, not knowing that they were undernourishing their children. Another feature that Higman points to in his book Jamaica Surveyed is an area on the layout of the plantation called the Negro houses, the Negro village, or the Negro kraal. I surmise that the people of Hazard were perhaps the remnants of the people who lived in the Negro village adjoining the sugar plantation.

Another memory of slavery and emancipation evident in Carron Hall was the growing of a large variety of ground provisions: yams, sweet potatoes, cocoas, dasheens, coconuts, plantains, and bananas. It seems that these provision grounds were the only spheres of control for slaves, and they continued to flourish after emancipation as a way of providing sustenance and income. Those ex-slaves who could acquire land became peasant farmers. The Presbyterian Church capitalized on their abundance and hard work through the celebrations built around the church's harvest service and through community auction after the service.

As a little child attending the Carron Hall Infant School, I can remember going to the harvest services in the middle of the day. The little children had to huddle and sit quietly, while the minister and his choir walked triumphantly into the church and approached the church altar. The altar would be filled with the display of the best food grown by each farmer. I remember singing these words of a hymn: "Bringing in the sheaves, we shall come rejoicing, bringing in the sheaves." As I sang this hymn as a little infant-school child, I remember hearing "bringing in the sheep." I looked expectantly to see sheep following the procession, for there were no sheep that I ever saw in the neighbourhood. They did not bring in the sheep, and no sheep came. I understood that not everything said in church could be taken literally.

Another memory that became evident in Carron Hall is of the mission schools and the free village development that came after emancipation. The purpose of the missions was to "rescue" souls from sin and damnation and to "civilize" the illiterate poor. In fulfilling these goals, the missionaries taught their flock to read the Bible, to sign their names, to manage basic arithmetic, and to learn to farm. Obedience to authority was encouraged, and courtesy and personal deportment were stressed. Cleanliness was next to Godliness. It is beyond the scope of this study to examine the role of the missionaries, for credit or debit. It is sufficient to note that in post-emancipation Jamaica making a rapid, and even dangerous, transition from slave labour to farm and domestic labour, and requiring significant improvement in the hygienic conditions, missionaries were among the few influences that were in a position to effect change.

In this first real-life story, I have pieced together vivid memories of my early childhood years. I have taken the reader with me to engage with my family, the landscape of the sugar-cane fields, and the marginalized communities of black people. I have woven memory, a history of slavery, and the plantation economy in a fabric where each thread, if it ever could be unravelled, is a twisted yarn of many episodes. I have referred to other sources of literature and tried to find explanations for the features of the landscape in Carron Hall and Windsor Castle.

— *Chapter Two* —

Louisiana Blues,
circa 1950-54

❖❖·❖❖·❖·❖❖·❖ ❖·❖❖·❖ ❖❖·❖❖ ❖·❖·❖❖·❖ ❖·❖ ❖❖·❖ ❖❖·❖·❖❖·❖

EUTEDRA MUST HAVE GROWN TIRED of Cee's lying and bullying. She must have resented the way in which Cee brought his three children into her dwelling as if he had brought three gifts. For her purposes, the only way they could be gifts was if she could have worked his children like the pickney gang of slavery days. This proved to be difficult because Trevor and Sonia rebelled in every way that they could. Trevor exacted pay for milking the cows and transporting the milk pans to the roadside before the crack of dawn. He did so by pointing the cow's nipple into his mouth while he squeezed each of the four teats in turn. Only when he had his belly full of raw cow's milk did he point the teats into the bucket.

It was so early in the morning that I would say that we were sleepwalking in the cold and dew as we untied and herded at least three cows to the cowshed to milk them. The first cock would crow at approximately three o'clock and the second cock would crow at about five in the morning. As a reward for keeping him company on those early mornings, when we were awakened between the first and second cock-crow, Trevor would feed me my share of milk. But he also fed me so that I would keep his secret. Since the cowshed was located close to the drinking water spring, he would use the water, which he scooped up using the gourd that he was suppose to use to transfer the milk from the bucket to the milk pan, to pour into the milk and replace what we had drank. I, of course, had to swear to secrecy. This was difficult to do since I had been sent to watch over him.

The Bybrook Milk Condensery had been paying Eutedra Williams less than she expected. The reason that they gave her was that there was a high percentage of water in the milk. She accepted this explanation because, after all, she had been watering the milk before Cee's children arrived, and she continued to water her milk after Trevor started doing the milking. She must have gotten wise to the fact that Trevor was following her example because she began to test the milk for water by looking at how blue the milk was. Trevor and Miss Eu sometimes had loud arguments about the weak blue milk that he was bringing home in the milk pans. Trevor also had to make adjustments to accommodate Eutedra's need tò water the milk, so he drank less and put less water in the milk. In a situation such as this one, the folk would say: "Tief from tief God laff" (a thief steals from a thief and God laughs).

Eutedra was clearly not benefitting from our pickney labour. Sonia was too sickly to carry a load of dirty clothes to the river to scrub and bleach on the river rocks. She did not even have the strength to carry the produce on her head from the provision grounds. With any exertion at all, her heart would begin to palpitate. When this happened, she would shake all over until she was exhausted and turn white as if her heart had pumped all her blood out of her body. My brother and I were always afraid that her heart would stop beating and she would die. Since she was so frail, she often got away with beating up my brother and me.

My father said she was born with a weak heart. All of the bush medicine that my father had the obeah man concoct did not help her

My beloved brother, Trevor.

condition. Years later, with the benefit of education, I often wondered how much poison was being fed into the poor child's body. In those days, doctors were few, and folk medicines were the only cures for some illnesses. In addition to being sickly, Sonia was full of "back-chat" (to answer back daringly) and "lie and story" (tell a barefaced lie and tell a story that is untrue). There were times when Miss Eu swore at Sonia saying: "One day, de obeah man ah go tun yu mout back a yu."

I was too young to be of much use beyond sweeping the yard and carrying small pans of water. As small as those pans were, my assistance was helpful because Eutedra would not let us go off to school until we had filled three big tar drums of water for her cows and for her domestic use while we were at school. The tar drums full of water were perhaps the only things that she had to show from Cee. As well as being too young to be of much help, I was also prone to asthma attacks and fretfulness due to the heat, hard work, and long walk to school. I caught "fresh cold" from the dust and, no doubt, from sleep deprivation. I was further debilitated by the rounds of laxatives and purgatives I had to take to get rid of intestinal worms caused by drinking stagnant rainwater or pond water when the spring had dried.

Ultimately, Eutedra had a farm to run to make money for the independence she so loved. She did not need Cyril. Eutedra had no children of her own and had never been married up to that point in her life. Why should she put up with a violent unreliable drunkard and his three children? Although his children were of some use, two were sickly and the third was given to acts of sabotage. Raiding the best sugar canes and eating them was a favourite prank. Trevor would cut the fattest and sweetest purple-stripe cane and leave the leaf tops propped up to make it seem the cane was still there. Until the leaves began to wilt and turn brown, it would take days to discover that the canes were missing. Another trick of his was to make fires in the field and roast the choicest sweet potatoes and yams before he took home the basket full of ground provisions.

When I met him at Eutedra's, Trevor, who was age twelve, had already learned the art of loading donkeys and carrying loads on his head. Life was hard, and he lacked for affection and care. We lived and breathed sadness and distress. We ate far too much to earn our keep, and we were about to eat this lady out of house and land, as the folk would say. Where was our mother to protect us from such a wicked father and his exploitive paramour?

Cee would not change his wicked ways. As far as Cyril John Shorter was concerned, his manhood and his brown skin were enough for any woman to whom he took a fancy. However, his brown manhood was no competition for the ebony-skinned butcher who began to call on Miss Eu, bringing the choicest cuts of rump roasts. The folk called the butcher Maas Manny, for he was indeed a fine specimen of a man and probably made Cyril John see himself for the midget that he truly was. Cyril John could no longer impress Eutedra with his empty promises and drunken railings, which were aimed at intimidating his children to work harder to appease her. The children had a troublesome habit of being children. Children consume more than they produce, and Eutedra had no use for "parasites."

My father moved us to a place called Louisiana—to a very nice three-room house constructed of board, with three concrete steps leading to a wooden veranda. In every room, the house had sash windows, which opened and closed by cords sliding on a pulley. We delighted in pushing the windows up and down to open and close them. We were glad to leave the thatched hut behind. The floors were maroon red from the logwood dye that was used to stain them. (Women chipped the bark of the logwood trees that grew all around and boiled it in a special dye pot to extract this dye.) The shingle roof was a haven for the croaking lizards, which took on the colour of the shingles and crawled across the ceiling to catch moths and other night insects. I did not like them because they walked upside down across the roof. I was always afraid of them falling onto my bed. Surprisingly, they never did.

To one side of the house was a big oblong concrete barbecue, sectioned off into about eight sections. It was the kind of barbecue that had been used to dry either cocoa or coffee beans and pimento. There were very few blighted coffee and cocoa plants in the area by the time we got there. In fact, the only cocoa trees I saw were on Miss Eu's property. All around Lousiana, for acres on end, there were dwarfed, stunted sugar cane, which no one either planted or reaped. They simply grew new shoots from the old stock left in the ground, "ratooned," each growing season until the roots died off and the leaves turned brown, dried, and rotted. Only the children and the stray cows ate the remnants of these canes. The logwood trees were planted in abundance in the area, so that logwood bark could be chipped and exported to England, converted into dye crystals, and then brought back to the island and sold for dying floors, straw, and sisal for crafts. I was seeing, although I did not realize it at the time, a patchwork of failed cash crops.

Two gourd trees grew in the front yard. One stood to the left as you entered the gate and the other stood just to the right, a few feet away from the steps. My sister was always looking towards these gourd trees on moonshine nights and telling me that she had just seen our mother walking by. It was a great mystery to me because I never saw anyone and if it had been a ghost of our mother I would not have known how to recognize her. I still did not know "what's a mother."

An abandoned kitchen garden lay beside the barbecue. My father chose a spot close to a stream to plant his own kitchen garden. We were grateful for this because it shortened our trips to fetch water to water the plants when there was no rain. He planted black-eyed peas, red beans, cabbage, sweet potato, callaloo, tomatoes, and corn. Trevor, Sonia, and I used to raid our father's garden and pretend that it had been done by other people. We liked especially to raid the corn because he grew the corn to feed his pigs and various varieties of birds that he began to bring home. We enjoyed the taste and smell of roasted corn very much and resented the corn being fed to the animals. We could count on our sister Sonia to lie convincingly to allay our almighty father's suspicion.

At the back of the house was the outside kitchen with a fire hearth fitted with an iron grid set over sturdy rocks. My brother liked this fire hearth because he could cook with more than one pot at a time.

There was a wooden table and a wooden window, which was great for letting out the smoke. At some distance below the kitchen was the pit latrine, which the sanitary inspector came from time to time to inspect for cleanliness and to determine when a new pit was to be dug. I remember that the sanitary inspector was the butt of unsavoury pranks carried out by neighbours who seemed to have resented any government representative. The tax collector was another hated government representative who harassed the poor people for money that they did not have and who was alleged to appropriate the best of their ground provisions.

The house was located on the top of a knoll between the main road and the parochial road. The main road was downhill at the back of the house. The important part of the main road was the stretch that led from Windsor Castle, via Louisiana, the Old Post Road, to Rio Magno, where my father's head office was. On his way to do road work at Windsor Castle or Carron Hall, my father would sometimes drop off bunches of bananas at the foot of the hill on the side of the track leading up to the house. Every morning, Trevor, Sonia, and I had to walk along the track leading downhill from the back of the house, go passed the soursop tree and through the scrawny little sugar canes to get down to the main road. We would cross the road with our kerosene tins to fetch water from whichever spring had water still running from it. There was a little stream in the vicinity, and we would strip off our clothes and bathe, before returning with the pans of water to fill the tar drums.

We were spared the water-fetching chore when the rains came and fell heavily for days. The house had eavestroughs made of zinc, which were mounted along the front and back slopes of the roof and tilted slightly to one end, so that the rainwater could collect in the drums. It was fun when the rain clouds gathered and started to move in like a beaded curtain of raindrops. Sometimes thunder and lightning would also come. The thunder and lightning would scare the little kids who would run and hide under their beds. Adults, mostly women, would shout helter-skelter to the older children from all of the households in the neighbourhood: "Rain a come. Set out de drum dem. Put out de wash pan. Lawd! Tek up de close dem ahfa de line. Quick! Quick! Befo rain wet dem up. Shet de winda dem, ar else de rain a go blow een."

Opposite our house was a flourishing banana walk. The folk always talked about the good quality of the Lacatan and Robusta bananas. They bore six and seven hands of up to twelve fingers. I would overhear talk about the high prices that the United Fruit Company of New Jersey paid for the bananas if they passed the quality test when they reached Port Antonio. It was important for them to reach the port in perfect condition or else they would be rejected. Rejected bananas were sold off cheaply in the marketplace, and the banana producer would lose the profit. The bananas were therefore carefully reaped and transported. When the bananas were fit (but not yet ripe), the banana men would cut the bunches and pile them carefully by the roadside. They would also cut a lot of dried banana leaves before they severed the soft trunk of the tree from which they had cut the banana bunches. Cutting down the tree at this point permitted new banana plants to shoot from the roots. The dried banana leaves were laid out on the truck bed to form a soft pad. The banana bunches were then carefully placed on the bed of leaves in preparation for their transport to Port Antonio for sale to the big banana boats. The banana boats would transport them to markets in North America and Europe.

We children always curried favour with the banana men to see if they would give us a bunch of ripe bananas that were too ripe to be sent to the boats. They knew enough to be kind to us or else the big boys would simply raid the bananas at night. I remember vividly how Hurricane Charlie blew the whole banana walk flat and how the children raided the ripe bananas and the adults raided the green bunches. The overseers threatened to prosecute everyone for this theft.

There was a cow pasture that stretched from Windsor Castle to Louisiana, and it reminded me of those big fat brown cows at Hazard. There were always little boys driving the cows to water and to other grazing pastures. These boys were armed with slingshots. Birds followed the cattle to pick the ticks off their back, so the boys had a steady target of birds at which to shoot.

My father collected birds for food and sport. For food, he had a collection of leghorn fowls and Rhode Island reds. He claimed that they were the best laying fowls. In the mornings before he left for work, he would call up the fowls and throw out handfuls of corn or chopped up coconut. The birds' beaks would all converge on the grains in one mass of clucking feathers. My father would swoop down and catch a laying hen. Then he would hold the hen in his left hand and insert the middle finger of his right hand up the hen's anus. Years later, in my high school biology class I learned that the correct name for the orifice where my father had searched the laying hens was the cloaca, not the anus. The chicken struggled and squawked out loud and then my father would let her go. He repeated this feed, catch, feel-up-and-let-go routine with every laying hen. He would then announce to my brother and sister that he expected them to collect a set number of eggs—say, ten eggs. This meant that they had to follow the fowls stealthily while they ran around looking for a place to drop their eggs or else they would have to go around after school looking in all of the likely places in which the fowls would have scratched out a nest.

Sometimes the dogs would find the eggs first, leaving the empty shells as evidence that a fowl had laid her eggs. When my father built a fowl coop, it was easier because most of the hens would lay their eggs in the coop. I remember helping to collect the soft eggs that were still warm from the chicken's body. We would watch the shells harden in our hands. We had to outsmart the dogs, which had the same idea as we did about eating the eggs. When my father got home, one of the things he would check in military fashion was the number of eggs that we had collected. We would pay with our hides if we collected noticeably fewer eggs than our father expected.

Like the dogs, we also liked eating the eggs. Invariably, the chickens laid more than their quota, and my brother had a system of hiding the surplus until he had enough for a feast of eggs. It was my brother's job to cook the pigs' feed after dinner. He would boil the eggs at night with the pigs' feed. The feed consisted of corn and other leftover peelings cooked in salted water in a kerosene pan over a big wood fire. Trevor would put the eggs on the top of the pig feed, submerged enough to boil evenly. When they were boiled, he would fish them out with a large spoon. One night my sister discovered my brother's ploy. They made a deal to share the spoils, and Sonia promised not to tell on my brother. However, Trevor had no intention of sharing equally, and the two fought over their fair share. Two of the eggs got shoved to the bottom of the pigs' feed.

When my father went to feed the pigs in the morning, he upended the kerosene tin of food into the pigs' trough. Out rolled the hard-boiled eggs. Sonia and Trevor swore to my father that they did not know how the eggs got into the pan. My father asked: "Are you telling me that the fowls laid the eggs in the hot boiling tin at night after they had gone to roost?" At times such as these, my father spoke perfect lawyer English. They, of course, had no answer, and my father then descended on them with his belt, speedily pulled out of his pant loops.

Sonia pushed my brother in front to take the licks and took off to a neighbour's house for the night, leaving my father to curse and swear until he literally fell asleep. When he cursed her, he called her the little wench. When he was really vexed with her, he would call her the "little black wench." It was difficult to cheat after this exploit because my father would brook no error in his egg count, even when the chickens did not lay. This chicken and egg game was expanded to include the ducks, game hens, and pigeons.

For sport, my father brought home barble doves and baldpates. Once, he even brought home an ostrich egg and buried it in the sand to wait for it to hatch. It never did, and he was so disappointed and embarrassed that his bright idea had failed. The gamecocks had to suffer my father clipping their wings, beaks, and spurs. When he took his cocks to fight he would come home drunk and bloodied just like his cocks. Behind his back, we would laugh hard at his misfortune. We knew full well that if he caught us mocking him he would have no difficulty clipping our wings as he did his birds. Between the maintenance of the pigs and the ducks, we had to carry a lot of water before we went school in the mornings. When the sun was hot and the water was scarce, the ducks would wander away to find streams of water.

There was a Mr. Peart, who lived in the neighbourhood and who owned seven of the fiercest pit bulls. He could not afford to feed these dogs properly. He had them tied up most of the time, and they would bark and whine from hunger. They were so ferocious that children dared not tease them. We came home from school one day when we did not have a maid and found that Mr. Peart's dogs had eaten all of the ducks and drakes. There were duck feathers and blood everywhere.

My father blamed us for this occurence, refusing to believe that all of his ducks had been eaten. He speculated that they had followed the stream that they sometimes escaped to. It was about this time that my brother ran away from home, leaving my sister and me to cope with my father's wrath. Sonia and I searched for days and could not find the eaten ducks. Shortly after this incident, my sister also ran away. I was left alone in the house for an unknown amount of time. It seemed that my father had not shown up for some days. I walked back to find Miss Eu. She took me in essentially as her pickney field hand to help drop the cane tops for planting. I was about eleven years old at this time. I did not go back to school for what must have been months.

In my father's room was a double Simmons spring bed with a coir mattress—that is, a mattress stuffed with coconut fibre. I liked the nice mahogany vanity with the big round mirror and stool. I was fascinated by the mirror and would play with my image appearing and disappearing until I got ferocious headaches and then I would fall asleep. In the big drawers of the vanity were some elegant woman's blouses and skirts and a very special black vest. This ladies' vest had beautiful cloth loops and buttons spaced close together. My sister and I would dress up and play in the clothes and put them back neatly before our father staggered home to do a military inspection of our housekeeping.

The inspections were terrifying occasions because he was bound to find dust in some remote place or declare that the mats were laid at some angle that mattered only to him. Then he would proceed to examine the table, which we had set for his food. We had to be up to serve him when and at whatever time of night he chose to come home. The maids had usually gone home by the time he arrived. Again, some implement or dish would be found to be out of place. He would then start to question us about why this and why that. I would remain quiet, trembling from fear, and ready to relieve my bladder or bowels. My sister Sonia would talk back to daddy. She was "a bare face pickney." He would take her backchat as an affront and an outrage, and scenes such as the following would invariably follow.

DADDY: Why is the fork placed like that?
SONIA: Because you moved it, daddy.
DADDY: Are you calling me a liar?
SONIA: But, daddy, I saw you when you moved the fork.
DADDY: Girl, don't but me. I said, are you calling me a liar?
SONIA: No, daddy, but...

Daddy would start to flush red as a tomato. His eyes would swivel from side to side in rapid fire as he grabbed Sonia by the arm with his left hand while his right hand began to remove the heavy leather belt from his waist. All the while, daddy was unable to stand up straight and Sonia would take advantage of his drunken state with impunity. Sonia would try to get away by dragging him along as he staggered to stay on his feet. His breathing would speed up and he would exhale strong fumes of Captain Morgan rum, his favourite. He would manage to drop a few licks over Sonia's back, but they are too light to appease his rage. Besides, Sonia would always dress every night for bed in several layers of clothing to protect her skin from the blows. Daddy, knowing this, would come down as hard as his drunken aim allowed. He would grit his teeth as he looked at her with the fire of hatred in his eye. Sonia and Daddy would struggle for the upper hand.

His intention was to beat the daylights out of her, while hers was to get free and humiliate him. It was a battle between sober and drunken wills. On cue, I would cry out: "Daddy, daddy, don't lick her." My sensitive brother Trevor would stand by, calculating his own escape when Sonia had cornered Daddy strategically, giving Trevor time to grab me and run. Sonia would break loose and run, hollering to me: "Come, Yvonne!"

Thus defeated and humiliated, Daddy would hurl obscenities at my sister and warn my brother of the "murderation" (severe beating) that awaited him when he was caught: "You little black wench. You are 'facety' just like you black mumma." "You, Mister Trevor, wait until I catch you; I am going to bus' your ass." Even when we were safely at a distance, we could hear him cursing and swearing. Meanwhile, the three of us had to plan which neighbour we would have to ask to let us sleep for the night. The neighbours were usually accommodating because they were powerless to interfere directly in my father's abuse. Somehow they expected better of this red-skin man. Some of the mothers would cup their palms to their chin and mutter: "Missa Shaata gaan mad." Others would say: "Him a tek disadvantage a de poor dead ooman pickney dem."

In saying this, the folk were acknowledging a profound truth about Jamaican mothers. They would not stand by and tolerate anyone abusing their children—not even their father. Another truth is that the worst fate that could befall children in Jamaica is for their mothers to die before they "pass the worst," meaning the point when children were old enough to take care of themselves. Taking care of themselves meant having not only economic independence but also the ability to take care of their integrity enough not to let anyone violate it. Our mother died before we had passed the worst. Reading Lucille Mathurin-Mair's (1998) article on women field workers in Jamaica during slavery helped me to understand the protective tradition that black mothers inherited from slavery. When I was a child if you did not have your mother or grandmother to stand up for you, anyone could put you to work and treat you disrespectfully. Hence, the "dead woman pickney" was to be pitied.

Daddy had his morning routine. He would rise just after the second cockcrow, dress himself, then wash his face in the face basin that the maid set up for him the night before. He made lather from a special tablet of shaving soap, spread it all over his chin, and then scraped off the foam with a Gillette razor blade. Then he would shake some salt from the salt jar in his palm, dip his index finger in the salt, and rub his teeth and gums. He gulped a mouthful of water from the full glass sitting beside the water goblet and held his head up to gargle his throat, swishing the water around in his mouth and then spitting in the basin. He would repeat this several times. Then it was time to comb his hair. He used Palmolive Brilliantine, which was a green paste in a squat jar. He scooped some out with the index finger of his right hand, placed it into the palm of his left hand and rubbed the palms together before spreading it evenly over his mop of curly hair. By the time he finished combing with the fine-tooth end of the comb, his hair was one flat shiny skin drawn over his scalp. At one time, I loved my father's hair. That was when he thought I was cute and harmless, and he used to tickle me and throw me up above his head and look at me with love in his eyes. Then he allowed me to play in his hair and even to twist it into what I thought were plaits. They were not anything but great knots that he had to get out before he went to work the next morning.

As soon as I could talk back and ask questions that showed that I was becoming "too ripe," everything changed. I had become "the stiff-necked child," which was to say I had started to ask questions and demonstrate my ability to think logically and truthfully. This meant that he had to either beat things into or out of me, as he did with my brother and sister. For a short while, when we lived with Miss Eu, my father became my Daddy. This relationship of Daddy versus the brown man was never fixed or stable. It was like a seesaw. At approximately fourteen years of age, I disowned him so that I could take charge of my life and destiny.

On another night of terror, it was Trevor's turn to be picked on to explain some silly detail about the care of the stinking pigs in the pig-sty and whether their feed had been boiled and set aside. It was always his turn after Sonia's sassing, struggle, and escape. Sonia was always there to attack and defend her brother against the tyrant. When he got up, my father usually woke up my brother, so that he could make the fire, set the water to boil, and help feed the pigs. By the time Daddy had finished his ablutions, his coffee was boiled and ready to be filtered and strained through a cone-shaped coffee bag made of flannelette. When the coffee had boiled to the proper strength, Daddy would select a fire stick that had burned to charcoal and stick it into the pan of coffee to settle the coffee grounds. Then he would pour the coffee through the coffee bag to get a clear brew. This strong black coffee is all that he would have before he fed the pigs and left for work.

As soon as Daddy boarded the bus for work, shortly after the second cock-crow, we would start to do our chores of feeding the pigs, if Daddy had not done so, fetching water, and cooking our breakfast and lunch for school. The maid, when we had one, would come in after we left for school to wash and iron our clothes and to cook the evening meal. For a time, we still attended Carron Hall School while we lived in Louisiana. When we moved to Louisiana the distance to walk to Carron Hall School was much farther. To be there in time, we had to watch the position of the sun as it moved from east to west across the sky like a clock. When we trotted to school in the hot morning sun, we were constantly watching our shadow to see its length. As the shadow shortened, the time got closer to midday. If Trevor and Sonia were late for the big school, the headteacher would be waiting to drop licks with his strap or cane for being late.

The most intriguing thing in my father's room was a grey tin case, stored under his Simmons bed. I would pull it out and spend time exploring its contents. In this tin case were my favourite things. There were exercise books with double and single lines, children's storybooks, yellow lead pencils with rubbers on one end, purple indelible pencils, ABC books, and other papers. I would play for hours with the magic of the pencils and the rubber. I discovered the meaning of indelible by trying to erase my scrawling that was done with the indelible pencil. When I could not rub it out with the rubber, I applied my finger with my spit and discovered the pencil marks produced a purple inky mark. In time, the dye on my finger and tongue would let my father know that I was playing in the tin case. I cannot remember that it was ever cause for his anger.

My brother read me a story called Dick Whittington and His Cat, and he also showed me how to write my ABCs in the single-lined exercise books. As I learned to read, I read some of what was written in the exercise books. When I was studying to become a teacher, I had a flashback in which I recalled reading one of the lesson plans in one of these books, with certain sections underlined and headings such as "aims and apparatus," "introduction," "development," and "drill." I longed to return to the contents of this grey tin case to learn more— most of all to learn to whom this case belonged.

Living in Louisiana was filled with times of great terror because of my father's bad temper and his drunken violence. The event that marked the date of our arrival in Louisiana was Hurricane Charlie, which blew through in August 1951. I remember the hurricane very well. The sky turned black and red, the thunder rolled and clapped, the lightning flashed in rapid succession, and the rain clouds burst. The howling winds were, it seems, travelling at speeds between fifty and one hundred miles an hour. Branches of trees broke off and sailed into windows, smashing them. We were both excited and afraid. My father came home in a rush and covered the bureau mirrors and boarded up the windows. The sheets of zinc flew off the roof of our neighbours' houses and travelled like spinning plates through space. As the storm became fiercer, my father knelt down and prayed hard and begged God to save his house. I cannot remember him praying for us kids. He may very well have. On this occasion, he promised God solemnly that if He spared his life he would surrender his soul to Jesus. His life was indeed spared, but he never kept his promise to God. In fact, we never saw him pray again. For years afterward, however, the three of us had a wonderful time acting out our father's dramatic show of reverence and laughing at him cowering in the storm.

When we were in Louisiana, my brother, sister, and I got the blues often and thoroughly. At those times, my brother and sister would talk about Mamma, a person who still had no meaning for me. Trevor and Sonia then would break out singing popular songs. One of my brother's favourites was Nat King Cole's melody whose lyrics went: "Show me the river, take me across, wash all my troubles away, For the lucky old sun has nothing to do but roll around heaven all day." This song must have been for him the lament of a lost childhood—a childhood that revolved around work, not play. Another of my brother's favourite lines was: "Those far away places I have been reading about in a book that I took from my shelf." The three of us loved to sing Patty Page's "Cross Over the Bridge" and "How Much Is That Doggie in the Window." We knew nearly all songs by Nat King Cole and Patty Page. In his good mood, my father would sing to himself:

"South of the border, down Mexico way" and "We were waltzing together in a dreamy melody." He too must have had his longings and his sorrows. My father, my brother, and my sister knew my mother and were obviously conscious of her loss. I felt the loss too, but I did not know who or what I had lost.

Now, when I recall these times, I have to ask myself how we would have heard those songs when we had no radio, no concerts, and no choirs? The messenger was none other than Bernice, the smooth, ebony-skinned good-looking young woman who used to live with and work for Mr. Stewart. Mr. Stewart was a very proud upright black man, who owned a house and property. He was what Jamaicans call a "respectable black man." He had a provision ground with a lot of fruit trees: avocado pear, ackee, mango, soursop, yellow-heart breadfruit, lime, orange, and pimento. He planted an equally wide variety of ground provisions such as yams, cocoa, dasheens, and greens and had enough to sell to his neighbours. There was no marketplace close by, so he must have set up his own way of generating an income from his provision ground. I remember that my father would buy breadfruit and avocado pears from him. Bernice was neither Mr. Stewart's wife nor his servant, nor was she any relative of his. It seemed a unique relationship, wherein Bernice came and went as she pleased. I loved Bernice. I would cuddle up to her at every opportunity and stroke her skin and admire her thick eyebrows and solid white teeth.

Bernice was an adventurer. She met Babsy and Clara, two "boasy" (boastful) young black women who visited the yellow-skinned man named Eric in his little two-room house from time to time. Every one called him Eeric. Bobsy and Clara boasted to Bernice about life in Kingston working at the Myrtle Bank Hotel. Since I loved Bernice so much, I would follow her around like a puppy dog and listen to all of the conversations that were not whispered or communicated in gestures that I did not yet understand. Babsy and Clara regaled Bernice and all who would listen to their tales of bright lights, rich white sailors, lots of money, and fun with the sailors who just loved black girls. Poor yellow Eeric had a big sore foot and a heavy bandage that smelled "high," as the folk would say. He seemed to resent their boastful talk, and when they got on his nerves he would call them harlots, whores, and Jezebels. In turn, they would tell him to go and mind his syphilis. There was a time, during slavery days and for some time after, when these women would be called wenches and would be expected to kowtow to the likes of Eeric or risk a flogging with a cowhide or a tamarind whip. At least, they would have gotten a swift box in the mouth or on the jaw. Now, they could insult him with impunity, and he could do nothing about it.

Bernice must have seen great prospects for herself in these stories that Clara and Babsy told her because one day we found out that Bernice had packed her grip and left for Kingston. When she returned months later, she made a grand entrance as she disembarked from the Sunshine bus that plied the route from Carron Hall to Kingston. She was dressed in a lime green taffeta circular skirt with a see-through white nylon blouse revealing her bra and her slip. This outfit raised eyebrows and set tongues wagging among the older moral Christian women. I am uncertain of the effect on the young teenage boys such as my brother and his friends Barry and Eucal. The hem of the taffeta skirt swung with Bernice's gyrating hips and went swish, swish, swish as she strutted on her high-heeled shoes, and the skirt went left right, left right to the rhythm of her walk. She wore bangles and necklaces, and her hair was straightened and styled in an upsweep. Bernice had returned to the village as a glamour gal, as the folk would say.

My brother Trevor, my sister Sonia, and I loved the good times that we had when Bernice came back from Kingston because she brought back the latest songs and the latest dances. This one time that I remember, she brought back an exercise book in which she pasted all of the lyrics to the songs that she had cut out from the *Star* newspaper. She must have rehearsed them thoroughly because by the time she arrived back in Louisiana, she knew both the words and the tunes by heart. My brother especially loved this song: "Up in the morning, out on the job, work like the devil for my pay but the lucky old sun has nothing to do but roll around heaven all day." Bernice also taught us dances such as the yank.

She would bring fancy cigarettes such as Du Maurier, Winston, and Royal Blend, for Eeric. She would also bring him fancy liquors such as Johnny Walker whisky or Captain Morgan rum. These gifts gave Eeric something to boast about after Babsy and Clara left again for Kingston. Eeric would boast that he was the only man in the district who could afford to smoke "dem kinda cigarette" and drink Johnnie Walker whisky. I remember looking at the bottle and at the man on the label in the red pants, white shirt, and top hat and thinking that that must be Johnnie Walker.

While the girls stayed with Eeric, he would try to be fresh with them, and they would take turns to "trace" him. In slavery days when some people had uncertain lineage, especially on the father's side, given the prevalence of rape and concubinage on the estates, some people delighted in telling others that they were so and-so's bastard picknies. As such, they were a nobody and came from nowhere. In retort, the persons who so traced would attempt to describe their lineage to show that they had better pedigree than their aggressors, and the argument would thus go back and forth in an attempt to reduce each other to nonentities. This kind of quarrel could last for hours or even days.

I remember some of the things they said to Eeric: "Go wash yuh stinking sore foot." "Clear aaf wid yu syphilis." "Yu too stink feh anybady feh want yu." These insults were sure to make Eeric hopping mad. He would flail his arms up and down, right and left, as he chopped them into pieces with special Jamaica expletives and sexist put-downs such as harlot, whore, Jezebel, and Delilah. He would spit in the dust or spit at them, catch his breath, and start the insults all over again, reminding them of parts of their body which he said stank more than his sore foot.

How do I make sense of the relationship that Eeric, Babsy, Clara, and Bernice had? My guess is that Eeric was perhaps a pimp for Babsy and Clara at the Myrtle Bank Hotel before he contracted syphilis. Since there was no prospect of a good life for Bernice in the district of Louisiana, she must have joined Babsy and Clara in Kingston to become a prostitute herself. The Myrtle Bank Hotel up until the 1960s was the most famous big hotel that dominated Harbour Street on the wharf in Kingston. It was the hotel for the rich and famous who had landed on the island by United Fruit Company steamers or by cruise ships. Kingston and Port Royal, since the heyday of the buccaneers and the slave and sugar trades, were entrepots for trade with Britain and North and South America. During the First and Second World Wars, Jamaica was of strategic military importance for America. The hotel must have been one of the places where the American sailors and European businessmen came to stay.

In addition to my adoration for Bernice, I will always remember her for the gift of three plastic bowls, as I recall in yellow, green, and blue, that she brought for us on one of her visits. They were so beautiful, and she told us that she bought them especially for us to drink our porridge from. We made a big pot of cornmeal porridge, nicely spiced with brown sugar and nutmeg. When we dished out the porridge into the bowls, they flattened out like pancakes right before our very eyes. At first, we were horrified because our good porridge by this time could not be drunk. It was mixed with plastic, which smelled strange. After we got over the shock, we howled with laughter. I have told this story over and over about how the hot porridge melted the beautiful plastic bowls. I was never to see plastic again until the 1960s when Melmac and melamine plastic plates, bowls, cups, and saucers appeared on the scene. These were hard, could withstand heat, and melted only if they were placed in an open fire. Bernice and Eeric live on in my memory.

It was not only the people in Louisiana who stand out in my memory but also the antics of what the folk call the "country pickney"— children who would perhaps have never seen a city or whose life was circumscribed by the cycle of the cash crops—pimento, coffee, cocoa, and especially sugar canes.

Country children went to school in gangs, much like the pickney gangs of slavery days went to the cane fields. Then, the pickney gang was comprised of children ages six to fourteen who worked in the cane fields to weed and carry canes on their heads. Aggery Brown (1979) speaks of these children as going from the cane fields to the classrooms. It is interesting that the schools they went to were only for that age group.

The pickney gang on their way to Mango Walk All-Age School would listen for the groaning engine of overloaded cane trucks and wait in ambush at the foot of the hill, ready to hop a truck and pull a cane.* On approaching a hill, the driver of the British Leyland or Fargo engine would gear up and accelerate to take the hill with a force to overcome the gravity of the load as it ascended the hill. The sugar canes were laid horizontally on the truck bed and tightly packed some eight feet high and perhaps as wide. I estimate that the truck bed was some ten to twelve feet long. As soon as the truck began to labour on the hill, one boy would shout, "Hap aan." Another would command, "Pull a cane." Then dozens of little "wooligans," as the folk would say, would descend on the ascending truck whizzing, sputtering, and firing to clear the hill with its sugary load intact. The first one to pull would aim for a cane or two in the dead centre and pull and run out of the way. In pulling the cane, it would loosen the tight pack and before long, the sugar canes on the ascending truck would come cascading down the hill. The rest of the wooligans would descend like vultures onto dead meat, grabbing the fattest sugar canes and skittering away faster than a mongoose. Thus relieved of his load of sugar cane, the driver would glide up the hill quickly, park the truck, get out, hands flailing, and utter a trail of Jamaican expletives. Along with these curses would come insults about "dem wutliss mumma" and the worst put-down of all, which was to be called "no-good black naygas."

---

* The name Mango Walk All-Age School is a pseudonym chosen by the author.

Without knowing it, the school picknies had taken their revenge on the sugar cane. It was for this sweet crop that their foremothers and forefathers had tasted the bitterness of exile and slavery on the sugar plantations. In the bush, their incisors peeled the canes and their molars did just as good a job as the sugar mills in grinding out the juice. By the time these boys got to school, their teeth were shining and their thirst was quenched. They had enough sugar in their blood to keep them energetic for hours.

Any driver who had the wooligans hop his truck and pull his canes was in deep trouble. The sugar factory to which he was carrying the canes had an insatiable appetite for grinding the canes round the clock. The sugar factories depended on the small farmers to grow the canes and provide a constant supply to meet their manufacturing quota. Both the farmer and the driver had the responsibility of delivering several hundredweights of sugar cane.* Arriving at the sugar factory with a load lighter than intended would be sure to raise the wrath of the "busha," the white man in charge of productivity at the sugar factory. At the top of the hill, many drivers would draw their brakes, get out of the trucks, and curse "de lickle thief dem." They would surely "pap dem neck if dem couda catch dem. But dem gaan like de bloody rat dem."

Sometimes there were disastrous consequences for the little wooligans when the cane fell too fast and pinned some of them under the weight. There were other times when the driver, expecting the ambush, would accelerate as soon as he saw them through his rear-view mirror. This sudden speed would sometimes shake the little boys off the truck, and their heads would hit the asphalt as they fell. There were a few times when little boys fell to their death. Such was the life of a "poor country pickney." Such was the scene during crop time—county children walking through cane pieces to school, their lives

---

* In British imperial weights and measures, which were used in the sugar-cane industry, one hundredweight equals 112 pounds, and 20 hundredweights equal one ton.

dominated by the cycles of sugar-cane planting, weeding, fertilizing, cutting, loading, and transporting to the sugar mills.

In 1951, after Hurricane Charlie, my father registered Trevor, Sonia, and me at the Mango Walk All-Age School. Virgil Bullock (pseudonym) was the headteacher of Mango Walk All-Age School. He had a reputation that preceded him. The people said he was a good disciplinarian. Many respectable parents felt good in handing over their children to his discipline. My father had full confidence in him. They were friends of a sort.

Mango Walk All-Age School was situated on a hill on the bank of a major river, right in the fork where a tributary joined the mainstream of the river on the other side. The landscape in the area was terraced, and at this spot there were three terraces rising from the riverbank in order to prevent the soil from eroding during the heavy rains. The playground was on the terrace closest to the river, along with the school garden plots. The schoolhouse was located on the second terrace, and on the uppermost terrace was the teacher's cottage, where the headteacher and his wife lived. Each of these locations has special memories that both delight and haunt me.

The playground was like a brown plateau of clay and sand. Dancing and skipping feet of boys and girls had ground the earth into dust. The wind blew this dust into our eyes, on our books, and into the classrooms. The dust turned to mud when it rained. The big boys and girls played complicated quadrille clapping games with up to sixteen squares. I remember watching them clapping, singing, and changing places, observing how a couple could end up at the opposite end of where they had started and then make their way back. I loved to watch the grace and precision of the dancers. I especially loved the ring game "Jane and Louisa will soon come into this beautiful garden." This singing and clapping ring game was like a mating ritual. Troublesome little boys and girls would watch the dance to figure out which big boy liked which big girl. We would giggle with delight that we had figured out their secrets. The big boys and big girls played this game during the morning and evening recesses as long as the dry season lasted.

The little boys would stake out a corner to play "marble and ta" or "marble and cashew." They would have loud arguments about who "tief de game" or who could play "real bad," meaning skilfully. The pockets in their khaki short pants were always weighted down with lots of glass marbles and a few of the coveted expensive steel marbles, called steelies. Winning steelies in the game of marbles was prestige personified. "Me win de mos steelies mon" was the victory cry at the end of the game, when the cussed school bell rang.

The little boys lived to play marbles and to run their wheels to school. The wheels were either tireless old bicycle wheels or barrel hoops pushed from behind with a long-handled wire hoop shaped somewhat like a tennis racket and bent back to cradle the arc of the wheel. The barrel hoops were more common because the boys could get them from the shopkeepers after they had sold all of the pickled mackerel, shad, and red herring that were shipped in from Newfoundland and New Brunswick. Old bicycle wheels were really hard to come by. The bicycle had not yet replaced the humble shanks pony or the donkey as transportation. The idea was to push this wheel continuously while you increased your running speed. It was a pleasure to push the wheel over the "nylon road," which was the smooth road of new asphalt. Gravel roads such as the short cuts were a nuisance. In order to get around the bumps and potholes, you had to slow your speed and interrupt your concentration.

While the little boys played their marbles, the little girls would occupy another corner of the terrace to jump rope, which was commonly called skipping. They cut large "withies" from the big overhanging branches of some of the big flowering trees growing nearby. The trees could have been the beloved poinciana. These "withies" were nature's rope. They grew in many widths and lengths. I loved the old man's beard and the love-bushes, which also hung alongside the "withies." These hung like tinsel on a giant Christmas tree. At infant school, I had learned that these were adventitious roots. I delighted in the way this big word used up all of my mouth to pronounce.

We skipped alone, in twos, or in groups. The group skipping was the most fun. We skipped over large "withies" swung by two strong girls. It was fun to have a group of twenty girls running and jostling to skip in and out of the swinging rope. We played such games as "Room for rent, apply within, when I run out you run in." This was a great game of turn taking, which required agile strength and skills in high jump to "jump over the moon" on the upward swing of the "withie" without being caught in the rope. If the rope caught you, besides getting a bruise from its blow, you annoyed those whose rhythm you broke and those waiting with concentrated aim to jump in before the bell rang. Those waiting their turn would shout "Pepper!" With this command, the rope swingers would swing so fast that the unwary child would be tripped and pushed out. A fresh lot would crowd in quickly before the rope started swinging again. All of the little bodies would tune into each other in order to establish and keep the rhythm unbroken for as long as they could.

The really aggressive girls would not take their leave without a fight. The fight would start in this way. One girl, usually older than most, would put on an ugly scowl, stand astride the rope with her arms folded tightly, and declare: "Me nah go no whey. If anybody tink dem bad, dem cyaan come tek me out." This would spoil the game for everyone, and invariably she would meet her match by another virago, who would haul her out by her frock waist. One day, this ritual took an embarrassing turn when one of the bullies insisted on jumping in out of turn. She waited until the rope was about to clear its maximum height on the upward swing, and she jumped with all her might, cleared the rope, and landed in time. Everyone gasped and shouted in unison: "Lawd gad, Hartense baggie drop offa har!" While we all howled with laughter, Hortense stepped out of her baggies (underwear), picked them up and ran to the toilet with them in hand. A bunch of us ran behind Hortense to the toilet. We had to see if she was wearing elastic or string baggies. No self-respecting girl of a certain age wanted to wear open-leg calico baggies tied at the waist with a string. Every girl boasted that she wore the new style, jersey, elastic-waist panties, whether she was wearing them or not. It became a game to creep up stealthily behind a boastful girl and quickly lift up her dress to show everyone what kind of baggies she was wearing. The boys would join in this embarrassing game too.

At the next round of skipping we would be fighting, jostling, and quarrelling about who should go first this time and whose turn it was to swing the rope. I was too puny and short to be a swinger. This was the only yard game that I was welcome to play since I was no good at softball or at catchball.

On the same level as the playground, a little further up the river, were the garden plots assigned to each class. Each class in the school had to cultivate a garden plot. Instead of going for nature walks as I did at infant school, I was taught to be a farm labourer in the school gardens. When I was in "A" class, I learned to dig holes, plant red beans correctly, fetch water from the river to water them, watch the beans grow, and harvest them at the right time. All of this activity was done under the teacher's supervision.

On the next terrace going further up the hill from the playground was the schoolhouse. Somewhere between the back of the school-house and the garden plot were the boys' and girls' pit latrines and a zinc lean-to urinal for the boys. After one of Virgil Bulloch's "mur-derations" of the big boys (a very violent beating, within an inch of the child's life), they would go behind the lean-to and peel off the bloodied shirts that stuck to their backs and compare weals, black and blue blotches, and lacerations. My brother Trevor was among the big boys who suffered from these contusions and lacerations.

I would only go to the latrines when my bladder was about to burst or if I had to empty my bowels without delay. The stench of urine and faeces made me feel nauseous, but I could hold my nose or my breath long enough to get my business done. It was the smiling lizards with the multicoloured bulbous jowls crawling stealthily on the toilet seat and walls that kept me holding my belly and doing a dance outside the door, until they were out of sight. When the lizards were out of the way, I had to face the brown cockroaches that were seen running around when I looked into the pit. What is more, I was scared of falling into the pit in trying to crouch on the seats. One never sat on those seats. When flush toilets came to my home in the fifties, I thought they were the best invention. I am still scared of pit latrines, even in campsites.

In the front of the schoolyard was a gravel playground that skinned many of the knees of baseball runners and catchball players. On the concrete steps leading into each division, girls played jacks. These were not the commercial jacks sets. We made our own, composed of ten pebbles and a lime scalded in hot water to make it bounce like the rubber jacks ball. In the front yard facing the main road, the boys and girls would play baseball with coconut-frond bats and hard rubber balls.

There were a few shade trees under which some classes were kept during the dry hot weather. Reading and singing lessons for the junior grades were often conducted under the shade of a tree. When classes were held under the trees, some boys had to transport the blackboard and easel as well as the teacher's chair. The girls would take along the box of chalk and the duster. The teacher would take along her book and her tamarind or guava switch or leather strap. Children in the lower divisions would carry their slates and pencils and reading books. The middle division classes would take their Caribbean Readers, Book One, Two, or Three, along with their double-lined exercise books and lead pencils. The Nesfield's Grammar Book was the standard grammar text used by all of the teachers.

At the very top of the hill was the teacher's cottage, where the headmaster and his wife lived. Fields of Guinea grass grew on the surrounding hillside, in abundance to feed the cattle. When the Guinea grass grew to maturity, it hid the cottage from sight of the school. Part of our learning to labour was to pull up these grasses when they dried. On the selected afternoons, the whole school was let out like the "pickney gang" of slavery to root up and bundle the grass. I never knew whose horse or cow it was reaped for. I do remember rooting up these grasses, which were much taller than I was. They were so deeply rooted that it took two or three little ones pulling together downhill with the full weight of our little bodies to dislodge them. Usually we would be sent rolling down the hill with the clump of grass when we managed to uproot it. At such times, we would be indecently exposed because we had no hands free to keep our skirts down. When our sweat mixed with the grass on our skin, we itched and scratched so hard that the skin on our arms and legs bled.

Just past the front of the school was a ford over which motor vehicles could cross the river during the dry season. A wooden footbridge built some distance from the ford allowed pedestrians to cross at all times unless there was a flood that washed out the bridge. When the heavy rains came and the river was in spate, the water would rise like a sea tide up the terrace. We would be dismissed early at the first sign of the river rising. During the rainy season, we sometimes stayed away from school for days until the river subsided. Virgil Bullock would issue a stern warning to stay away from the river when it rained. One day, he had to haul a boy who had disobeyed his orders out of the swift turbulent flood. Virgil Bullock did not let the boy free until he flogged him over his back in his wet shirt. I daresay the boy may have wished that he had been left to drown.

As I think back to the schoolhouse and recall some of the teaching that went on there, I hesitate. The memory of it brings back some of the fear to which we children were subjected. I recall the physical layout of the school. It was one big open room divided into three equal spaces each separated by a step. At the lower end was the lower division, where A, B, and C classes were held. The next step up was the middle division, where first, second, and third class sat. From there, the next step up took you to the upper division, where the fourth, fifth, and sixth class were. Virgil Bullock's desk was placed on a dais in the centre of the upper division from where he could overlook everything. He was in charge of standard six, and his sweet wife was in charge of standard five.

The founders probably named the school for the abundance and variety of mangoes grown in the surrounding villages. Children loved the mango season. The higglers brought hampers full of mangoes loaded on donkeys to sell at recess and lunchtime. There were many varieties of mangoes: number eleven, milly, black mango, hairy mango, kidney mango, and Julie mango, to name just a few. I now wonder if this place was an experimental station for the mangoes brought from Mauritius to Jamaica in 1782, when Lord Rodney stole them from a French ship taking seedlings to the French West Indies.

The children played tricks with the vendors. We would eat half of a really good mango, then take the black node of the stem and sink it in the flesh and return the mango half eaten, claiming it had worms. The vendors were glad to give us fresh mangoes to replace the "wormy ones" until they got wise to our tricks. When they caught us, they would punish us by limiting our choice to the puniest fruit.

Those children who were given lunch money bought their lunch at the gates or went out to the Post Road village centre to buy from the shops. The "flaa-flaa" (codfish fritters) sellers came with their glass case full of annatto-coloured salt-fish fritters and fried dumplings. For sweets, they sold grater cake and drops. These were not as good as Mrs. Phipps's jackass corn (hard coconut biscuits). The jackass corn that Mrs. Phipps made were so hard that they were a challenge to chew and could dislocate jaws or shake teeth loose.

Virgil Bullock and my father shared many beliefs about child rearing. In this respect, I had two fathers. They believed that they could get children to learn by beating things into and out of them. Children should be made to fear them. Like the patriarchs of the Old Testament, they did not believe in sparing the rod and spoiling the child. I was beaten a lot, and I learned to fear both Virgil Bullock and my father equally. The good book admonished parents in these words: "Train the child in the way he should grow and when he is old he will not depart from it." When I was old enough, I departed from much of this brutal upbringing. They also believed that children were twigs to be bent because as the adage says: "As the twig is bent so the tree inclines." They must have been unmindful of trees, such as the guava tree, which would not incline as their twigs were bent. I was as obstinate and resilient to bend as the guava tree limbs that I tried to bend to get the sweetest guavas at the top of the tree. "Children must be seen and not heard." "Children must only speak when they are spoken to." "Children must be kept occupied and useful; the devil finds work for idle hands." I learned to be useful in whatever way garnered praise and spared me the wrath of the adults who raised me.

Under this child-rearing regime, I learned to fear male adults and stern females in authority. I looked and listened hard because I should be seen and not heard. As a consequence, I believe I became an acute observer of human behaviour. With my father, this keen observation sometimes saved me from a licking because I was able to observe the subtle changes in his mood and facial muscles and predict his behaviour. With this sixth sense, I could anticipate what was coming and was sometimes able to disarm his hostility.

I often wondered how the female teachers could be so docile. I could not tell what these teachers thought about Virgil Bullock. He seemed to have bullied them into silence and submission. Only his wife's face gave her feeling away. She always had a merciful look for any child being victimized and a "cut-eye" for her husband when he was not looking to show her disdain. I came to learn that adults did not betray each other by criticizing people in authority in front of children. They closed ranks to uphold blind obedience to authority figures such as headteachers, parents, elders, and parsons. They would even uphold and imitate cruel and unfair treatment of their children by the Virgil Bullocks of the community. The folk held Virgil Bullock in very high esteem. So much so, that when he died they gave him a hero's funeral and eulogized him as a man of upstanding character and an outstanding teacher. In their words, "the community has lost a strong disciplinarian." I must have been in teachers' college when he died. For my part, God had finally answered my prayers and taken the tormentor of children away.

As a child, I understood a disciplinarian to be like my father, someone who instilled fear. A disciplinarian was someone who could make your heart beat in your throat in his presence; someone who made you want to empty your bladder and bowel when you heard his voice coming; someone who made your knees knock as you trembled with fear; and someone who caused your palm to sweat and your skin to go cold and clammy. This is how I remember Virgil Bullock. At school, he was the lone raging bull in a pasture of calves and heifers. Instead of horns, this two-legged bull charged with canes, straps, and switches. The silver-tipped cane and leather straps were part of the educational equipment that the Department of Education supplied to all headteachers, together with regulations on how to strap and cane. The folk alleged that some power-crazed headteachers augmented the regulation width of the strap with their own made-to-order lengths and widths. These were designed to meet the challenges of any big boy who they believed needed to be shown who was the boss man. Certain big boys were designated to maintain the supply of tamarind switches, which teachers and headteachers used or kept on their desks to deter the chatterboxes and the skylarkers. There were no plantation pen keepers to tame the bull or to put a ring in his nose and lead him to a bullpen.

As if his arsenal were not enough, Virgil Bullock never hesitated to box someone from cheek to cheek with either the back of his hand or his open palm. His sole reason for being in this school seemed to be to bully the female teachers and the pupils and to bust the flesh and "whale" the children's backs. The big boys most feared the silver-tipped grey cane. They would go to great lengths to destroy it. The most well-known sabotage was to break into Virgil Bullock's desk and use a sharp knife to score invisible rings at regular intervals. When he dropped licks, as the boys would say, the cane would break in many places and lose its tensile strength to deliver a painful blow.

One day, I witnessed an episode that is etched in my memory, even fifty years later, for its abominable cruelty. Virgil Bullock called a boy from the middle division up to his desk one afternoon because he saw this boy talking or, more likely, moving his lips after he had commanded silence from the whole school. This act of speech was an enormous challenge to his authority. For when Virgil Bullock banged the cane on his desk to get everyone's attention and bellowed "Silence!" no one talked until he or she was called upon to answer one of his general knowledge questions or, worse yet, to give the answer to one of his mental arithmetic sums. Sometimes after ordering silence, he would cast a roving eye throughout the school to see that no one was speaking. Woe betide the child he saw even moving his lips. It was on one such occasion that he caught the boy either talking or just moving his lips. In order to avoid a beating for getting the wrong answer, children coped by whispering the answers to each other. In so doing, they reduced the incidents of terror and anguish. They saved their skins, literally.

This particular boy victim was wearing short pants, as was the custom for boys under twelve, I believe. As soon as the boy came up to him trembling, Virgil Bullock grabbed him by his pant waist and heaved him up off the ground. So tight were his pants drawn up that the seam sharply divided and exposed his two buttocks just the way Virgil Bullock liked to prepare them for the blows.

I can only imagine the pain that this "draping up" caused to the boy's testicles and what damage may have been done. As Virgil Bullock took the cane in hand, the boy struggled to get away, begging: "Do, teacha no lick me. Me na do it again." Virgil Bullock was deaf to the child's plea and apparently unsympathetic to the pain he was already inflicting with the draped up pants. He must have known he was causing great pain—after all, they both shared a similar anatomy. As he raised his arm to strike the child, the boy let out a blood-curdling scream in anticipation of the sting on his bottom. Virgil Bullock snorted and struck down hard. The cane crackled to pieces as it hit the boy's buttocks. We held our breath, torn between horror and comedy. Without missing a beat and still gripping the boy by the pant waist, Virgil Bullock pulled the boy along as he reached into his desk drawer for the skinniest strap. He pelted the boy harder with every scream. The big boys alleged that the skinny strap was soaked in urine to increase its weight to deliver the worst sting. Virgil Bullock let go of the boy when his own face turned red like a big tomato and he began to pant like a tired bull. His sweat gathered in beads of water on his forehead. He grabbed his handkerchief out of his trousers pocket and mopped up the sweat. By this time, his big fat bull neck, with veins bulging and throbbing, ballooned over his white shirt collar and necktie. The amazing thing is that the whole school sat in an uneasy silence and watched the spectacle of this raging bull "murdering" a child.

After such episodes of "murderation," the big boys and big girls would hold a verbal post-mortem, a palaver, out of Virgil Bullock's earshot. It would be time "fe tek bad tings mek laff." They would improvise a drama, which I now see would follow three acts. The first act would recreate "how Big Boy late de teacha man," meaning how the big boys beat Virgil Bullock at his bullying tricks. In this act, the big boys would enact how they believed the big boy broke into the school, picked the lock on the teacher's desk, took out the cane, and screwed it. They would demonstrate the careful way in which the cane would be laid down, just as it was found, would be done with great finesse. At this time, the audience would laugh and clap while exclaiming: "Yes mon, de bwoy dem late teacha, good good."

Act two would begin when the role play turned to the draping up and beating. There were no shortages of volunteer actors willing to play the bull and the bull-bucking scenes with frightening accuracy but with a difference. No one would actually drape up any boy, only pretend to do so. To the mock screams and pleas for mercy, there would begin hissing of teeth and shaking of heads and looks of recognition when someone said: "Teacha tek disadvantage of de likkle bway." Someone would shout: "Teacher so bex im beat de bwoy til im neckstring naly bus." Another would follow with: "Ah how come de teacha man so wicked?" This comment would herald a change of mood from humour to outrage.

The need for retribution and revenge could only be expressed in words. The powerless children could only imagine what they would have done to address this brutality. Act three would follow when different child actors began to shout: "If ah coulda, ah would ah jump up an grab teacha by im seed and drag im aafa de platfaam." Another child would pipe up: "Me woulda jump back ah im an lick im in ah im neck back." Then another: "Ah woulda give 'im a tump ina 'im sola plexus." Still another: "Ah would ah trow a rock stone in ah im winda."

After this palaver, the children would scatter in all directions to return home to their humble abodes to ponder in silent loneliness all of the brutality that they had experienced. If some of them dared to tell their parents who had blind obedience to authority, their parents would turn on them and beat them, saying that the headteacher was right. Sometimes though, a fiercely protective mother had been known to go to the school to confront the headteacher. She would go to the door closest to the head-teacher's desk and call him out. He and the whole school would rather try to ignore her presence than go out to address her. The headteacher certainly knew better. If he did address her, he would run the risk of being pulled out the door and draped up by the virago. She would trace him loudly and ignominiously until she was tired. To top it off, before she departed, she would stick her head in the door and make two promises. She would either set obeah on him or tell him that she would ambush him and return the beating if he ever set foot in her village.

In re-enacting this episode, the children would come to realize the trauma of such gratuitous violence. Although they were powerless to do anything at the time, in their imagination they had verbalized what they would have done if they could. I cannot help but recall victimized powerless folk in the village calculating opportunities for revenge and wishing for divine retribution on the mighty. I wonder now what that little boy and others like him grew up to be. Have they drowned their repressed anger and pain in rum? Do they live in a state of displaced rage? Have they become abusive husbands and fathers? Have they become disciplinarians like Virgil Bullock, who taught them so well by example? Judging by the men in my family, I can answer yes to all of those questions.

Sadly, my brother whom I expected not to repeat the sins of his father grew up to physically abuse his children. I too am guilty of repeating the pattern. When I became a mom and started to beat my children, I flashed back to the agony of my childhood and relived the pain in my body and saw the horror in my children's faces. It devastated me to realize that I was beginning to do the very thing I vowed not to do my children. I locked myself in the bathroom and cried my heart out at the horrible spectre. I obtained counselling with the help of my family doctor. I broke the cycle.

Virgil Bullock did not spare the girls. I was one of the victims of one of his mass beatings. It was not unusual for Virgil Bullock to line up a whole class or even the whole school and beat every single child. Indeed, I had a doomsday of my own—one that I shall describe shortly.

Sanitary conditions at Mango Walk All-Age School were deplorable. It must surely have been one of the condemned school buildings described in the West India Royal Commission Report (1945). The report, which was also called the Moyne Report, was a result of an inquiry into the social conditions in the British West Indies. The sanitary conditions at our school were very bad. I caught head lice, worms, chigger, and yaws while in attendance. My father had to delouse my sister, brother, and me with dirty black engine oil. When he combed the engine oil through our hair, the lice would fall out by the dozens. The white nits or eggs stood out and were destroyed by squeezing them between the two thumbnails. Picking head lice was a ritual shared between women and children. In school, I remember watching lice crawl along the collar of girls sitting in front of me. When the lice bit me on my scalp, I would sometimes scratch and catch some lice between my fingers and place them between the pages of my reading book. I would wait for them to crawl out from between the pages.

One day as I was watching the lice crawl out and not paying attention, the teacher came over and whacked me across my back several times with a tamarind switch. I both feared and hated that teacher. I think her name was Miss Lewis. She is the one who sat me in front of her, with my back towards her, and got me to read aloud from my Caribbean Reader. I remember that I was reading fluently until I came across the word "imagine." I sounded it out as "imagain." The word was barely out of my mouth when I felt the pelting on my calves. She shouted "Imagine!" while she beat my calves with her cane.

Worms of all sorts were common, picked up from contaminated water and mud. Intestinal worms came from drinking impure water. Of these, the Guinea worm or "negro worm," was the most serious. It manifested itself on the scalp in rings the size of a sixpence. It was also the hardest to get rid of. Medicine to get rid of intestinal worms was regularly given both at home and by public health nurses at special clinics in the districts. Hookworms would enter the soles and between the toes when we walked in the mud after the rains and cause ground itch. Hoofed animals also got the ground itch from the mud during the rainy season. The surface of the toes and between the toes would itch so badly that we would scratch until the toes bled. Hot poultices were used to treat the feet in the hope that the worms would fall out. I remember how badly my toes would itch and how I would scream when the hot poultice was applied. With this home remedy, it was believed that the hotter it was the better.

Chigger or jigger was transported to Jamaica with the enslaved Africans. It was an insect infestation in people who walked in their bare feet. The shoes that I brought with me from my Aunt Joyce were well worn. Everything was done to extend their life. The shoe toes were cut with a razor blade so that my toes could hang out. The backs were also cut to accommodate the protruding heels. The rock stones of the gravel roads bored holes in the soles. When there was no way of extending the life of the shoes, I went to school barefooted just like all of the other children. Our soles developed thick calluses that had the appearance of the inside of a grater from walking on gravel. Most poor children went to school without shoes and therefore caught chigger. Chigger flies would lay their eggs in the sole of the foot, between the toes and especially around the nails. This malady is said to have caused most of the general infirmities of Negroes during slavery days. Infestations could also cause deformity of the toes and feet. Children who were badly infected walked on their heels or hopped on the side of their feet.

My father was good at picking "chigga" from my toes with needles that he sterilized with a burning match. The chiggers appeared to me like a tiny head of garlic encased in a thin transparent sack that took on the colour of the soles and white skin between the toes and at their base. Only the tiny black head helped to identify where the chigger was located. My father said he had to dig out the sack whole. According to him, if the sack burst the chigger would grow again. To be sure he got it all, he would squeeze the infected areas until bleeding occurred. Then he would disinfect the areas with Jeyes' fluid. The pain was inflicted relentlessly. When I squirmed and whimpered, he would tell me that if I did not stop my crying he would give me something to cry about. By this response, he meant that he would either box my face or remove his belt and strap me. At times like these, my father may just as well have cut my vocal cords. He would not have to hear my screams, and he could have inflicted as much pain as he liked.

When my father was not delousing our hair, or picking chiggers, he was breaking the blisters and washing the sores caused by yaws. All I can say about my father's treatment of the yaws sores was that he used the methods of a plantation veterinarian, until he had no choice but to arrange for me to go to the drugstore some ten miles away to get injections in my hip. It took five such painful injections to cure. Although the sores dried up, traces are still in my blood. I cannot donate blood to the blood bank, even after a second set of antibiotics, which I took when I was in college. During routine medical tests I had to take before entering college, the nurse got my blood test back and thought I had something more terrible than yaws.

According to Richard Dunn in his book Sugar and Slaves (1972), "yaws, clinically similar to syphilis, was a common affliction among the slaves on the English islands. The repulsive skin ulcers characteristic of yaws could develop into bone lesions and destroy or deform the nose, lips, hands, and feet." No wonder the college nurse was so alarmed and concerned about my blood test results. Luckily, my doctor had studied tropical medicine and ascertained that I had yaws when I was a child. Besides the trace of yaws that still exists in my blood, I have a three-inch square scar below my left ankle. This lesion caused me to walk on my toes until the five injections cured the yaws. Thankfully, the blisters on my face and body left no scars.

In addition to these maladies, there was pink eye and the perennial fresh cold, which we contracted from the heat and dust. When the cold ripened, and we had to blow our nose the girls used their dress tails for handkerchiefs in which to blow the awful green goop that tickled our throats and tied up our chests.

Rat bats lived in the roof of the school. When the children arrived in the mornings, the rat bats would fly away to come back when the children left in the afternoons. In addition, Hurricane Charlie must also have done damage to the building for, some time around 1953 or 1954, construction for a new school began some distance away from the old school. The children who lived close to the construction area came to school one morning to describe in fantastic terms how a caterpillar was knocking down trees and uprooting them with just a touch. Now there was only one caterpillar that I knew. It was the one we put in a bottle at infant school and watched as it turned into a butterfly. So you see, I had to go and see how a caterpillar could do this great magical thing. My head was filled with the magic of fairytales. At Carron Hall Infant School, I learned and loved such tales as the Wicked Step Mother, Hansel and Gretel, Billy Goat Gruff, Three Little Pigs, and Little Red Riding Hood. I loved the world of fantasy. With such a miserable childhood, I could imagine families in which I wished to live. In my fantasies, I could love, hate, laugh, grieve, and control the forces of oppression that were incomprehensible to me.

To our amazement, it was not the sort of caterpillar we were expecting. It turned out to be a bulldozer that felled the trees and with its great big jaws picked them up and moved them to the side. A large number of us forgot time since we were so intrigued. When someone looked around and saw his shadow lengthen in the afternoon sun, he hollered: "Lawd Gad we late." With this realization, we would pick up our feet and run as fast as we could to get back to school. We would wish we could erase our shadow. When we arrived, Virgil Bullock had all of the doors locked, except the front door before which he lined up all the latecomers to beat. The line was long. Virgil Bullock was shouting and dropping licks while he watched our every move lest any one of us tried to escape. If we escaped that day, we would have got the licking the next day because the attendance was taken in the mornings and afternoons. Those who were missing in the afternoon would surely be called up in the morning to get their dose of punishment.

I thought that I could use my smallness to outsmart Virgil Bullock by crawling swiftly on my hands and knees past him while he was busy dropping licks. I managed to get under the long desk, which ten to twelve children shared. I wormed my way to my space on the overcrowded long bench. My seatmates would shift their little bottoms to keep me out. If they had let me onto my seat, then one of the children who had come early would not have had a seat for the rest of the afternoon. In the pushing and shoving to secure a space to shuffle into, my seatmates would laugh out loud. This drew Virgil Bullock's attention, and he paused to look at what was happening. Just as I raised my head to see if it was all clear to slip onto my seat, our eyes met.

His response was like a bull running at a red flag: "Come here, Shorter girl: You think you are smart. I am going to show you who is smart." With this said, he grabbed me by the hand and dragged me out over the top of the bodies of my seatmates, dropped me to the ground at the same time that he struck me several times in quick succession across my back. I can still feel the stings on my back and the sensation of warm water running between legs. When I looked down, I was standing in a pool of my own urine rising between my toes. By this time, I was going to school in bare feet since I had worn out the shoes that I had brought with me from My Aunt Joyce. My flesh stung all over. My cotton baggies were cold and uncomfortable to sit in for the afternoon on the bench. When I got up a wet mark showed on the wooden bench. The wet baggie chafed my skin by the time I walked the three miles home. On the walk home, the children jeered and called me "the pissing tail gal." The teasing and name calling stuck for as long as I attended that school, much to my lifelong humiliation. The new wales across my back just added to the old ones, which my father had delivered perhaps the night before to vent his drunken rage.

I stayed away from school for days. Instead of going to school when I left home in the mornings, I would take unsupervised nature walks by myself along the secondary road leading to the school. I would hang out in the mango and rose apple trees and watch the big tree lizards blow up their bright orange and yellow balloons to attract the smaller lizards that they would pounce on, grab, and wrap themselves around. Later in life, I learned that this was the mating ritual of lizards. I always felt sorry for the little lizards because I thought they were being beaten up. I most feared the green lizards with the saws on their backs. They were as green as the leaves among which they lived and caught their prey. I was so fascinated with lizards that I would spend a day following their movement in the trees and on the ground. I was so excited when I found out that lizards laid eggs. They did not build nests like the chickens but, instead, burrowed into the sandy soil and laid their eggs in there. As I did with chicken eggs, I broke some of the eggs to let out the baby lizards. Bird's nests were another fascination. I would watch the mother bird feed her young and raid the nests and take the baby birds home. The mother bird never failed to find her babies and demand them back. Some birds were so fierce that they would pick at me with their beaks. When my shadow told me it was afternoon, I would walk home as if I had come from school. I had no mother to check on me.

School life at Mango Walk All-Age School was hell. It was in direct contrast to Carron Hall. The time following lunch was the most terrifying at the school. This was the time when Virgil Bullock either led the whole school in singing or in general knowledge—important subjects in the curriculum. I cannot recall any musical instrument, not even the piano, which seemed to be in all of the schools. We practised a lot of "doh-rayme-fah-soh-lah-tee-doh" before we were taught a song. Of course, I saw no relation between these endless scales and the lyrics that were to be sung. Having us sing rounds was interesting to me. A regular one was:

Kookaburra sits on the old gum tree.
Merry, merry King of the woods is he.
Laugh Kookaburra, laugh Kookaburra laugh
King of the woods is he.

Virgil Bullock would count to three, after which the lower division would start. At the end of the first line, he would bring in the middle division with a wave of his hand, and finally the upper division would come in with the first line. When the whole school had sung this round in perfect harmony, Virgil Bullock would bring the singing to a sudden halt.

The year was 1952. The telegram man had arrived at the school and rang his bicycle bell at the gate. The telegram man always brought news of death from afar. Virgil Bullock went out and came back with an envelope. He brought the whole school to a standstill. He told us that he had just had very sad news. We were told that King George VI had died. He pointed to the picture of this white man that hung on the wall of the upper division looking down on all of us. Virgil Bullock told us that we had been the king's subjects and now that he was dead we were henceforth to be his daughter's subjects. His daughter's name was Elizabeth, and since there was a Queen Elizabeth the First this queen would be Queen Elizabeth the Second. He then introduced the whole school to the Latin word regnum. It meant reign and that the queen's title will be EIIR. This then turned into one of his famous general knowledge sessions. Virgil Bullock asked the whole school to tell him what EIIR meant. There was a long pause—no one put up their hand. He went strutting from division to division piercing our brains with clues to get the right answers. In a rare moment of generosity, Virgil Bullock parsed the E, then the II, and then the R, imagining that we would be able to put it together more easily. This parsing and cajoling for the recognition of this royal title must have gone on forever. He finally had to capitulate and tell us what EIIR meant. It meant, he said, Elizabeth the Second reigns. Thereafter, the whole school plunged into a preparation for the queen's coronation the following year. I remember the whole school practising "I vow to thee my country" and "Rule Britannia" for Queen Elizabeth the Second's coronation in 1953.

Some children, including my sister, went on an outing to the coronation to join in the mass choir of school children that were taken from all over the island to sing these anthems in Sabina Park in Kingston. The rest of us got to go to Carron Hall for a local ceremony where we lined up in military fashion and sang both of these songs and joined in the "hip hip hoorah" to the queen. "God save our gracious Queen" replaced "God save our King." After this ceremony in the hot noon-day sun, we drank lemonade, and all of the adults and children were given a little aluminum cup, in pink or green, with the queen's face on one side and EIIR on the other, which we were told was her insignia. From that day forth, the symbols of the king began to be replaced by those of the queen.

The new free issue exercise books, which children in the All-Age schools got, bore the queen's portrait on the front cover and the tables of imperial measures on the back cover. The official government stationery said "On Her Majesty's Service" instead of "On His Majesty's Service." Some time soon after, a portrait of the queen and Prince Philip replaced the king's portrait. This portrait was to stare at me in every school I attended until independence in 1962, when these symbols of empire were replaced by the local governor general and prime ministers.

At the age of ten, this whole fuss about the queen left me puzzled and worried about my sister who had gone off to the coronation on the school outing without my father's permission. I had to carry the horrible burden of knowing about the scheme to deceive my father. My sister plotted every step with precision. She asked permission to go to the coronation. My father flatly refused, and so my sister ignored him and resolved to go without his permission. She knew that she needed a new dress and shoes and socks to go. She also needed a packed lunch and pocket money to buy aerated water and a snowball, the latter being a concoction of shaved ice and syrup that was a must in the heat of Kingston. She waited until my father's payday when he would come home drunk either with his pockets empty of money or unaware of how much money he had. When he was sound asleep, she took down his pants hanging on a nail on the door and took out most of the money that he had.

She performed this routine several times during the year of preparation so that she could acquire all that she needed including the truck fare. She bought some light blue rayon fabric and red rickrack braid to make her dress herself. She was then thirteen years old, had passed her first Jamaica local examination, and had the reputation of being "bright." She was also, in my opinion, very talented. She learned to sew at the Friday classes at the Practical Training Centre when she attended Carron Hall All-Age School. She learned how to hand sew because there were no sewing machines and the girls were taught to be useful with their hands. I saw my sister lay out the fabric on the floor and cut out the dress with my father's razor blades. She backstitched the whole dress together and trimmed the frock tail and sleeves with the red rickrack braid. She also bought herself a pair of shoes.

On the morning of the coronation, my sister got up at the first cockcrow and quietly snuck out of the house before my father knew what had happened. He thought she had diligently gone to fetch water as we were supposed to be doing so early in the morning. By the second cockcrow, he would be getting up to ready himself for work. My father realized that she was gone only when he came home from work and could not find her. I think either my brother or I confessed the secret that we had known for months. I remember distinctly asking my sister what she would do when Daddy found out and her answer had been: "I will just take the licking."

I could not comprehend her response, since Daddy's beating for being outsmarted was a "murderation." In her indomitable style, she would reply: "What no cost life, no cost nuttin" (What does not cost life does not cost anything). I remember these lines to this day at times when I am feeling cowardly. This attitude of courage in the face of danger is one of the many gifts I received from my sister, even though it was this very attitude that eventually cost her her life.

After the coronation was over, we began to prepare for the opening of the new school, which was to open in a few months. We had to practise "Bless this house, oh lord, we pray / make it safe by night and day / bless the roof and benches all / let thy peace lie overall" for the opening. I was not around when this finally happened.

There were turbulent times at home, and my schooling was interrupted for I do not know how long. As I mentioned earlier, both my brother and sister ran away from Louisiana, leaving me alone to face complete abandonment. I knew the way to Miss Eu, so I went to her. She really had no space or time for me in her life. She had scaled down her farming and was getting ready to marry a Mr. Ellis who had just bought a big house on Spanish Town Road. This place was so big that I think it was a tavern and lodging. It had a sign that read "Western Sports Park Tavern and Lodging." A Chinese family with about six grown daughters lived upstairs, and an older Chinese man kept a grocery store downstairs. When she moved from Windsor Castle to her new residence on Spanish Town Road, Miss Eu carried me along. She suited me out with some new clothes. I attended her wedding, which was held in the tavern.

I was so unhappy and lonely there. The scenes in front of the tavern kept my senses alive. I would stand by the windows facing the busy Spanish Town Road. On one side, I would watch the motor vehicle examination depot where learner drivers knocked over the drums during their test drive. On the other side of the examination depot was a grass yard and an open-air market. This market sold mostly charcoal and ground provisions. The market trucks, which came in on Thursday nights loaded down with produce, heralded three days of hustle and bustle among mostly black people who were loud in their hawking and selling. The fisher woman with her pushcart filled with fresh fish on ice would push along, crying with a nasal pitch: "Feesh, fresh feesh. Dacta fish. Buy yuh dacta feesh, parat feesh an goat feesh. Buy yuh feesh, me wih scale it feh yuh." She had a hand scale and knife ready. The sea was close to this spot. Handcart drivers snaked around speeding trucks and cars, while the drays loaded down with grass plodded along, oblivious to the dangers that surrounded them. The drivers of the city and the country buses sped by, depending on their horns to avoid knocking down jaywalkers. School children dressed in uniforms that were a rainbow of colours milled around in the morning to wait for buses to take them to school. Donkey milk carts and bread trucks were part of this pedestrian, quadruped, and motor traffic that spewed exhaust and smoke.

Huge flatbed trucks carrying stainless steel cylinders roared by with such power that all vehicular traffic gave them the right of way.

On the sides of the cylinders was the legend "J. Wray & Nephew Ltd, Distillers and Blenders since 1825, Monymusk Limited." Only many years later did I learn that these cylinders were filled with rum from the Monymusk, Clarendon, and Frome, Westmoreland, distilleries. They were bound for the ships at the Kingston wharf. From there, they would be shipped to England to supply the British Navy. This rum trade between Britain and Jamaica was to last for some three hundred years. The trade came to an end only in the 1970s with the decline of the British Navy and the end of the sailors' rum ration.

Other scenes at this busy intersection of Spanish Town Road and Waltham Park Road remind me that there must have been a significant Chinese presence in this area. I have already mentioned that the tavern, when Miss Eu and her husband bought it, had Chinese people living in it. Behind the tavern on the Waltham Park Road was a shop and dwelling in which a Chinese family of three lived. The son who was about my age went to a private school. Every morning, he would join the long line of little uniformed Chinese children who were waiting for the "chi-chi" buses to go to school somewhere in Kingston. On Saturday mornings, this same group lined up to catch the bus to Chinese school. A few times, my curiosity drew me to follow the elaborate Chinese funeral motorcades to the Chinese cemetery that was located some distance up on Waltham Park Road. White, gold, and red colours on the grand, ornate tombstones stand out in my memory.

Nailed to the wall of every house and business in this area was a rediffusion box that was never turned off while the Radio Jamaica and Rediffusion (RJR) network went on and off the air. I spent a lot of time close to this box trying to figure out the mystery of the voices in it. At first when I heard the voices, I would try to talk back and was quite puzzled that the voices could be so near and yet not be able to talk back to me. I was so fascinated that I tried to pry the box off the wall to find the people inside the box. I was caught before I could accomplish the task. RJR played the latest American tunes and broadcast American radio dramas such as Doctor Paul and Life Can

Be Beautiful. A voice would say: "It is twelve o'clock and it is time for Doctor Paul." There would be an endless stream of jingles advertising detergents, washing soaps, toilet soaps, alcoholic beverages, aerated water, and travel dates of passenger boats leaving for Southampton, England. These jingles were brought to listeners courtesy of such names as Unilever Limited, Procter and Gamble, and Canada Dry.

Miss Eu enrolled me at Greenwich Town Elementary School, which was located just behind the examination depot. I missed my brother and sister so much that I think I almost went mad. At school, I discovered a girl around my own age that had the same last name as me who lived at 2A East Avenue, the address to which my brother Trevor had run away and left my sister and me. He used to write to my sister from this address. In time, I discovered that indeed my brother lived with her family. Her father, Uncle Tom, was my father's first cousin, which would have made this girl my second cousin. I do not remember her name now, but I did follow her home one day in order to visit my brother.

Trevor and I were both so surprised to see each other again. He was living with Uncle Tom and learning the carpenter and cabinetmaking trade as a kind of apprentice. I wanted to stay with my brother, but there was not enough room in Uncle Tom's house, and he telephoned my Aunt Emily (Auntie Black) to come and take me back to May Pen. It was the first time that I had ever seen anyone using a telephone and talking through a mouthpiece and a wire. Uncle Tom was a contractor and carpenter—a real businessman. Mr. Black, Aunt Emily's husband, my uncle-in-law picked me up from Uncle Tom's house. He was quite friendly with me. I sort of liked him because he dressed well, drove a car, and spoke to me politely. I grew to like him more as he praised me for being such a useful child, for, indeed, by the time I was twelve I had learned to labour. The year was 1955.

— *Chapter Three* —

Life and Schooling in May Pen, circa 1955–62

✥✥✥✥✥✥✥✥✥✥✥✥✥✥✥✥✥✥✥✥✥✥✥✥✥✥✥✥

I CAME BACK TO MAY PEN IN 1955, some eight years after that unhappy day when my father snatched me away. Some of the old places remained, some were new, and others were gone. I recognized several buildings instantly. These were the places that my Aunt Joyce would have taken me to or were the places that would have been the subject of overheard conversations. I recognized the May Pen Market, Shagoury's Haberdashery, the Hardware Store, and Mr. Black's grocery store. Mr. Levine's Dry Goods Store, which had been next to Mr. Black's, was gone. I missed seeing Mr. Levine again. He used to give me sweeties and talk to me when I was little and accompanied my aunt on her outings to buy cloth, trimmings, and notions for her dressmaking.

Philip Young's supermarket was new. This Chinese merchant family also had a cloth shop on Main Street. In these premises, he made the finest *bullah* cakes. At lunchtime, those of us who did not spend our lunch money in the soup kitchen went to the supermarket to buy *bullah* and cheese. My friends and I used to sneak behind the store and watch the bare-chested black men, skin glistening with sweat, who were mixing and kneading together the big bags of flour, baking soda, ginger, sugar, and molasses. We would gasp and exclaim that we would never eat Philip Young's bullah cakes when we saw the men wipe the sweat from their forehead with their index finger and shake it into the dough. Of course, during the avocado pear season, we would forget about this and buy the *bullahs* because they were the best-tasting cakes to eat with avocado pear for lunch. When the pears were out of season, *bullah* cake and New Zealand cheddar cheese was eaten instead. This lowly *bullah* cake was sold for about a penny. It was about the diameter of an old-style singles record, about one inch thick, and looked and tasted somewhat like ginger bread.

I watched Mr. Black quarrel about how Philip Young was squeezing him out of business. His supermarket was glamorous, and the prices were lower than Mr. Black's. Shoppers could help themselves and not wait to be served as they had to when shopping in Mr. Black's shop. At the supermarket, some shoppers thought they could literally help themselves and not pay. Mr. Black, who allowed his customers credit, was left with unpaid debts as many of his customers switched to buying with cash from Philip Young's supermarket, which did not carry credit. There was a section of the supermarket that carried such items as foreign dolls, cameras, sets of fancy hairbrushes and combs, and small mirrors. Although Mr. Black struggled to stay in the grocery business until the mid-1960s, he was among the last of the small grocers. His heyday was in the late forties and early fifties when the market people could buy their salt provision, sugar, condensed milk, and Milo (an instant chocolate powder) after they had sold their ground provisions in the market. In those days, people bought groceries on credit.

Storks De Roux's Hardware Store seemed to cater to the wealthy few. At Christmas time, he created a Toyland in his store. The windup trucks and cars intrigued the boys, while the girls loved the blonde and auburn-haired dolls with their pretty clothes. Toyland brought toys from a white world far away in England and America. I always wondered who bought these toys because none of my friends' parents could afford to buy them. They were simply unaffordable. We assumed that Mr. De Roux, a white man, must have sold the toys to the other rich white families who lived and worked on the nearby sugar estates of Sevens, Yarmouth, and Monymusk as well as those who worked for the Sharp Citrus Company. At lunchtime, we children would literally swarm the Toyland to play with all of the toys. Mr. De Roux would get mad and have his sales clerks call us little thieves and chase us out disgracefully. We took to going into the store in smaller numbers and made less noise as we wound up fewer toys.

In terms of hardware sales, the Shagoury Hardware Store that was almost next door drew more customers. I think these Syrian owners were better sales people who mixed with the folk and bargained with them. I believe they even sold on credit to trustworthy folk. The De Rouxes were regarded as aloof and hoity-toity and were never seen mingling with the common folk.

Lubsey's Drug Store on Main Street was new and trendy, carrying a wider assortment of drugs and toiletries than the old drugstore on Baugh Street. This drug store carried cosmetics and all sorts of feminine products. Lubsey's Drug Store was where the moneyed people shopped. Poor people stood outside and looked in at the attractive displays.

Places that would have been there when I first lived there as a baby were the two banks—Barclays Bank, Dominion, Colonial and Overseas and the Bank of Nova Scotia—the police station and the jailhouse, the

Clarendon Theatre, and the Texaco and Esso gas stations. I have memories of the Clarendon Theatre. My Aunt Joyce used to go to "picchas" and talk about the film stars. The most troubling memory I have of the Clarendon Theatre is of a neighbour named Allan, who loved to go to see the moving pictures of "cowboys and Indians" but who would invariably have an epileptic fit while he was watching. Someone would bring him home, frothing at the mouth with his tongue all mangled. The next day, everyone would be down on him to stop going to "de piccha show."

I ask myself now why there would have been a movie house in this city during the 1940s. My best guess is that there was a movie-going population drawn from an American army base in Vernam Field, which was located about twenty miles to the south, not far from the West Indies Sugar Company. May Pen was, and still is, the capital of the parish of Clarendon, where all of the institutions that served the many sugar estates were located. The Clarendon Theatre became a place of enchantment for my sister. She dragged me along to see such epics as *The Ten Commandments, Ben-Hur, The Robe, South Pacific, Samson and Delilah,* and *Seven Brides for Seven Brothers.*

Boys would watch the westerns and re-enact scenes of gun battles between cowboys and Indians. They would also collect cards with pictures of their favourite film stars. I would overhear the boys discussing the acting abilities of actors such as Howard Keel, David Niven, Charlton Heston, and Yul Brynner. Sometime around 1960, the new Capri Theatre opened, and the old theatre was demolished. When I worked in the bank, I would go on paydays to see movies at the Capri Theatre with friends. We would sit in the open-air balcony where the most prestigious seats were. Couples could be observed necking in this semi-private part of the theatre.

Of all the old places, the May Pen Market and the associated grass yard held particular fascination for me. When I was a babe in May Pen, I was not taken to the market. I lived cloistered behind the grass yard commons. I returned to find that the market was still there as the centre of petty trading from Thursday evening until Saturday night. It was situated on a triangular plot of land bounded by three roads. The market was huge. On one side of the triangle was Main Street, which ran east to Kingston and west to Montego Bay. May Pen is situated on the banks of the Rio Minho, which is right in the middle of the route from Kingston to Montego Bay. It is said to have been a resting place for horse-and-buggy traffic in the early days of settlement.

According to Olive Senior in her *Encyclopedia of Jamaican Heritage* (2003), May Pen was once a sugar estate named for its owner, the Reverend William May, who was rector of Kingston Parish church for some thirty-two years. The "Pen" part of the name indicates that a cattle pen was attached to the estate. Since cattle were a necessary part of the sugar production, cattle pens were as important as the cane fields and the sugar mill. Cattle were used for transportation, to turn the sugar mills, to provide manure, and to provide meat for eating.

May Pen became the capital of Clarendon, where a large number of sugar estates are located. I remember a few of the names of these estates: West Indies Sugar Company, Monymusk Limited, Yarmouth, Halse Hall, Sevens Sugar Estate, Longville, Suttons and Danks. May Pen was the commercial centre for all of these sugar companies as well as for the Sharp Citrus Company.

In front of the main gate of the market was a wide parking lot where the buses and trucks stopped on their way to and from Kingston and other places. On the other side of the triangle, travelling north to south, Sevens Road forked from Main Street, leading to the Sevens Sugar Estate. Muir Park Road joined Sevens Road due east at the corner that divided the elementary school from the market along Sevens Road. Muir Park Road ran like an arc around the northeast side of the market rather than following the straight line of the triangle.

The clock tower, which was one of the many symbols of the empire and was built from the finest stone masonry, rose above every other structure and stood like a sentinel watching over all from its four faces. Each of the four round white faces was etched with

Roman numerals, one to twelve, in black. Every hour, the clock struck the exact number of strikes to indicate the hour of the day or night. It struck only once on the half hour. A little park surrounded the clock tower in the fork of Main Street and Sevens Road.

The folk from up country cared not a bit about clock time. They could not read the Roman numerals anyway and even if they could count the number of strikes it did not matter to them. Their day began with the first cock-crow at about 3:00 a.m., followed by the second cock crow at about 5:00 a.m., and followed by dawn and sunrise. They have been telling the time of day for as long as the sun has risen in the east and moved across the sky to set in the west. They have worked in "backra" (white man's) cane fields and in their provision grounds from sun up to sun down. They can tell the time in the morning and in the afternoon by the length of their shadows. In the morning, the shadows would shorten as noon approached and would lengthen again in the afternoon. The lengthening and shortening of shadows before noon and after noon determined when children went to school and returned home. Country folk lit their lamps or went to bed when the chickens came home to roost.

On Miss Eu's farm in St. Mary, I often heard talk about planting certain crops in relation to the phases of the moon. Full moon and dark night were two phases that I enjoyed. The full moon was for playing out at night with my shadows and the shadows of the trees and leaves. The dark nights were enchanting for the ghost stories that some elderly people told us kids and for the light of the "peeny wallies" (fireflies) among the leaves and the night sounds of frogs and crickets. Some old women predicted imminent deaths, with spooky accuracy, from listening to dogs howling during dark nights. On moonshine nights, the barks and fights of mongrel bulldogs over the bitches in heat kept many mortals awake. Tomcats moaned like babies before a spat.

I loved the marketplace. The market people were different from the people I met at school and at church. Emasculated men and masculinized women, who were made equals in labour in the field gangs on the sugar plantation, continued to be equals in the marketplace. Higglers hired handcart men to transport their goods from the trucks to their stalls. If the men tried to put one over on them, they were capable of pushing them aside and heaving the loads onto their heads and transporting their loads themselves. I saw women in various states of emotions, hardships, and friendships. They spoke the patois unabashedly. The Jamaican *labrish* (gossip) abounded with pithy repartees about sex, religion, politics, cunning, bakra (white man's) business, "lie-and-story," misery, tragedy, and divine retribution. Satire, irony, and pathos abounded, and still abound, in the marketplaces where the elements of drama were performed in the theatre of the absurd with the best acts of improvisation. I saw men and women making a living from nothing.

The market was so interesting that I would run away from school on Friday afternoons to walk through the hustle, bustle, and hawking of the ground provisions and haberdasheries. Among these haberdasheries, customers could find cloth by the pound or by the yard, rubber tire sandals, ready-made dresses, and men's shirts, blouses, and underwear. There were also enamel and aluminum kitchenware and iron pots.

The ground provisions depended on what was in season and would include breadfruit, yam, cassava, bananas, dasheen, callaloos, oranges, mangoes, and much more. I remember gleefully how I would abscond from school frequently on Friday afternoons with friends to buy our favourite collection of fruits and repair to the logwood walk to sit under a logwood tree. We would gorge ourselves, tell lies and stories, and laugh uproariously. We would then collect five sixpence pieces so that we could punch five tunes in the jukebox at Mr. Morant's Restaurant and Dance Hall. I can still hear the tunes of Fats Domino's "Blueberry Hill," Elvis Presley's "Blue Suede Shoes" and "All Shook Up," and Chubby Checker's "The Twist." We would twist for hours until we were sweaty and exhausted and then we would disperse and run home to make up for the illicit time that we had spent in the market and dance hall.

Towards the back of the market near Muir Park gate were the butcher stalls. The butchers wore long white aprons. The carcasses of cows, goats, and pigs hung throughout the stalls both for display and for the food inspector. The butchers had to set aside the liver and light (lungs) from the freshly butchered animal for the food inspector to test before any of the meat was sold. The inspectors would stamp the carcasses with purple or red ink after inspection. Of course, the inspectors would be given the first and prime cuts of meats before even the Custos Rotulorum of the parish. As the queen's head of the local government, the Custos Rotulorum had the power to order all of the butchers' stock if he wished to. I had even overheard the butchers tell painful stories about how "bakra tek de meat an doh pay far it."

When I was old enough and the maids were unavailable, or my aunt did not want to be seen in the market rubbing shoulders with the higglers, she would send me with a list to a special butcher to get so many pounds of round and sirloin cuts. As I stood in the crowd waiting and watching, I would see poor people haggling with the butcher to put a piece of meat onto the bones and cartilage that they could afford to buy to make soup or stew. They were buying cheap cuts such as gooseneck and brisket, the former to make pumpkin soup and the latter to make stew. The middle-class housewives who dared to come to the butcher themselves would point to the choicest cuts of meats hanging on the hooks. The butcher would then walk up to the hindquarter of the cow, give it a bear hug, and heave it off the hook and onto the counter. He would cut off a piece of flesh, saw some bones, slice a piece of suet, and put it on the scale to gauge the weight. If the woman dared protest, the butcher would look to the next in line and say: "De meat married to de bone." With this said, the women would understand that they could either take it or leave it. Very often, they would take it and grumble because there were always more customers than meat to sell and even if they went to another stall the principle of sale was the same—"de meat married to de bone."

The poor people would buy the cow foot, cow tail, and cow head to "make up" with dry broad or lima beans or green Congo peas for their Sunday dinner. The rich only ate these dishes as an economy measure, not out of necessity. Also available to poor people was the washed and scalded tripe, which was called *offal* in my cookery class.

All sorts and conditions of humanity mixed and mingled on market days. In 1992, I was able to visit the Macola Market in Accra, Ghana, and the Onitsha Market in Nigeria and found remarkable similarities to the May Pen Market of my childhood.

In the marketplace, the smells of life and decay rose and diffused in the hot air that blanketed the spaces between the market and the grass yard. The broiling heat of the sun released odours, fragrances, and smells that both attracted and repelled. The fragrance of mangoes, jackfruit, oranges, and ripe bananas drew my friends and me like flies. After leaving the butcher, the women methodically followed the aroma of the thyme, onions, hot peppers, and garlic, obeying the unwritten law of Jamaican cooking that meat must have seasonings.

The human odours ranged from the agreeable smell of the clean and healthy to the foul smell of the dirty and unwashed. I could distinguish between the beads of fresh sweat that rolled off the backs and brows of men pushing loaded carts and the putrid smell of menstruating women sweating out their time sitting or walking around to hawk their wares. Those who were verbally offensive to their fellow peddlers or customers would sometimes be told with great vitriol that "yuh smellin high" or, worse, "yuh smell like seven day cabbage wata." Nursing mothers who had to leave their babies for two or three days to come to the market to sell their produce to earn the money they needed to buy condensed milk, Milo, or Ovaltine, salt fish, sugar, and bar soap would groan in pain as the milk engorged their breasts. I would hover around certain women to eavesdrop on their woman talk. I learned that they often had no alternative—that there were likely other children and aging parents at home depending on their labour and income. They carried the yoke so that their families could be fed, clothed and sheltered and their children would have a better life. There were no conveniences to take care of their needs for washing or bathing over the three market days.

On Sunday, the women would rise early to make breakfast and usher their children and men folk to their churches—Moravian, Pentecostal, Baptist, Methodist (but certainly not Anglican)—dressed in their Sunday best to offer thanks to their Lord and personal Saviour. The folk would clap and sing to unburden their cares onto Jesus, the only person whom their Christian missionaries told them cared about their lot of misery and suffering. He alone (their pastors and elders preached to their fold) could soothe their pain if they carried their burdens and laid them down unto Jesus. Jesus, they were told, was nailed on the cross to atone for their suffering and shame. He died for their redemption. When the folk sang "Nobody knows the trouble I bear, nobody knows but Jesus," they believed this from the bottom of their hearts.

When the reading from the New Testament was taken from the book of Matthew 6:25–34, which told them how important their faith in the Lord as provider should be, they would renew their faith in a just God and a place of heavenly rest. The parson in his care to comfort his weary ones would emphasize these verses in a confident, soothing, well-intonated baritone or bass voice:

> Therefore I say unto you, take no thought for your life, what ye shall eat, or what ye shall drink; nor yet for your body, what ye shall put on. Is not the life more than meat, and the body more than raiment? Behold the fowls of the air: for they sow not, neither do they reap, nor gather into barns; yet your heavenly Father feedeth them. Are ye not much better than they?

As if to exhort his flock to believe the incredible, he would remind them with words from Hebrews 11:1: "Now faith is the substance of things hoped for, the evidence of things not seen." Invariably, the parson would end by exhorting his weary souls to believe in miracles. And so they did.

In expressing their strong faith in their Redeemer, the folk would pour out their sorrows in their tears. Their hot salty tears would mingle with their sweat, the result of the heat from the broiling sun on the zinc roofs without ceilings. Some let their tears flow freely, others concealed them by looking up to Jesus, while others just wiped their tears away unashamedly with their white cotton handkerchiefs. Some released the inward pressure of pain and suffering of the hard life into spontaneous shivers and groans that echoed among the believers. This was called getting the spirit or getting into the spirit. People from the established churches mocked these ways of worshipping God. However, the established churches had no relevance to the lives of these folk. Believing that Jesus would redeem them from their suffering and pain helped them to carry on under the weight of slavery and its aftermath—of making a life after emancipation without reparations.

The grass yard was a place of intrigue and curiosity for me when I first lived with Aunt Joyce as a little girl before my father apprehended me. It was located on Sevens Road, opposite the Sevens Road side of the marketplace. I could only have observed the activities from a protected perch on Aunt Joyce's veranda. The grass yard was gone by 1955 when I returned to live with Uncle Harry and my Auntie. I saw many sights in the grass yard then that I would like to bring back to life, both as a chronicle of a way of life long gone and as a tribute to the capacity of my archival memory to yield so much information about a past I had lived unselfconsciously.

The grass yard was an open commons that provided a place to park drays and carts and to tie and feed horses, mules, and donkeys. On Thursday nights, dozens of horse-drawn drays and carts rolled into May Pen with produce and grass from near and far. Traders from as far away as Sevens, Kellits, Mocho, Porus, and Four Paths brought their produce in market trucks. In the backs of these trucks, men, women, children, live pigs, and chickens mingled together with ground provisions on their way to market. Some women higglers also brought their produce in hampers (basket panniers) that were loaded onto a wooden harness saddled on the backs of donkeys or mules. Most often, the women took turns riding the loaded donkey or walked beside it, beating it with a tamarind or guava switch to speed up its gait. The beating was part cruelty to the beast of burden and part expediency to get to market before their produce ripened and spoiled, losing its saleable value. I saw donkeys' legs buckle under the heavy loads, and I would shed tears over the pain of the beatings. At different times in my childhood, I remember feeling a deep pity for the donkeys and the mules. People would call them beasts of burden and seemed to think that they had no feelings.

This open commons had several poinciana trees whose blooms of bright red flowers provided beauty during the summer season. The wide leafy crowns shaded animals and people alike from the hot broiling sun as well as from the heavy rains during the rainy season. The draft animals were either tied to the tree trunks or to stakes driven into the ground. I would be kept awake by the braying donkeys and the whinnying horses. Looking back now, it seems as if the animals were talking to each other out of utter boredom and hunger, which was forced on them by their captive state. Sometimes two animals would pine after each other and finally get away to mate and play. I was particularly fascinated with the tube of dark purple flesh, which seemed to distend from the belly of the male horses and donkeys. When I stared at it and asked what it was, I would be shooed away with the words: "You are getting too ripe for your age." With age, I did figure it all out.

On one corner of the commons along the roadside was a busy blacksmith shop with a furnace of red-hot coals fanned by manually pumped bellows. The blacksmith and his apprentices made horseshoes, cart wheels, and spokes and also repaired all of these same items. One day, I remember a big noisy crowd gathering swiftly under one of the big poinciana trees. Aunt Joyce went to investigate and told the neighbours that a man had been found dead under the tree. He was taken to the almshouse morgue to be buried because no one had claimed to know him. I did not know then what dead meant. Later in life, I learned about the significance of the almshouse and what it meant to be buried by the almshouse or to end up in the poorhouse. The May Pen almshouse was located off the main road at the high point of Railway Hill. When I had to walk from Palmers Cross to May Pen All-Age School, I would observe the dirty water from the almshouse running down the roadside gutters. On part of the open commons where the grass yard was located, a big new post office building was located. Right across from the post office was May Pen School.

I was enrolled in May Pen All-Age School in 1955 shortly after my arrival in May Pen after Uncle Harry had picked me up from Uncle Tom's house. I was happy that my prayers for deliverance from my wicked father had been answered and that I was now with Auntie Black. Auntie Black was very special to me then and has remained so all my life. In the family, she followed my father, who was the oldest of six siblings, three boys and three girls. At the time of my writing this story, she is ninety-three. She reluctantly helps me make sense of what seems to be the mystery of my mother's life and death.

I have fragments of recollection of Auntie being very kind to me as a baby. My first vague recollection of her is of her bathing me and talking to me. She combed my nappy hair with the gentlest tug of the comb while she talked to me. She then fed me my "din din" (dinner), which must have been served in an enamel plate because I remember banging the spoon on the plate to hear the sound and her saying: "Eat your din din." From the stories I have heard from the family gossip, this must have been at a time when my mother was very ill and in the asylum or she may already have died. The story is told that when she died, I was a babe in arms and was terribly neglected because there was no one to take care of us children. My Aunt May said she was told to come and get me because I was crawling around and eating dirt. It was during the war when petrol was scarce and travel difficult. She tells the story of coming to rescue me on a bicycle. I have heard about my mother's situation with regard to my father's brutality as well as the illness of her own dearly beloved father shortly after my birth.

Mr. Lampart, the headteacher of May Pen All-Age School, played a very pivotal role in determining my future. A memorable episode occurred in my Uncle Harry Black's shop where I had to work to earn my keep after school and on weekends. Mr. Lampart would come on some Saturday nights for conversation with Harry and Millie, my aunt. I gathered that he and Millie knew each other in their youth. Only Mr. Lampart and Uncle Harry would call my aunt "Millie," which was short for Emily. Properly, my aunt goes by Elaine. Sometimes, Mr. Lampart would pick up typing that my Auntie had done for him or sheet music that she had purchased for the church choir, to which both of them belonged. At the end of their conversation, Mr. Lampart would invariably purchase a small tin of Nestlé or Betty condensed milk for Muffet, his baby daughter. She was such a beloved child that she had a pet name—one of the ways that parents demonstrate their special love. Oh, how I envied his children for the mother and father that they had and the cultured life that they led.

One Saturday night, on one of these visits to Uncle Harry Black's shop, Mr. Lampart asked a defining question, within my earshot: "Harry and Millie, what are you doing about Yvonne's education?" I can only imagine that a very intense discussion followed. I knew to obey the commandment to be seen and not heard when adults were talking. However, to hear this question was, to my mind, the beginning of my liberation through education. Uncle Harry had always said that the best thing for me in life was to be a helper in his grocery shop. No doubt, he believed that he could make me a servant for life, as white people could do during slavery days with a motherless black or brown child. I was totally vulnerable to abuse, and Uncle Harry felt able to take this kind of liberty with my future because my mother was dead and my father refused to support me. I heard my father tell Uncle Harry in that same shop: "Why are you asking me for support for her? You have her working in the shop!" I believe my father regarded me as his slave child. He was giving Uncle Harry licence to turn me into domestic labour. That was the day when I disowned my father.

Auntie always supported bright young people of all walks of life in their aspirations to higher education—her nieces and nephews among them. She had already fought the battle for Sonia, my older sister, but she seemed to be losing the fight for me. As a motherless child in this situation, I walked the invisible tightrope between Uncle Harry's expectations for me as a labourer and my aunt's desire for me to have a secondary education and a better station in life.

I have always known that Auntie respected my mother. She told me so many times when I was a very sad child in order to lift my spirits and to encourage me. I learned recently from her of the profound debt of gratitude she owed my mother's father, the Honourable Charles Archibald Reid, for the opportunities that he gave her in the civil service, from which she retired. I only learned of this in 1996 when I began to investigate the truth of the generous things that people had said to me as a child about a Maas Charlie Reid, who was supposed to be my grandfather but about whom no one in my father's family talked. I was never allowed to meet any one from my mother's side of the family. I still have not been able to find out why.

To get me started in my secondary education, Auntie seemed to need a hook—a lifeline—to save me from servitude. In asking my aunt and uncle about my education, Mr. Lampart had given Auntie and me the lifeline we needed. I worked in Uncle Harry's shop, and I also worked with the maids at home to compensate for my upkeep, to make peace at home, and to be allowed to go to secondary school.

Uncle Harry had quite a different attitude towards my ten cousins who had their mother and father to protect them and support them. He must have wanted to avoid the expense of sending another child to secondary school. He therefore decided that I could no longer live in his house. It was too much for him to have both my sister and me, so I was sent back to Aunt Joyce. This seemed fair enough since I had started out with her and had had a relationship with her eight years before.

The decision to send me to Aunt Joyce occurred at precisely the time I was admitted to the May Pen Comprehensive School. Aunt Joyce and her husband were reluctant to have me move in with them, and, this time, it was she who wanted to make a servant out of me. It was her husband who intervened to give me the twenty-six shillings necessary to purchase the textbooks I needed for the first year at the comprehensive school. I would have to lie and steal money from her shop till to get the money for the books I needed in future years. I could not read a book in her sight. I had to resort to using a flashlight under my covers to study when they had all gone to bed. She would have ironing and cooking for me to do after school, and she would have me scrub the floors of three rooms before I could leave to walk the three miles to the May Pen Comprehensive School. I was often late for school. I would be so tired by the time I arrived at school and embarrassed that I had not been able to do my homework. I would often steal time right after school to do my homework before I took the three-mile trek back home. Often my aunt would yell at me in a fit of rage: "You getting to be just like you black mumma [the derogatory form of mother] who thought she was better than me."

When I first came back to live with Aunt Joyce and Uncle Harold in Palmers Cross, where they now had their own property, she was still doing her dressmaking trade at home. Uncle Harold would ride his bicycle to his tailor shop in May Pen city, about three miles away. A couple of years later, they built a variety shop, with an adjoining tailor's shop for Uncle Harold. Being out of the city centre, Aunt Joyce had fewer customers and turned increasingly to being a shopkeeper. However, she still kept her sewing going and insisted that I be her sewing apprentice during the summer holidays. When I would grumble about other children having the summers to visit friends and family in the country or to go to the seaside and that all I did was work, she would give me a few swift boxes across my face as she said: "Every woman should have a trade, and one day you will thank me for this."

I later appreciated the wisdom in her words, but to this day I resent her method and motivation for trying to teach me her trade. I was to be a dressmaker and not a scholar. Now I have become both. "You always have you head in a bloody book," she would say. It would seem that Aunt Joyce must have resented the fact that my mother had had a higher level of education than she had. One of the conditions of slavery was to deny the enslaved any access to literacy and schooling. As soon as the missionaries brought formal schooling to the island, black people took to education just as the thirsty take to water. After emancipation, as many black people as could afford to, sought and obtained an English education, through missionary schools or by going to England. By means of education, black people addressed and refuted the subhuman qualities that had been attributed to their intellect and personhood during slavery. With the power of knowledge that they acquired from the knowledge regimes of the oppressors, black people asserted their intelligence. They could stand shoulder to shoulder with any white or brown person in argument, speech, writing, and political action as well as in the acquisition of the trades and professions formerly denied them.

Some black people acquired much higher levels of education than many white people on the island. The tables turned once proud educated black people were able to return the scorn of illiteracy on those who had denied them education during slavery. The moment of truth came when educated and wealthy black people sought and achieved legal equality of status. In time, the less educated white and brown sectors of the population resented the power, pride, dignity, and distinction of the growing sector of educated and relatively wealthy black people. This segment of the population was termed "respectable." My mother's family was among the respectable blacks. I have come to call this change in socioeconomic status after the emancipation of slavery the ascendancy of black over white on the island.

The turbulent situation at home made studying a challenge. Aunt Joyce did not value my education. Other children's parents valued secondary educational opportunities and provided them with unencumbered time from chores to allow them to study for the various exams that they had to pass. At school, to save face and to pretend that I was among the loved and cherished, I would smile a lot to cover up my misery and then would sob in my private moments. One morning when I flashed my grief-covering smile at him, Mr. Lampart said: "Yvonne, you have such a sunny disposition. Your smile is like sunshine, lighting up my day." Little did he or anyone else know of the oppressive home life that I was experiencing.

By contrast, my cousins' parents saw to their proper schooling and preparation for the common entrance examination that determined one's future prestige. Most parents tried everything within their means to give their children the best schooling that they could. Only the really poor people's children were left in the all-age schools to leave at age fifteen to take their place among the literate labourers. Auntie got my sister into Clarendon College after she passed her third Jamaica local examination while she was attending the May Pen All-Age School. I was languishing in the all-age school rudderless until one day some of my friends said: "Come mek we go tek de tes" (let's go and take the test). I did not know what the test was for, but I went in and wrote the papers. When the test results came out, I learned I had placed first.

I learned from reading Ruby King (1979) during my research for this book that this was the test that was given to children who were too old for the common entrance examination but who would be given an over-age scholarship. I had missed the opportunity for the eleven-plus scholarship, as my father did not care about my secondary education. Again, my mother was not around to champion her child. I remember Mr. Lampart going to the Ministry of Education to get permission for me to attend the May Pen Comprehensive School, which was about to take in its last cohort. I was too acutely aware of the difference between my cousins and me. They had responsible and caring parents, and I had none. I was also very disturbed by the inexplicable absence of my mother and the shame and resentment that I felt towards my father—the inveterate drunkard and abuser that he was. I truly felt the pain of parental neglect and the lack of care in my life. To this day, I feel the effects of my disturbed childhood.

To say that I was neglected is in no way to be ungrateful to my aunts. Auntie Black especially did her best. I recognize that each aunt tried within the constraints of her own life imperatives to take on the unexpected responsibilities of raising my father's lawful children. Yes, my father had many "illegitimate" children whom he did not maintain either. This was a very bad time of my life because I was old enough to reason things out. I contemplated suicide many times. When the Rio Minho was in spate, after a heavy downpour, I thought of jumping over the bridge into the river on my way to school. This was a common means of suicide in the area.

It was Mr. L.S.C. Lampart and the teachers at May Pen who gave me reasons to live. I can still hear the voices of my teachers, especially that of Mr. Lampart, principal of the May Pen All-Age School and the Comprehensive School, which I attended until I was age sixteen. He had studied in England and then had returned to give back to his country. Each morning at the school assembly, he would expound on a "thought for the day." He would select from the Biblical text as well as from the best of Western literature. As an exemplary educator, he would show many hundreds of poor children of illiterate parents their way to a worthwhile life through education.

Mr. Lampart and his teaching staff encouraged and inspired us children to believe in ourselves and to strive for a pride of place in our society. He often would remind us that we were to be the leaders of tomorrow. His inspiring words and ways comforted me and fired my ambitions. His exhortations continue to speak to me when I need to renew my belief in my self-worth and my abilities. These thoughts have carried me through many trials and tribulations. I excavate my memory to bring to the reader some of the aphorisms and thoughts that have sustained me through life:

Man! Study to know thyself. Knowledge is power.

Education is to cultivate a sound mind in a sound body.

Silver and gold may vanish away but a good education can never decay.

You are privileged to be given the gift of literacy; read to discover the world's great literatures.

In being given an education, you will be the leaders of tomorrow.

To whom much is given, from them much is expected.

You are expected to use your education for the betterment of society and mankind.

Love truth and justice.

To thine ownself be true, and it must follow as the night follows the day, thou can'st not then be false to any man.

Education is an antidote to poverty of the mind, spirit and material existence.

Do not hide your talent under a bushel.

To be an educated person is to be well mannered, having a sense of decorum, deportment and respectability and being able to walk with princes and paupers and not lose your grace.

The pen is mightier than the sword.

He has showed you, O man, what is good; and what does the Lord require of you but to do justice, and love kindness and to walk humbly with your God? (Micah 6:8)

Lives of great men all remind us that we can live our lives
sublime and departing leave behind us footprints on the
sands of time.

The heights of great men reached and kept / Were not
attained by sudden flight / But, they while their
companions slept / Were toiling upward through the night.

God could not be everywhere at the same time, so he made
mothers.

I spent five years at school in May Pen—two years at the May Pen
All-Age School and three years at the May Pen Comprehensive School
experiment. This time was highly important for me. I matured in my
consciousness and was old enough to begin to assert my independence and to try out different ways of being. In the next section, I take
time to paint a picture of schooling for me, in this significant time
and place, and look back at how I navigated my way to independence.

The school compound was located on Sevens Road opposite the
market. The May Pen All-Age School was housed in three buildings,
plus the buildings of the housecraft centre, the soup kitchen, and the
manual training centre. In a far corner of the school compound were
the pit latrines with stalls for the boys and girls on opposite sides
back to back. Close to the rundown school garden was a concrete
water fountain with four or five taps along two rows. A girl had to
wrap her skirt tail and tuck it between her thighs while she bent
her head to drink at the fountain or else the boys or the wind would
carry it over her head. One day, I witnessed a horrible fight at the
fountain when some boys attacked Enid Johnson, the prized girl warrior, and tried to pull her skirt over her head. They succeeded, but in

quick retaliation Enid landed a blow to the head of one unsuspecting wooligan with the sharp edge of her wooden pencil box. He let out a scream and held his head forward from which blood flowed. A crowd gathered around. A teacher took him to the doctor nearby, and he received several stitches. Revenge was exacted on Enid on the last day of school when some children brought bottles, sticks, and stones in order to participate in a "last day fight." Enid was prepared and put up a memorable defence with her teeth, fists, and trusty pencil box.

Lower division comprised A, B, and C classes. The zinc-roofed oblong building had classrooms that were open on the two long sides. The teachers' desks and a movable blackboard on easels divided the classes. The solid wall on either end of the long oblong building had a blackboard permanently mounted on each wall. Middle division comprised 1, 2, and 3 standards. The building and layout were similar to the lower division.

Upper division comprised 4, 5, and 6 standards, a classroom for students taking the third Jamaica local examination, which was appointed with cupboards for storing school supplies, and the principal's office. The building was secured with doors and windows fitted with locks. Break-ins were a problem. The classroom spaces within the building were for the most part open and divided by teachers' desks, blackboards, and easels similar to the lower and middle divisions. The housecraft building and the manual training centre had locks on their doors. Nonetheless, these rooms were frequently broken into.

Private lessons for the Jamaica local examinations were held in the upper division building and were given outside the regular school program. There were syllabuses for first, second, and third years. Students who passed the third Jamaica local examination could start teaching with the title of "pupil teacher." Each school was rated highly for the number of passes that it achieved in these exams. However good this level of education was, though, it was not seen as a lever of social mobility for the working-class children who attended but only as a means of increasing their abilities as prospective farm and domestic labour.

It was not unusual for parents of children who passed the Jamaica locals to sacrifice to send them to grammar school for at least two years to prepare for the Cambridge "O" and "A" levels. Attendance at a grammar school and obtaining the requisite Cambridge O and A levels offered some measure of economic advancement by providing entrance to civil service jobs and entry to higher education. Auntie sacrificed to send my sister Sonia to Clarendon College after she had passed the third Jamaica local examination at the May Pen All-Age School. There was no provision made in the family for my secondary education. I had passed the age for common entrance, and so I was to remain in the May Pen All-Age School until I graduated. It was explicit policy that these schools prepared literate labourers—girls that would normally become servants and boys that would become yardboys. My fate would have been to become a domestic servant had not Mr. Lampart intervened and helped to place me among the last cohort of the May Pen Comprehensive School experiment. I felt ready.

In 1954, the newly formed Ministry of Education, in its attempt to increase the number of secondary schools, amended the code of regulations to permit the experimentation of teaching secondary subjects in all-age schools. Three sites were selected—Kingston Senior School and Central Branch School in Kingston and May Pen School in Clarendon. The May Pen experiment took in three cohorts—1955, 1956, and 1957. Children took the first three years of a five-year grammar school program. The headteacher of the all-age school was also responsible for the comprehensive school. Selected teachers, usually those pursuing higher education, from the all-age school taught the subjects using the same textbooks that were used in the grammar schools. Children from both schools shared in the same morning devotions and cultural, social, and athletic events. The comprehensive school experiment became the model for the junior secondary schools, which proliferated on the island during the 1960s.

The May Pen Comprehensive School experiment was housed in a two-room prefabricated structure made of heavy gauge zinc mounted on a concrete base. I remember the heat in the all-zinc structure was like the heat in a convection oven. We sometimes had to go outside to have classes under a tree to find relief from the searing heat. The school was located in the eastern corner of the May Pen All-Age School compound, close to the Methodist Church and close to Sevens Road. We could hear the traffic of the sugar-cane trucks carrying canes along Sevens Road to the Sevens Sugar Estate mills during crop time. The majority of children who attended the May Pen All-Age School lived in the Sevens Sugar Estate settlement. This meant that their parents either worked on the sugar estate or in the cane pieces adjoining the sugar mills. The children at the May Pen Comprehensive School sometimes reaped the benefits of the sugar cane, which the wooligans from the All-Age School pulled from the passing trucks. The Comprehensive School children would not be seen pulling canes from a passing truck—we were expected to behave "respectably," befitting the secondary education that we were receiving.

This experiment offered the first three years of grammar school, the equivalent to first, second, and third forms in the grammar school. The May Pen Comprehensive School was the feeder school for Clarendon College. Students who attended did not have to pay school fees, as did their counterparts in the grammar school. My recollection of the curricula of both the All-Age and Comprehensive Schools will show the difference in knowledge imparted in each school. Of further note is the relatively small number of children being given opportunity for advancement through education.

As I mentioned earlier, the curricula for the all-age schools were designed to develop literate labourers and domestic servants. The following subjects were taught: English grammar and composition, reading, writing, spelling, recitation and choral speaking, scripture, arithmetic or sums and mental arithmetic, general knowledge, manual training (drawing and carpentry), school garden, arts and craft (potato printing, drawing, and sisal weaving), and needlecraft (embroidery and sewing). There were three subjects that have left vivid memories with me: singing, geography, and history. Singing of rounds, solos, quartets, choir with base, tenor, alto, and soprano to music of the piano or from the "doh-ray-me-fah-soh-lah-tee-doh" of the teacher's voice. In geography, we drew maps showing the wind systems of the world, the physical geography of the world, waterways, lakes, rivers, and mountain ranges. Our maps also showed the cash crops of the empire such as rubber, tea, coffee, cattle, wheat, sugar, cotton, and lumber. We made beautiful papier-mâché relief maps of the world and Jamaica and painted in the mountains, valley, lakes, and waterways. We were also taught some civics, hygiene, and, of course, the history of the empire.

I was always curious about the history that the students in the third Jamaica local private classes learned. I would hang around the big boys and big girls while they were studying in order to learn what they were learning in the hope that one day I too would take the third Jamaica local examination. I did overhear my sister and her peers studying a lot of history and literature of the empire. In history, they studied aloud the Magna Carta, the Middle Passage, and the wind systems of the world: the trade winds and the doldrums; the British seadogs: Nelson, Raleigh, Hawkins, and Morgan; the Spanish Armada; and the abolitionists Clarkson, Wilberforce, and Buxton. Some of the more important calculations that they learned of were longitude, latitude, and Greenwich mean time and how mariners used these data to travel around the world.

In literature, they talked a lot about imagery in poetry, Jane Austen's *Pride and Prejudice*, Thomas Hardy's *Far from the Madding Crowd*, and Shakespeare's *Measure for Measure, The Taming of the Shrew*, and *As You Like It*.

The curricula of the May Pen Comprehensive School were based on the first three years of the grammar school. A grammar school education prepared us for civil service and clerical jobs after O levels. After A levels, we could enter university to study for degrees in arts, science, or the professions such as law and medicine. When we entered high school, we were expected to pick up at fourth form and be ready to take our Cambridge examinations at the end of the fifth form. Those who could afford it would stay for two additional years for sixth form, at the end of which we would write the Cambridge advance level exams in various subjects. The curriculum comprised the following subjects.

BIBLE KNOWLEDGE was taught by Mrs. McLean, who was herself studying this subject at an advanced level through some form of extramural studies or external university such as Cambridge or London. I remember learning about the role of the prophets Amos, Micah, Hosea, Isaiah, and Jeremiah in a way that was different from learning about them in church and Sunday school. The study of the prophets in school had a resonant familiarity. Some children heard their family reading the words of the prophets and discussing the meaning of the prophesies in their life. The folk would draw on the books of the prophets and the Psalms to inspire them and guide their way, especially in times of great distress. The twenty-third Psalm, which begins "The Lord is my shepherd, I shall not want," is a favourite among the folk and gentry alike.

In this curriculum, we learned about the Maccabees and the books of the Apocrypha. We were introduced to the Hellenistic influences on the Bible. We had to study the Acts of the Apostles in great detail. Through the study of St. Paul's various letters to the apostles we were taught about the church as the body of Christ and the correct behaviour of men and women in that church. Without it being said directly, we understood that we were being given ethical principles by which to live.

MATHEMATICS was mostly algebra and geometry with Mrs. Harrison. This lady ran herself ragged drumming in theorems and proofs (QED), parallelograms, rhomboids and triangles, cylinders, squares, and angles. Our pencils were never sharp enough to draw the angles and arcs that our protractors had to measure with scientific precision. Solving simple equations and quadratic equations really set apart those who were and were not mathematically acute. I was definitely among the less favoured in this subject area.

It is interesting now to realize that I was using geometrical knowledge in dressmaking but did not know it then. In those days, a dressmaker drew her own patterns. All of the shapes that we studied in geometry were embedded in the drawings. The properties of the circle were inherent in the drawings of necklines, armholes, and circular skirts. Angles as well as perpendicular and parallel lines were all part of designing a garment. In geometry, the examples we used came from the construction of bridges, steeples, and cardinal points, which all had to do with the masculine world of conquest and expansion.

LATIN was with Mr. Lampart and then Mr. Griffiths, the only other male teacher I remember at May Pen Comprehensive School, apart from Mr. Brown, the woodwork teacher who was there for a short time. Latin—this was the dead language that we had to learn! We were made to believe that all learned and erudite people had to know Latin because it was the root of the Romance languages such as Spanish and French. Declensions of nouns, which were said to have many cases such as ablative, dative, nominative, numerative, accusative, and genitive all had their appropriate prepositions, affixes, prefixes, and suffixes. We learned to conjugate regular and irregular verbs. The construction of the proper Latin sentences with all of the appropriate parts of speech was of mathematical precision. And there was some attribute called the subjunctive mood, which I do not remember anything about now. It was vital to know the masculine, feminine, and neutral forms of nouns and pronouns. The ultimate test of the linguistic knowledge of Latin came when we had to translate the unseen passages from the *Odyssey* or the *Aeneid* or from the famous accounts of the Trojan or Gallic wars. There were chariots and horses decorated with magnificent regalia, celebrated heroes, and brave soldiers. The names, invariably of men, ended in "-us": Flaccus, Brutus, Augustus, Aurelius.

SPANISH with Mrs. Lampart was easy compared with Latin. We loved Spanish because the grammar seemed straightforward. In contrast to Latin, it was a living language spoken by our neighbours just ninety miles north. Furthermore, basic Spanish lessons were published daily in one of the newspapers. I believe it was the *Star*, because the pages were smaller than those of the broadsheet *Daily Gleaner*. We made a scrapbook of these lessons to complement our red-and-green-covered textbook and class drills. We even tuned in to Radio Havana and listened to the trilling "Rs," which we imitated for each other's amusement. Jamaica is only ninety miles south of Cuba and their radio waves came in very easily. We listened for the perfect Spanish phraseology of speech. We had our Spanish orals to prepare for in which our accents and the use of appropriate idiomatic expressions were key. Now that I think of it, we must have been hearing important news about the political life in Cuba, but since Jamaica was anti-communist we must have learned not to try to make sense of what was going on in Cuba in the 1950s.

ENGLISH GRAMMAR AND LITERATURE was with Miss Reid, Miss Broomfield, and Miss Miller at different times throughout the three years. All of these teachers also taught in the All-Age School. Miss Reid spoke the Queen's English perfectly but without the English accent or pretensions. She drilled us in every grammatical rule in sentence structures, punctuation, vocabulary—especially antonyms and synonyms—spelling, and figures of speech. We practised summarizing passages of varying complexities to one-quarter or one-third of their original length. Dictation of poetry and prose tested our spelling and comprehension. Miss Reid made known to us that she was already preparing us for the Cambridge examinations, which were some years away. Practice makes perfect was her adage when she sensed that we were tired of the drills. Miss Reid abhorred verbosity and sloppy expression.

We were introduced to English drama. Shakespeare, who was considered the greatest playwright, was the model of all plays. Shakespeare's language was so difficult for us—we hated the enormous effort that we had to put out to understand that far-off world. Our deliverance came when we found a book, in the May Pen public library, which was called *Lamb's Tales from Shakespeare*. The author had written the plays in plain prose. We were able to construct the story line as we studied the plays. The tests were based on being given certain passages that we had to memorize from the plays and then being asked to say which character spoke those lines and under what circumstances. Furthermore, we had to expound on the meaning. I remember studying *The Merchant of Venice*. We had to memorize "the quality of mercy" speech from this play as well as Lady Macbeth's speech from *Macbeth*. We had to learn certain of Shakespeare's sonnets by heart and were parsed for all of the conventions of the form. We studied *The Rivals* by Brindsley Sheridan. In this play, we revelled in the idea of "Malapropisms," which was the closest thing to "speeky-spokey"—the language that resulted when our unschooled folk tried to speak Standard English. We could identify with the ridicule that Mrs. Malaprop received in the play—the same kind of ridicule that folk who could not master Standard English, nor cared to, received from the literate. In addition to the study of English drama, we studied poems by Keats, Byron, Longfellow, Milton, and others. A group of us sat for days under the Bougainvillea bush and memorized all sixteen stanzas of the *Destruction of Senacharib* by Lord Byron, just for the fun of poetry and choral speaking. As far as prose went, I can remember only George Eliot's novel *Silas Marner*.

Around this time, in the mid-1950s, a new public library was built to serve the city of May Pen. It was located close to the school in the same direction that I walked home from school to Palmers Cross.

I often stopped to borrow a book and stole a secluded read at a special spot by the railroad tracks before I got home to the work that awaited me. Most of us signed up for membership in the library and took great pride in being frequent borrowers. Through the library, we discovered young adult fiction such as the Hardy Boys and Nancy Drew books. We enjoyed books by Enid Blyton and many more authors whose names I now forget. The boys read many books about explorers and talked with great excitement about the adventures of such men as Amerigo Vespucci, Pizzaro, John Hawkins, and Admiral Nelson. The girls read biographies of Florence Nightingale and Joan of Arc.

Stories about swashbucklers and buccaneers and their adventures in Port Royal, Jamaica, the world's wickedest city in the seventeenth century, fascinated us for reasons we did not then understand. After reading entries on Panama, Port Royal, and Piracy in the *Encyclopedia of Jamaican Heritage* by Olive Senior, I now understand that Port Royal was the strategic location from which the British plundered and disposed of the booty robbed from Spanish fleets and from settlements in the Americas and Caribbean Sea. From here, the booty was shipped to England. Henry Morgan was the most famous buccaneer of the time, notorious for sacking Panama City in 1671. When the English state ceased licensing privateers such as Henry Morgan to carry out their piracy, Morgan was knighted and given the position of lieutenant governor of Jamaica. In 1766, Jamaica was made a free port and the centre for trade with the Spanish-American colonies. Kingston replaced Port Royal after the 1692 earthquake, which sent 90 percent of the city under the ocean. The folk used to say that God sent the earthquake and the massive tidal waves that followed that year to destroy the city and to vanquish the sinners. Nine-tenths of Port Royal was lost forever. Since the 1950s, marine archaeologists have been excavating the area and retrieving artifacts.

I was to borrow and read four books from the public library that influenced me profoundly. The first one was called *Freedom from Fear*, the author of which I do not remember. Through reading this book, I came to understand how much my life was governed by fear and what I could do to relieve myself of fear to release my potential. Part of the book dealt with fear and dreams. The kind of fear I experienced manifested itself in dreams in which I found myself naked in public places such as schools, churches, and on the street. Another nightmare I had was that all of my teeth would fall out mysteriously just before I was to speak or that I had flown so high that I was afraid of being lost in the sky or breaking into pieces when I landed. A recurring dream about crossing muddy waters and being caught in quicksand was particularly terrifying. So was a dream about bulls chasing me up hill or about being entwined by giant lizards. Reading *Freedom from Fear* helped me understand how I could interpret my dreams to figure out what was causing the fears. Afterwards, I experienced a distinct shift of consciousness, in which I began to experiment with my autonomy and act as my own person. The other three books were by Dale Carnegie: *Public Speaking, Debating,* and *How to Win Friends and Influence People.*

Through reading, I created a rich imaginative world to carry me through my many hardships. Even while I did the chores, I could imagine a better life. The life of the mind has always been important to me ever since I could read. I spent so much time alone that I would have gone quite mad if I could not escape through reading and thinking. I wish only that I had understood the value of writing—I would have kept a diary.

BIOLOGY with Mrs. Murray introduced us to the perfect order of living things. Botany was not nearly as interesting as zoology. We learned about vertebrates and invertebrates, skeletal systems, and systems of locomotion in vertebrates and invertebrates. The various adaptations of feathers and fins to aid locomotion of birds and fish through air and water respectively fascinate me to this day. We marvelled at the anatomy and physiology of the human body and the various systems such as the circulatory and reproductive systems. It was at this time that I discovered a medical encyclopaedia in Auntie's home and saw the baby coiled up in its mother's body. I manipulated the colourful transparent overlays so often that they began to fall out of the book. We found a green book in the May Pen public library that we called Wyeth's Biology for short and I practically devoured its contents. This book and our own initiative sparked by our interest in biology increased our knowledge of our bodies far beyond what was taught in class. We learned biology solely from texts, drawings, and pictures. We had no laboratories, not even a hand lens. Mrs. Murray copied the diagrams from the books to the blackboard and labelled them as she taught us the anatomy and physiology of each plant or animal. We took notes or copied Mrs. Murray's own copy of the text on the board.

COOKERY with Mrs. Murray was interesting because she was taking an in-service education course in Kingston to upgrade her teaching certificate, and she taught us many English dishes such as white sauces, cream soups, casseroles, and one-pot dishes that she was learning in her course. We never cooked these things at home. We only cooked them for exams just as Mrs. Murray had to do. I did make cakes at home with Auntie Black, so the information on cake baking reinforced what Auntie Black taught me. Most of the children with whom I went to the All-Age and Comprehensive School did not have the type of range to bake in the ways that we were taught. In the 4-H Club, we were taught how to bake a cake in a Dutch pot with coals at the bottom and a zinc sheet on top—the cake tin was set on top of a coal pot sandwiched between these two sources of heat. Later, we learned to construct a homemade oven from a discarded coconut oil tin and wires. This oven had a door and a shelf on which to place the cake tins. The oven itself was placed on a pot of heated coals. I made one of these ovens and baked cakes for Aunt Joyce who did not have a range as Auntie did.

NEEDLEWORK and sewing were a bore for me. Beside the fact that the teacher could not sew, she had a vitriolic tongue and the most acid disposition. She must have thoroughly disliked children. I was already able to construct garments by the time I was thirteen years old and could teach sewing better than she could. I was not at all interested in learning to patch and darn and to make samples. The lady could not even make a decent hand-sewn buttonhole. I had no respect whatsoever for her teaching skills. She detested me as much as I detested her. Her class was on Friday afternoons, and I always did my work quickly and helped my friends so that we could abscond at recess time to go to the market, which was a much more interesting place than sewing class.

MANUAL TRAINING was for boys only. The manual training centre had lumber and tools such as planes, saws, and mitre boxes. After the manual training teacher, Mr. Linton Brown, left the school there was no replacement, and the boys had the time free when we girls had to go to sewing classes on Fridays. They did not miss much in terms of the curriculum that would continue at Clarendon College because woodwork was not one of the subjects taught there. The boys had to catch up on agricultural science when they went to Clarendon College.

I do not remember learning much general history at the Comprehensive School. I just remember Miss Broomfield engaging us with general knowledge about what was happening on the island and beyond. I remember us studying the progress of the West Indies Federation through daily reading of the *Daily Gleaner*. She read the published speeches about the West Indies Federation. Miss Broomfield was passionate about good speech and excited about the prospect of a West Indies Federation.

ATHLETICS AND SPORTS were attended by both schools together. We belonged to the same houses. The big boys played cricket. Volleyball was played by co-ed teams or by the big boys alone. Mr. Lampart took an active part in the sports after school. I can still see him in his white shorts and tennis shoes. An official coach named Mr. Anderson (affectionately called Mr. Andy) taught track and field, including such sports as pole vault, discus, relays, the mile race, 400, and 800 yards. I was mainly a spectator in the athletics and sports program. I remember a lone Indian boy named Herman Williams who attended May Pen All-Age School and was the best runner. He seemed to sail around the track as if he had no body weight. He won all of the races one year. He got a lot of respect for his athletic ability. Sports day comprised a colourful parade onto the sports ground under our house banner as well as an opportunity for girls to dress up in short shorts and go parading around the sports field. Boys whistled at the girls and flirted and teased them. At the end of the sports day after all the prizes had been awarded, the houses would line up again in winning order and march out of the sports grounds.

CHILDREN'S FREE PLAY consisted of many activities. Girl children skipped individually and in groups. When we skipped in groups, we took turns to the chant of "room for rent; inquire within; when you run out I run in." We played segregated and co-ed ring games and square danced. Boys played marbles and "tah" (cashew nuts) and rode the seesaw. Girls entertained themselves with colourful hoola-hoops. Or, with their right hand, girls took turns bouncing a rubber ball continuously through a hoop made with their "skirt tails" held up with their left hand. The aim was to keep up this in-and-out movement of the ball through the hoop through a count to ten. Onlookers cheered and sang the tune of "1, 2, 3, 4, O'Leary, 5, 6, 7, 8, 9, 10, post man pass." The single ball would change to another player when the ball failed to go through the hoop and stopped bouncing. Girls invented games such as "Mother Hen and Her Chicks" to ward off the hawks. I remember that the girls played in multi-aged groups. Young girls looked up to the older girls who would sometimes be like sisters. I had the affection and care of several older girls who protected me from those who picked on short people. Cultural events provided fun and joy where the formal curriculum did not.

CULTURAL EVENTS were numerous, and our teachers tried to engage us in all of them. We were consciously being groomed to appreciate culture beyond the mundane daily grind. The influence of the missionaries and agriculture were foundational to our cultural activities.

SCHOOL CHOIRS were coached by Mr. Lampart and several female teachers. Just about every class had a choir. I especially remember Mr. Lampart teaching us a Latin song entitled "Gaudeamus igitur," which translates as "Let us now in youth rejoice." I loved this song. Christmastime came alive with various carols and nativity plays. The words to "Good King Wenceslas" required some imagination to make meaning of the words such as: "When the snow lay round about, deep and crisp and even." There was no equivalent scene in tropical Jamaica where we had the rainy season and the dry and where the average temperature was well over eighty degrees Fahrenheit most of the year. The northeast trade wind blows over the island from November to February, and Jamaicans swear that it is cool with just a few degrees drop in the temperature. Equally strange was singing: "The holly and the ivy when they are both full grown, of all the trees in the woods the holly bears the crown." Even stranger were the words: "I dream of Jeannie with the light brown hair borne like a vapour on the summer air." The teachers were doing their job of teaching us English culture to the best of their abilities—even if much of it did not make sense. We children learned everything eagerly because we were told that we were learning to be cultured. Of course, we wanted to be cultured. We were striving for the British polish. After all, at this time we were still citizens of the United Kingdom and Colonies.

DAILY RELIGIOUS OBSERVANCES took place throughout the school day and involved all of the children. We began the school day with morning devotions comprising a hymn such as "All Things Bright and Beautiful," followed by a scripture reading, which was often done by a senior student or a teacher. Afterwards, the principal would make a commentary complemented by a thought for the day or a "golden text" from the scripture reading. Prayers would follow.

Me during Education Week, 1958.

The whole division said grace before they were dismissed for lunch. I remember the grace: "For health and strength and daily food we give thee thanks O Lord." A song such as: "The day thou gavest Lord is ended" ended the day. The ritual ringing of a large copper-coloured bell marked all of these moments in the day. A big boy usually had the important task of ringing the bell on time.

INTER-SCHOOL VISITATIONS became a regular annual event. For example, a group of us visited Mr. Griffith's school when he was appointed its head-teacher after he left May Pen. If my memory serves me correctly, the first Education Week in Jamaica was held in 1958. On this occasion, a group of us from the Comprehensive School experiment went to visit the Mocho All-Age School north of May Pen up in the mountains. This visit was memorable because I think it was the first official Education Week announced with great fanfare by the Honourable Edwin Allen, who was then minister of education. I came into my own as an effective speaker and leader during this trip. This visit gave me a significant view of myself, as I represented the May Pen Comprehensive School. The teachers at Mocho complimented me on my spoken English. They thought that I was a very courteous child. I enjoyed the classroom displays, the food, and the social activities.

SCHOOL CONCERTS took place sometimes, especially at Christmas and at the Comprehensive School graduations. I remember the dance that Mr. Lampart choreographed to the tune of "Lavender Blue" for my Comprehensive School graduation ceremony, where I was the valedictorian. We prepared and sang "Gaudeamus igitur" in Latin for the occasion. I still remember the great honour and the equally great expectations of me. Mr. Lampart had this way of making memorable rituals and ceremonies out of life in school.

HOUSE COMPETITIONS were a regular feature of school life. We had house captains and secretaries and competed in sports, clubs, and school-work. The houses bore the names of prominent wealthy white and brown persons such as Sharp House, which was named for the owner of the Citrus Company in May Pen and for Terrier, who was a wealthy landowner. The house system brought children of different age groups, talents, and interests together.

SCHOOL OUTINGS were something special. Most of us did not have parents or guardians who were able to take us on outings. Mr. Lampart rented a market truck and took a truckload of us to a trade fair in Kingston around 1959. I believe American manufacturers and exporters put this fair on. The animation of the little Pillsbury flour mascot intrigued me. We stood transfixed watching the operation of machines and assembly line techniques of the industrial mass production of bottled and canned goods. The Lannaman's Confectionary put on a fine demonstration of candy making that I remember to this day. Sweeties (candies) were made into an art form. We kids would drool as we stared at the beautifully coloured red, pink, and green sweeties wrapped in cellophane paper and stored in very large glass jars. Some were flavoured with mint and ginger and some were made from molasses. These sweeties were sold by the dozen. We had very little or no pocket money and could not afford to treat ourselves to any of these sweeties. We bought them later when we saw them in shops in May Pen where we could afford to buy one or two at a time.

4-H CLUBS were introduced onto the island from the United States and took root in the rural farming areas. The four Hs represented the head, heart, hands, and health. 4-H members had to apply the pledge as a way of life. We repeated the pledge at every meeting:

I pledge
My head to clearer thinking
My heart to greater loyalty
My hands to larger service and
My health to better living
For my club, my community, my country and my world.

Once per year all active clubs in the whole island assembled for a week of competition at the All-Island 4-H Show, which was held at the Denbigh Agricultural Show Grounds. During the year, members practised various farm skills such as raising small animals such as pigs, chickens, goats, and rabbits. Some even raised calves and were taught to judge cattle. As farmers-to-be, the male members had to be able to identify various grasses and animal feeds. Those who specialized in crops had to know the qualities of soils and the art and science of cultivation. The female members specialized in various cooking, canning, sewing, and embroidery projects. The schools that could afford the canning jars bottled mangoes only for the show. Often they were stored to be shown the next year. I never saw anyone eat any of these canned fruits, but we were taught how to can them.

I won a prize the summer before I started Clarendon College for cooking fricassee rabbit. This fame earned me the election by acclamation to be the captain for the Clarendon College 4-H Club team in the 1960 Denbigh show. I had only been at Clarendon College for six months, but my reputation as a leader had preceded me. Mrs. Stuart, who was our examiner for cookery, was very impressed with me and sang my praises. She also saw to it that four of us were promoted to the fifth form, thus skipping the fourth form, which was the place for us after the three years at the Comprehensive School experiment. I did not seek the honour of being captain. I was just trying to find a place in a school, which I should have entered three years earlier, had things gone as they should have and had I had parents who were charting my future. I was frankly uncomfortable in the place where everyone seemed to know that they belonged. My older sister Sonia had earned a place as a "brain" in biology and chemistry, and everyone knew she was on her way to becoming one of the future surgeons on the island. She loved dissections in biology and titration in chemistry. I lived in her shadow. I was always Sonia's little sister.

Teachers were expected to act *in loco parentis* to the children in their charge. For many children, such as myself, schools were home places. Health, nutrition, and hygiene were of uppermost concern. The public health nurses visited us regularly to give vaccinations, especially during the years of polio. They would also talk about personal hygiene, particularly in relation to germs and contagious diseases. We were encouraged to wash our hands before meals and to keep our nails clean. The school dentist had scheduled visits every Wednesday to extract rotten teeth. The United Nations Food and Agricultural Organization augmented the local government child welfare programs. From this organization and other agencies in the United States came powdered milk, cheese, butter, and food yeast.

A soup kitchen was located right beside the housecraft centre, and two cooks were employed to prepare hot lunches and to mix the big vat of powdered milk. A senior girl collected lunch money every morning and turned it in to the teacher in charge. This money was used to purchase produce from the nearby market. I remember a large store of milk powder, butter, and food yeast that was sent to the schools as part of the school-feeding program. Some parents contributed ground provisions, while others contributed firewood. I did not eat from the soup kitchen because I went home for lunch for the first two years when I lived with Auntie Black. The next three years when I lived with Aunt Joyce she gave me lunch money. With my lunch money, I bought *bullah* and pear and Canada Dry aerated water, when avocado pears were in season. The more stylish thing to do was to go to Uncle Sam's Ice Cream Parlour and buy cocoa bread and patties and banana splits with lots of chocolate sauce. Those of us who could afford to buy lunch were in an enviable position.

For school uniforms, we wore navy blue tunics and white blouses, while the boys wore khaki pants and white shirts. There were long pants for the boys over twelve and short pants for the boys under twelve. Those who did not have uniforms wore what they had.

School supplies consisted of free issue exercise books with the queen's face on the front. The multiplication tables and table of weights and measures were printed on the back cover. They were available in both single- and double-lined versions. These were provided to all children, along with slates, yellow lead pencils with a rubber on one end, indelible pencils, and crayons. The Caribbean readers and workbooks in grammar and sums were available to be used and left at school. Other supplies included white and coloured chalk, blackboard rulers, compasses, and Parker and Quink's Ink in blue and red. There was a supply of pens with the cursed G nibs, which would drop gobs of ink on the paper that had to be blotted up with blotting paper, for cursive writing. Only the teachers or those children whose parents were well off enough owned fountain pens with rubber bladders. Auntie had many, so I would sneak one from time to time to show off at school.

Arts and crafts supplies consisted of plaster of Paris and oil paint for making paper covers for bookbinding, which the seniors did. Newsprint was used for writing out songs and poems from which the whole class would work. With the plaster of Paris, children would design and make wall hangings, which they would take home. Irish potatoes cut in half and dipped into mixed paints made prints on calico cloth or on paper. The paper was used to wrap book covers when they were dry. The cloths were used to make garments or tablecloths.

The class on either side of it shared the two-sided blackboard. Being on easels and on wheels, it doubled as a classroom divider and could be flipped over for use on both sides when not in use by the other class. It could also be wheeled outside under a tree when we needed more room or when it was too hot to be inside. Each teacher wrote on the side facing her class. On occasion, teachers in adjoining classes would share singing class and agree to use both sides to write out the words and sometimes the notes to songs. They would agree to spin the other side by just tipping the lower end of the board and it would just spin around.

The school bell was a regular feature of the school. There was one for each division. A senior boy was assigned the task of ringing the bell for the start of school, morning recess, lunchtime, afternoon recess, and dismissal at the end of the day.

The school furniture for the All-Age School consisted of long benches and desks, which seated ten to twelve kids in the lower grades, depending on the size of the child. The upper division had an attached desk and bench combination that seated three or four children, depending on the size of the child. There were inkwells spaced along the topmost ridge of the desk, which sloped slightly from this ledge. There was a shelf under the desks for books and slates. Kids at the Comprehensive School had individual desks. These desktops opened up so that you could store books inside them. We could put padlocks on these desks and had stacking chairs to go with them. We thought it was something special to have our own desks. The inkwell was still built into the desk, but I believe ballpoint pens were coming into vogue at that time. Most of us had bought the popular Sheaffer or Parker fountain pen with the rubber bladder.

In listing these subjects and activities, I have tried to chronicle what was taught and learned, and what life was like, in schools at this time. In excavating the details of my schooling, I have provided a partial record of schooling towards the end of the empire and as the country was moving towards independence and education was being transformed on the island. The comprehensive school experiment of which I was a part provided the model for mass junior secondary education in the 1960s.

I had a reasonably good school life at both May Pen All-Age and May Pen Comprehensive School between 1955 and 1959. I matured and took charge of my life and decided that life was going to be what I made it. My teachers held me in high esteem. They showed me that I had talents that I should develop and share to make this place better for my having passed this way once. I learned much and passed my exams at the end of my comprehensive program and was promoted to go to Clarendon College for January 1960. Yet when my achievement should have been a time of rejoicing, things took a bad turn at home. I still longed for my mother. Where was my mother?

Chapter Four

Clarendon College, Chapelton, January 1960–July 1961

❊❊❊❊❊❊❊❊❊❊❊❊❊❊❊❊❊❊❊❊❊❊❊❊❊❊❊❊❊

IN JANUARY 1960, my dream to attend Clarendon College in Chapelton came true. I was happy. Certainly, I would have liked to attend a more prestigious high school, such as St. Andrew's or St. Hugh's, but this was never to be. Passing the eleven-plus examination with the requisite high scores gave students a choice of attending a prestigious high school. Being a motherless child with a neglectful father, and living in unstable and transient home environments, I had no one to ensure that I prepared for this exam nor anyone prepared to pay for my secondary schooling.

The opportunity to attend the May Pen Comprehensive School experiment, where no fees were charged, changed the course of my life for the good, and I am eternally grateful to Mr. Lampart for rescuing me in time. For the entire three years that I spent there, I thought of myself as a Clarendon College student-in-waiting.

On that first morning, I needed to pretend no longer, I was an authentic Clarendon College student. I left behind the navy blue, pleated tunic and white blouse uniform of the All-Age School, to which the Comprehensive School was attached, and donned the sky blue, pleated *tobralco* tunic and white poplin blouse that Auntie and I had made. Black leather pointed-toe Bata shoes and navy blue nylon stretch socks complemented my outfit. In those days to wear nylon stretch socks meant that you were wearing the latest in fashion. I thought I was dressed even more smartly than my sister Sonia who was known for her elegance. My hair would have been hot combed and brushed high up into a plaited pony-tail and held in place by a ring comb. The brand new navy wool flat beret would have been moulded over the ponytail and held in place on either side with curling pins. In time, the flat plate of a beret would be broken in to fit over our bulky kinky hair rather than the straight flat hair for which they were designed. I joined the sea of billowing sky blue tunics and stiff khaki that symbolized the sartorial splendour of the college. I fit right into Clarendon College—I had rehearsed all of the mannerisms and affected speech that were characteristic of the Clarendon College students whom I knew and wanted to be like, including my sister.

My sister was equally well-decked out, except that I remember her swollen ankles. Her congenital heart problem caused intermittent bouts of serious heart palpitations that left her white as a sheet and sometimes caused her ankles to swell. Auntie Black would keep a constant supply of Oxo beef soup cubes to make her an instant drink in order to restore her colour after one of these crises. When Sonia ran away from our father's house and found her way to Aunt Joyce, she was badly in need of medical care. Auntie Black took Sonia from Aunt Joyce to get her proper doctor's care and to rescue her from Aunt Joyce's cruelties. In other words, my sister and I changed places. The doctor started her on a course of big green pills. We emptied the bottle and counted one hundred and forty-four of them.

When I was forced to join them that Christmas holiday in 1959, I could see that Auntie loved and adored Sonia. They both delighted in talking about public affairs and about the details of her courses of study. Sonia was headed to her final year of sixth form, at the end of which she would take her general certificate of education at the advanced level in zoology, botany, and chemistry—"zoobotchem" as the combination of subjects was known. Students who were in the science stream enjoyed considerable respect and veneration and were generally considered to be "brains." Sonia had always lived up to this expectation, to the envy of my brother and myself. She was also good at acting out her future career as a doctor. I do not know where she got a stethoscope, but she always wore one around her neck.

The white lab coats, stained and holed with spilled reagents, gave us the aura of scientists at work. Mr. Gunter's business-like procurement and display of specimens—plant and animal cells, live cockroaches, frogs, and guinea pigs for observation under the microscope or for dissection under the bell jar—added to the mystique of the sciences. The big scientific words of anatomy and physiology and the long chemical formulae of organic chemistry were enough to intimidate the insecure or to attract the gutsy and curious.

On that particular bright sunny cool morning in January, Sonia and I had to be ready to join the throng of students at Fernleigh Avenue and Main Street, from where we walked downhill to the May Pen train station. At seven o'clock, we caught the Kalamazoo—a two-coach train that was attached to the sugar-cane cars—to take us some twelve miles to Chapelton.

The city of Chapelton in the north used to be the commercial capital before the parish of Vere, to the south, was amalgamated with the north to form the parish of Clarendon. According to Olive Senior in her *Encyclopedia of Jamaican Heritage*, the parish of Clarendon came into being during the seventeenth century, when King Charles II awarded land grants to former Commonwealth troops who had established sugar estates along the Rio Minho valley. Place names such as Sutton, Pennant, and Ballard Valley are reminders of these original owners. The city has served the commercial needs of several major sugar estates in the north such as Suttons, Danks, and Longville, which was owned by the historian Edward Long. The Danks Sugar Estate is alleged to have been a gift from Sir Henry Morgan, the famous buccaneer and first lieutenant governor of

Jamaica, to his German sweetheart. She named it Danks for the German "danke"—thanks.

Chapelton had a clock tower, a market, an Anglican Church, a courthouse, a jailhouse, a sub-branch of Barclays Bank, as well as several bakeries, dry goods, and grocery shops. It also had a hospital, which May Pen did not have. There were also many fine big houses that took in Clarendon College students as boarders. Auntie Black tells me that during the war, Summerfield, which was about fifteen minutes further north by the same train that took us to and from May Pen, was a marketing centre for ground provisions, grown by peasant farmers in the far north of the parish. The Marketing Board would purchase produce in bulk and ship it by train to May Pen to join the main railway line bound from Montego Bay to Kingston.

We could get off the Kalamazoo at the Chapelton Station, from which we walked uphill for another mile or so to get to the college. If we wished, we could get off further up the line at the side stop, which gave us a short cut up a three-terraced hill to the campus. The college was situated on a hill that provided a panoramic view of cane fields, meadows, and citrus groves. Try to imagine us gripping the dirt and gravel to walk up hill in a pair of pointed toe shoes. By the end of the week, the toes were upturned and grinning at us. We had to resort to stuffing the toes really tight with cotton batten to try and keep them straight. My toes were pinched together into a painful cluster that in the long run damaged my tarsal, metatarsal, and my phalanges. I am sure that many children from that era have bad feet now. Pointed toe shoes and crinolines, which were both the height of fashion at this time, were the cause of painful self-consciousness, given my short stature. I seldom went to the popular teenage dance parties. For me to dress up and dance in two and three crinolines under my skirt and to wear spiked heels and pointed toes shoes made me look like a bobbing little mushroom. I must have been a sight because the unflattering comments were humiliating and hard on a short girl's self-image. I did go to the parties that were held once a week between three and five o'clock in the building adjoining the playing fields, which was close to the Kalamazoo stop. Everyone was in uniform and virtually indistinguishable, so we were able to lose some of our self-consciousness.

By the time we made it to the top of the hill, we were panting, hot, thirsty, and sweaty. The white cotton or linen handkerchiefs were soaking wet from mopping up the beads of sweat from our foreheads and necks. Every blouse and every shirt had sweat marks under the underarm. Some marks were pale and others were light yellow or light green. The most embarrassing thing to happen to any of us was to slide and fall as we navigated our way up hill. During the rainy season, it took a great deal of skill to get up and down the hill without falling and sliding on our buttocks in the slippery clay mud. The big boys and girls helped the handsome little form-one boys in short pants get up the hill as well as the cute little girls who still wore ribbons in their hair. How well I remember the exquisite tingling of joy when the boy on whom I had a crush helped me up. His behaviour was consistent with the chivalric codes of romantic love, the stuff of our literature and deportment classes. By this code, the gentleman should rescue the damsel in distress, while the lady was never required to rescue the lad in distress. There was so much affection and respect among age groups. I miss those moments.

In the time before the bell rang to start the day, Sonia took me around to introduce me to her best girlfriend, Eleth Gibbs, and to several boys whose eyes lit up and whose ears perked up to give me a completely flirtatious welcome. I do not remember feeling flirtatious at all because I had just spent one of the saddest Christmas holidays of my childhood.

Aunt Joyce had opposed my secondary schooling ever since I started the May Pen Comprehensive School experiment. As I matured and became more sophisticated, our relationship deteriorated, and I had come to feel that she disliked me. In November 1959, I really provoked her wrath. I told her, somewhat boastfully perhaps, that I had passed my final examinations and was to start at Clarendon College in January. I bubbled with happiness and told her that I had done so well that I was one of four students who would be allowed to skip a grade and sit for O levels in one year rather than two. Her face clouded over as I spoke. I added that it meant that I had to board in Chapelton because I could not do the chores and walk the three miles in time to get to the Kalamazoo for seven o'clock. She turned red, flew into a rage, and demanded: "Ah who de hell yuh tink a go do de housewuk and help in a de shap? Meh na pay one red cent fe yuh ga a dat school." I was shocked and hurt that she did not find my achievement praiseworthy and a source of parental pride. The parents and guardians of my other three classmates boasted about their achievements and were ready to sacrifice everything to make sure that they did well in school. Secondary schooling was of such prestige that all parents and good guardians wanted it for their children in order to gain social mobility and respectability. I could not, and did not, answer her.

I just walked away like a wounded dog. At that moment, I was consumed with hate and resentment for her and for my father, which burned a hole in my soul. I felt totally and utterly alone in this decision of whether I would go to secondary school or not. I racked my brain trying to think of someone to whom I could run. But there was no mother, no father, and no family. Hot tears burned tracks on my cheeks. I withdrew into a surly silence and mock obedience, while I continued to be submissive to the slave-like labour regime. I had no choice. I often wondered if my mother were somewhere up there, looking down on what was happening to the baby she had left when she died.

The folk would say I could not win because in this fight Aunt Joyce held the handle of the sword and I held the blade. Looking back now, I can see why people used to say that the worst thing that could happen to a child is for her to lose her mother. Even to have had a caring grandmother would have been the next best thing, but I had neither.

From that moment on, I could do nothing right. I guess I had beaten Aunt Joyce at her game and done well in school, despite her refusal to buy me books and to provide me with time to study at home. I had defeated her by being "a sneakin pickney." I paid rapt attention in classes because I knew I would not have much time for revision before tests. I did my homework before I left school to walk the three miles home. My textbooks were stored in my padlocked desk at school. I did not take up a book in her presence because she was bound to find more work for me to do. If I was seen reading a book, she considered it idleness and would find work for my idle hands. She believed in the adage "The devil finds work for idle hands." I regarded her as the devil. Only after the evening chores, such as doing the family's weekly ironing, which would sometimes keep me up until ten or eleven o'clock at night, would I be able to read under my pillow with a flashlight. It was work, work, and more work. She was determined to make a servant and dressmaker out of me.

Aunt Joyce continued to try every mean trick in the book to dissuade me from going to Clarendon College. She piled on more housework in the mornings before school and in the afternoons after school. Sometimes she would play sick, take to her bed, and have me stay home to wait on her. Once I caught her laughing to herself as she was setting herself up in bed to be served the chicken soup that I had to make for her lunch. When she saw my resolve, she would say: "You just like yuh black mooma. She did tink seh she betta am me. An ah it mek me get me bredda feh box har dung. Ah hav a mine fe box yuh dung, jus like how yu faader box yu mooma dung."

In writing this story, I have tried to figure out why Aunt Joyce hated my mother so much. Was she upset that black Jamaicans were ascending socially and eclipsing the power that white and coloured Jamaicans held exclusively before emancipation and for generations after? Was she jealous that my mother, a black Jamaican, had a better education than she had and that she was the daughter of an influential and powerful black man in Jamaican politics? My mother's father had been elected twice to the legislative council and was later awarded the Order of the British Empire. In the process of doing this research, I learned from Auntie Black that "he was the first Negro to be awarded this honour in Jamaica." All of this would have been hard to take if you believed in the white supremacy ideology that justified slavery and the empire and secured ill-gotten gains for a few people like yourselves. The loss of status, prestige, and sense of entitlement must have been humiliating.

Things came to a head one Friday morning as I was on my way to school. Aunt Joyce gave me a blue-seam crocus bag (a sack made of unbleached jute used for shipping sugar), with instructions to go to do the marketing that the maids used to do. She gave me a list of items and told me how much I was to spend on each. She refused to include money to pay for a handcart man to take the bag around as I bought the food provisions and to carry the loaded bag to the bus. She insisted that I carry the bag of food by myself on the bus. This was an assault on my dignity. I was a teenager, struggling with my emerging sense of self, and this self-dignity depended considerably on the esteem of family and school. I refused and walked off and left her and the bag standing there. None of my schoolmates' parents would ever do this to them. I often envied the affection and high regard with which their parents held them. So many parents of lesser means expressed their vision of a bright future for their children, especially those whose "brains could tek book learning." I am sure that if my mother were alive and well, Aunt Joyce could not have taken such liberties. My observation was that the poorest mother would not have allowed any one to put her children to work the way that Aunt Joyce did me. Even her maids would not have allowed their children to do housework. Did Aunt Joyce regard me as a slave child because my mother was black and I had the kinky hair to mark me?

When I came home from school that evening, Aunt Joyce was waiting to pounce on me like a tiger. In a drunken rage, she turned on me, reeking of rum and cigarettes, and scratched my face, grabbed me, and thumped me all over my face and body. Finally, she grabbed a plait of my hair and held it tightly near the roots. I fought back and tried to get away from her. In the tussle, I bit one of her fingers that she had in my mouth trying to rip my cheek. When she saw her blood, she screamed: "Yuh draw me blood!" I had literally bitten the hand that fed me.

She became a deranged woman, as though she was out to kill me. In that moment, the hate between us was like a blazing fire out of control. She fell on me again with her full body weight, and I only escaped from the pounding when I pulled hard enough to leave my plait of hair in her hand. As a result of this appalling episode, I was left with the left side of my face swollen, my eye looking like a slit in a half-baked breadfruit. My body was black and blue all over.

It was a Friday night, the busiest night of her business and the inconvenience of not having my labour to serve the crowd of customers added to her fury. My labour was valuable to her. On Friday nights and all day Saturday, I would weigh and wrap pounds of flour, sugar, and fine salt. I would chop and weigh out pounds of dried salted codfish and pickled mackerel to dozens of customers. I would measure and pour coconut and kerosene oil in pints, quarts, and gallons. At the end of the day on Saturday, my back and pelvis were always ready to break and the soles of my feet were sore and blistered in places. On Sundays, I would not even be able to get dressed up and go to church. I would have to spend the day scrubbing down the counters and mopping the floors in the shop. Ours was a noticeably ungodly household in the community—no prayers, no Bible reading, no church going.

Aunt Joyce locked me out that night. I was too exhausted and sore to walk the three miles to Auntie Black's house, so I slept in the kitchen, which was a separate building from the main house. On Saturday morning, I walked the three miles to Uncle Harry Black's shop and was told that Auntie had gone to her half-day work. Uncle Harry asked me what was the matter, but I would not tell him. I walked away to Mrs. Martin's house. Mrs. Martin was one of my May Pen All-Age School teachers. She was, and still is in my mind, the kindest, gentlest teacher, wife, and mother I have ever known.

She pulled me into her arms and gave me one of those memorable protective hugs that I imagine mothers give to their children. She made me some tea and tucked me into bed. I spent Saturday night with her family and then walked to Auntie's house on Sunday to arrive after church services.

After this episode, I vowed I would never speak to Aunt Joyce again for the rest of my life. It is interesting how I came to break that vow. One day, when I was working in the savings department of Barclays Bank, Dominion, Colonial, and Overseas in May Pen, Aunt Joyce arrived at the counter all dressed to the forty-nines, as the folk would say. I was quite surprised to see her because her bank had always been the mattress or the dark corners in her shop. I respectfully said: "Good morning, Aunt Joyce." She smiled and came close to the counter and heaved up her purse on the counter top. It was weighed down with money. She said that she wanted to open a savings account. I directed her to lodge the money with the teller who would then give me the lodgment slip to open the account. She looked at me with that dancing eye as if she expected me to personally take the money from her and lodge it. I watched her shelling out the money at the teller. There were five-pound notes, one-pound notes, ten-shilling notes, five-shilling notes, and bags of silver and copper. I cannot remember the total lodging, but I remember being surprised that she had so much money to deposit. As I was filling in the section of the account holder, she said: "Put yuh name pon it." I replied: "I do not want to, Aunt Joyce." When I refused, I saw her right eye begin to swivel from side to side and dance. Her temper rose and her face and neck became flushed. She gritted her teeth and said with her hand akimbo: "See Yah, yuh put yuh name pon it far when me ded and gaane me no have nobady fe inherit de fruits af me laaba." I reluctantly put my name on the account and forgot about the account for some ten years or more.

Aunt Joyce and Yvonne, 1961

Months after Aunt Joyce died, I received the bank book by registered mail from Auntie. On her deathbed, she gave Auntie the passbook to give me. I do not remember the sum of money, but it was enough for me to buy my first car. Before she died, she was also working on buying me a plot of land.

Although I did speak to Aunt Joyce again and did some nice things for her, the way in which she had treated me caused scars and rifts so deep that they never healed and never enabled me to reconcile with her before she died. She tried many reconciliatory moves over the years before I left Jamaica, but my formerly warm heart for her had frozen cold. The memory of her life haunts me.

Nevertheless, I cannot deny Aunt Joyce's tremendous influence on my life. I will always remember that she insisted on beating her dressmaking trade into me. She boxed me up and told me when I grumbled about having to spend my holidays sewing buttonholes and doing dress hems: "Every woman must have her own trade, and her own money. One day you will thank me for this." I have thanked her many times. The lessons of my life have led me one step further to say that every young woman should also have her own shelter, unencumbered, whether she has a partner or not.

I have benefited from learning the dressmaking trade in many ways. In the first place, I was able to make elegant school uniforms and clothes for myself. I have made most of my clothes since the age of thirteen when I first started as Aunt Joyce's apprentice. Then when I went to teacher's college, I was able to earn my keep and pay for my textbooks from the money I earned sewing. I did this by using my old 1890s Singer hand machine. When I was leaving for college, Auntie Black talked me into buying it for my own use. When people in college saw how well I sewed, they would ask me to sew custom-made dresses and to design graduation dresses. They paid me handsomely. This meant that I was relatively well off and could support myself when I was in college. This was very important because I had no other means of financial support. Most of my class-mates were supported by their families because jobs for students were few or non-existent. I also had fun sewing because the old ma-chine generated much humour. It had no cover as hand machines usually do. The shuttle cover had even got lost so you could see the shuttle moving back and forth as I turned the handle. My friends teasingly referred to it as "the portrait of a machine." This was after a poem by Louis Untermeyer that appeared in our textbook *Rhyme and Reason*, which we called "crime and treason." By designing patterns on brown paper or adapting commercial patterns, I was able to supplement the government-paid tuition and room and board that I needed to become a trained teacher. I was and still am very proud of how self-reliant I was.

When I graduated from teacher's college, Aunt Joyce gave me a top-of-the-line Singer sewing machine as a gift. By doing so, she gave me the skills and the tools of the trade. I gave the old Singer to a very promising student in my clothing and construction class at Vere Technical High School, where I had taught before leaving the island. At different times in my life when I have fallen on hard times, I have been able to set up a cutting table, get out my block patterns, my scissors, tape measure, common pins, and iron and go to work in my trade. When I was a young teacher in Jamaica, I began to earn more from dressmaking on the side than from my full-time teaching job.

When I became a mother, I made three-colour dresses for my two beautiful daughters just the way Aunt Joyce had made them for me when I was their age. They loved these dresses as much as I had loved mine. I would tell them the story of how My Aunt Joyce had made me dresses just like I had made theirs. By having these skills, I have been able to adorn my body inexpensively throughout my life and have even appeared well off when I am far from it. Now, I only sew for myself as a creative outlet and as a means of therapy. I sew something beautiful for myself when I am troubled or angry. With every stroke of the scissors, I slice through my rage. I make the pus of life ooze out with every prick of the needle through the cloth. I join the seams of experience together as I stitch the fine textures and colours to make a well-crafted suit. My frowns change to smiles as I emerge from my absorbing world of creativity and beauty. Every day as I get dressed, I remember Aunt Joyce with loads of compassion and regret.

It is clear that I have lived to appreciate the truth of Aunt Joyce's philosophy about a woman's autonomy and self-reliance. She was absolutely right. I have come to accept that she meant well, but the memories of her cruelties still make me weep. I weep also for the terrible marriage that she had to endure to her death. After reading much of the history and sociology of the making of Creole society in Jamaica, I weep for the brutal history into which we were born—that of a racist slave society in which families sorted their children and kin by their physiognomy: clear skin and black skin, "good" hair and "bad" hair, straight noses and flat noses, and all the tricky combinations of interracial mixing that were such ammunition for racist abuse. A family with one white and one black parent could produce children in all colours of the black–white spectrum, from those who were unquestionably black to those who could pass for white. The social and psychological consequences of this variety were our obsessions with complexion, hair texture, and the shape of the nose. Colour prejudice manifested itself in the stratification of class and opportunity based on skin colour. The scale of preference placed the highest value on white skin and straight or "good" hair and the lowest on black skin and kinky or "bad" hair. The mixed or "coloured" or "brown skinned" people were in the middle. This led to the perverse situation where a person who was passing for white would be reluctant to acknowledge dark-skinned siblings or other relatives in public.

We were born into a society that inherited the worst forms of brutality against man and beast. Sexist brutality was tolerated in the society where men could beat women with impunity. Adults could abuse children, in the family and in schools, with no accountability. We have allusions here again to the Biblical saying "Spare the rod and spoil the child" (Proverbs 13:24) and discipline with "the rod of correction" (Proverbs 22:15), and, therefore, they believed such actions were in keeping with God's directives.

Aunt Joyce died within months of my moving to Canada, and I was unable to return for her funeral. One of the nice things that I had hoped to do for her was to give her a trip when I settled in and could save up some money to bring her to Canada on a holiday. I had even thought that I could eventually get her out of the hell she lived in. But by a cruel twist of fate, she developed cancer in her neck at the very spot where her husband used to choke her during their fights. I learned that her husband withheld the painkillers and other medications from her when she went home after the surgery. This news, although shocking, was not surprising, given the unspeakable brutalities I witnessed when I lived with them. My grief at her death was unbearable. She had asked me, when we were on friendly terms, to be sure to prepare her for her burial. She asked me specially to do this for her because she did not want to be taken to an undertaker when she died. I had no idea that she would die so young. She died a horrible death after years of battering. She was buried at the back of the property, which she and her husband owned. I have visited her gravesite on a couple of occasions, but at those times I was too suffused with rage and sorrow to contemplate the meaning of her life and death.

In 1998, when I went to lay flowers at her tombstone, I was mellow enough to note what was written on her tombstone. It read: "In loving memory of Joyce Hylton, born March 31, 1916, died May 21, 1970." That was all. She was not a loving mother, a loving wife, a loving daughter, or a dear sister. She belonged to no one, and no one belonged to her. In writing these autobiographical stories and doing the research to find meanings and answers to my life history, I can now say that a great-great-granddaughter of the British empire had been abandoned in the colony—just another bastard of empire. She was unprotected, brought low, tortured, and perished at the hands of a monster that slavery had bred. She had lived out the worst nightmare of the planter class. When she sang "Guide me oh thou Great Jehovah pilgrim through this barren land," she was singing for all of those like her family who could not return to England or Scotland after the fall of the sugar and coffee plantations. She had gone native and consorted with the descendants of the people that their ancestors enslaved. In so doing, she had become one of their intimate enemies. While Aunt Joyce and her siblings could "pass," more or less, and regarded themselves, as "Jamaican white," the skin colour and nappy hair of my father's children, whom he had sired with the "black wench" constantly reminded the family of sexual transgressions with their "inferiors."

This brutal history of enslavement, colour prejudice, racism, and class pretension poisoned every relationship in my beloved country. As Simone Schwartz-Bart writes in her novel *Bridge of Beyond* (1982), Martinique had had a history similar to Jamaica's and "people are still dying from slavery." I am to this day grievously sorry about how bad my relationship with Aunt Joyce became. In spite of the hardships and pain that enveloped us, Aunt Joyce taught me so much and did so much for me. She had saved my life. At a more profound level, I have come to understand how certain forms of brutality hold some women in captivity until they are killed in a marriage. I have kept my promise to myself. I swore when I was growing up with her: "I will never, ever, let any man control my life and brutalize me like that." I have never allowed any form of brutality to continue as soon as I have realized it was happening. Through her suffering, she gave me the insights and skills to avoid and escape these traps.

If it were not for the generosity and ingenuity of Auntie Black I may never have made it to secondary school. She saw the gravity of the situation, swallowed hard, and decided to do what she had to do. Perhaps she was acting out of gratitude to my mother, Lucy May Reid, and her father, Charles Archibald Reid. I say this because when I was researching my mother's family background, as part of this project, Auntie Black reluctantly revealed that the Honourable Charles Archibald Reid had given her the civil service job with the Trade Board, which became the Ministry of Trade and Industry. She therefore had a secure job with a pension until her retirement. He even paid for her to go to learn Pitman's shorthand and typing. This was an important educational gift for any woman who did not go to secondary school or earned a pupil-teacher certificate. These skills obviously allowed Auntie Black to escape from earning her living as a dress-maker, which is not to take away from the very hard work that was necessary to maintain her position, especially in the late 1950s. It was a time when young black people with degrees from the University College of the West Indies began to displace coloured and white people who held patronage appointments, based on colour and family background in the landed gentry or the merchant class. These were people who had very little education and were not entitled to the positions that they held. Maas Charlie's largesse also extended to my father whom Auntie said had been provided with accommodation. Auntie said that my father was such an abusive and disrespectful drunkard that Maas Charlie had to put him out. In disgust, she once said: "That man should be whipped, you know!"

Auntie Black never hesitated to take me in, a second time, and to make preparations right away for me to be ready in January for Clarendon College. I believe this was around late November or early December 1959. Auntie was so proud of my achievements, especially since she had cooperated with Mr. Lampart to give me my chance at secondary education. She was the person who had had to pay for my birth certificate and to get all of my papers in order for me to qualify to take the over-age scholarship. This had not been easy, as it would seem.

Auntie Black always gave me a view of my mother that was opposite from the one given me by Aunt Joyce. She held my mother in very high esteem. When I lived with her earlier, she would remark whenever I did something disappointing: "Your mother would be so disappointed that you did that." Auntie told me that she and my mother were good friends and that my mother was the finest seamstress and milliner. She said when they were young they had had a dressmaking business together in Kingston. They went out of business when the big stores in Kingston started selling ready-made clothes, which had resulted in less demand for custom-made clothing. At these revelations, I would get bouts of melancholy and depression and cry myself to sleep. When I prayed, I would ask God why my mother had to die and leave me to suffer so. My aunt kept everything surrounding my mother's death a secret during my childhood and for most of my life. I got no answers from God or man. Eventually, I stopped praying for answers.

In my senior years I confronted Auntie Black about my right to know my maternal origins. I informed her that I had the right to know about my mother. Her answer was: "She is dead and gone already, why you want to know." I have never been able to understand completely her indifference to my need to know about my roots. In fact, Auntie said to me in 1998: "You come to find out your Negro roots! I have Negro roots and it has done me no good." Was she expressing the shame of sexual transgressions and the social and material consequences in that society at that time? Or were some things too painful to remember? The so-called stain of black blood was still a social and economic handicap in Jamaica at that time.

When Aunt Joyce came to get me back, I could taste and smell the scorn in Auntie's demeanour. After listening to her and entertaining her, Auntie sent her away and prevented me from returning to such an abusive situation. I will never know what words passed between them. Auntie Black was very proper and restrained in her words and actions. Auntie's way of dealing with me was to expect the best of me. She never beat me or verbally abused me. She was by no means perfect in my eyes, but I loved and adored her very much. She had, and still has, her class and colour prejudices, which I have had to live with.

When I became an adult, we had several arguments about the way in which she played up to some people and patronized others. One day after we had had an argument about the way she treated her maid, she said to me: "I know you don't distinguish among people but I do." I could see in her eyes that she wanted to explain so much about how the social history of the island had brought her to that way of relating, but she did not attempt to. I can only now imagine that it was too messy and confusing even to try. Both sisters had always been estranged. Aunt Joyce winced with pain whenever she spoke about how her sister Mrs. Black came to her wedding in a black dress, which was the colour for funerals in Jamaica. In those days, one would never wear black to a wedding. This was a sign, perhaps, that she may as well have been attending her sister's funeral because her death started with her wedding when she defied conventional wisdom and married down in class and colour. Her older sister saw ahead, foreseeing that Aunt Joyce would come to a bitter knowledge as she lived in the unholy state of matrimony. Auntie Black, without saying so, had no use for the life choices and temperament of her sister, Joyce.

Auntie Black had to pacify her husband's outrage for having to shelter and maintain, yet again, one more of Cyril's neglected children. I can only imagine how my presence had disrupted a peaceful, stable relationship. I knew instinctively what the tacit bargain was. I would willingly put in many hours of child labour in Uncle Harry Black's grocery store and in the household in order to earn my entitlement to a school uniform and train fare. I was quite aware that I would have a better standard of living in spite of the work. I shared a room with my sister instead of sleeping in a corner of Aunt Joyce's dining room. Clearly, Aunt Joyce had lesser means, but her husband, who had come from a lower class than she had, also curbed her desires to raise their standard of living when they had the means to do so. This was especially evident when electricity eventually came to Palmers Cross, and they could have replaced the icebox with an electric refrigerator. When electricity and running water came to the village, Aunt Joyce and Uncle Harold had many fierce quarrels about remodelling their house to bring the kitchen and toilet under one roof. He relented with the bathroom and toilet but not the kitchen.

The standard of living in both households stood in stark contrast. Housework in the Blacks' household was easier than in the Hyltons' house. For one thing, Aunt Joyce and Uncle Harold lived outside the city limits where there was no electricity or piped water in the house long after May Pen had had electricity. Therefore, the bathroom, kitchen, and toilets were in separate detached buildings throughout the time that I lived with them. Auntie's house, by contrast, had all of these facilities under one roof. The kitchen range graduated from a big iron woodstove, first to gas and finally to an electric stove. Meanwhile, Aunt Joyce kept her charcoal pot and paraffin stove even after the village of Palmers Cross got electricity. It was delightful to cook without having to cope with bad wood, charcoal, soot, and smoke. By the same token, it was easier to scour the pots with white Vim Dutch cleanser than with grey and black ashes. Dutch cleanser was less corrosive to the hands and nails. At Auntie's house, there were outside showers for the maids and yardboys as well as sleeping quarters for the maids. These were never used by the time I came to live with them and were eventually demolished, so that several rooms made of concrete and steel could be added to the older original wooden house. I loved the labour-saving devices that Auntie steadily bought, even despite Uncle Harry's protests. He became furious when he realized that Auntie used the appliances to save the maid's labour and that she had no intention of doing the housework herself with these appliances.

Auntie sewed for herself, my sister, and me until we were proficient enough to do so ourselves. She taught us touches of haute couture, such as piping, trims, bindings, and tatting. Fabrics and fitting had to be perfect. Auntie had exquisite taste in clothing and accessories. It was a charm to sew on the electric Singer Zig Zag sewing machine rather than the Singer treadle straight-stitch sewing machine that Aunt Joyce had. The treadle was so hard to pedal and there was always the nuisance of avoiding backward pedalling and breaking the wheel belt. I learned to cut garments out of commercial patterns from *Vogue* and *McCall's* rather than the freehand patterns that Aunt Joyce used. It was from Auntie that I learned of such famous designers as Christian Dior because we cut dresses either by using his patterns or by copying his style from stylebooks. Knowing the two ways of cutting garments has been very useful. The pinking shears and the zig-zag stitch took the drudgery out of hand-finishing seams.

The electric washing machine reduced days of hand washing, scrubbing, boiling, and bleaching clothes. The electric iron replaced the solid irons that had to be heated on hot coals in the coal pot and cleaned with quailed banana leaves before applying to the garment.

These irons had to be routinely greased when hot before storing to prevent rusting. The electric mixer made baking cakes a pleasure for me. I did not have to cream the butter and sugar with the wooden spoon for what seemed like hours. The pressure cooker made cooking stews and dried beans a breeze. Aunt Joyce was still parching her coffee beans over an open fire, pounding them in a wooden mortar and pestle, and then brewing the grounds with charcoal to get a clear brew. Auntie was using a percolator or instant coffee.

The floors at Auntie's house were cleaned with mops, commercial floor wax, and the electric polisher. Aunt Joyce still used a floor dye boiled from logwood bark and applied with rags and bare hands to stain the wood floors. Beeswax was then applied to a coconut brush, and I had to kneel on hands and knees to shine the wooden and terrazzo tile floors with the brush. Blackened knees and dye-stained hands were a sure sign that you were a domestic servant. The dye stains on my hands were a source of embarrassment when I went to school. I seemed to be the only one among my schoolmates who scrubbed floors. I yearned to be indulged in the ways that they were. Inasmuch as Uncle Harry tried to eliminate the maids, Auntie always insisted on having someone to wash and iron the clothes, especially during the times when they kept boarders in the new rooms that replaced the maid's quarters. I did not mind helping with the housework, but I resented bitterly doing shop work for Uncle Harry who seemed to think that that was the work for which I was born. He did not believe that my sister or I deserved any privileges for living in his house.

Auntie, for the most part, treated her maids well. They generally liked and respected her, but they detested Uncle Harry whom they complained was mean and who tried to pay them less than a fair wage. He was always paying them short, and Auntie had to make it right with the maids in order to keep them. He was also in the habit of arriving at the house when Auntie had gone to work and ordering the maids not to use the labour-saving devices, which he maintained should only be used by Mrs. Black. Auntie had a cordial social distance between herself and her maid, while Aunt Joyce worked side by side with them and was in frequent quarrels about social distance and deference. She often said after some of these quarrels: "Familiarity breeds contempt." Or she would say: "You lie down with dogs, you get up with fleas." Of course, it was easier for Auntie to keep her distance because she went to work outside her home, while Aunt Joyce worked at home and in her shop, which adjoined her dwelling.

There were many other ways in which the standard of living was higher in Auntie's home. Auntie stressed balanced meals and formal dining every night at supper. She loved to make beautiful salads and tasty custards. I enjoyed making Christmas fruitcake with her. During the course of this research, I learned that this cake was originally made by the king's chef from the fruits and spices of the empire and therefore called Empire Cake. The recipe is displayed in the Maritime Museum in Greenwich. I enjoyed Auntie's company. She did not talk much but took obvious pleasure in whatever she was doing. I admired the artistic way in which she arranged food on the plate when she served it at the table. Uncle Harry would not serve himself. He insisted that she make up his plate for him. Discounting the fact that he was a very lazy man—too lazy even to pour himself a drink of water—I believe that he appreciated her art of serving. She took pleasure in serving him, to the extent that she would even put out his clothes for him and run his bath. They had a ritual of greeting each other warmly when Auntie came home from work in Kingston, a journey of thirty-six miles in the heat. He would peck her on the forehead and say: "Hi, Putsy, how was your day?" She would smile coyly and say something like: "So-so." Then he would make them a drink of rum and orange juice or whisky and soda.

Auntie sang in the church choir at Saint Gabriel's Anglican Church and always had my sister and me dressed up to attend church with her and Uncle Harry. When she succeeded in getting me to take catechism and confirmation, she gave me a beautiful little Bible in which she wrote, "You are bought with a price. Your body is a temple.

Be pure in mind and spirit." I have lost the Bible, but the words have remained with me.

The school fees and books were much harder to come by than the uniforms. Auntie, Sonia, and I sewed the uniforms together over that Christmas holiday. Auntie Black had to go to the bank to arrange for an overdraft to pay for the school fees for my sister and me. My unexpected arrival brought on a crisis in the Black household and added another layer of melancholy to my feelings of abandonment. One Saturday, when Auntie was at her civil service job at the Trade Board in Kingston, and I was helping Uncle Harry and the shop helper, he got into a really foul mood. He was sitting on his high stool at the counter in his favourite corner of his shop doing his crossword puzzle and pausing occasionally to stroke the two big spoiled cats. Suddenly, he left his crossword puzzle on the counter, got up, did a little jig, as if he were having an anxiety attack. Then he flushed red, broke out into a sweat, and yanked off his glasses and reached into his back pocket for his white stiffly starched handkerchief that I had ironed for him. He unfolded it and wiped his face in jabs. Still holding the crumpled up handkerchief in his right palm, he put the back of his hands akimbo and turned to me. He pointed at me and then laid down the conditions under which I could live in his house and attend Clarendon College: "When you come from school in the evenings and on weekends you have to come and help in the shop. You get holidays today; the maids will be gone tomorrow. You will have to do the washing and the cooking." He did not stop there. "When the time comes for you to board, you can only board from Monday to Thursday. On Fridays you have to come home for the weekend to work in the shop." His reference to the time to board referred to the practice of many parents of day students of having their children boarded for the term just preceding their examinations. This would allow their children to study intensively in order to do well. Sometimes, it could make the difference between passing and failing. A child's examination result could determine the future of their life as well as the family's fortune. I said nothing. I just held my head down and the tears of humiliation just fell to the ground. I continued to work in a sombre mood. At the end of the day, he fired the shop hand.

Uncle Harry treated Sonia differently from me. Although Sonia worked in the shop when she was at home, Uncle Harry did not lay down the same demands. This was perhaps due to her frail health or to the fact that he was willing to indulge Auntie's pleasure in having Sonia as a surrogate daughter. Auntie made the financial sacrifice to board Sonia fulltime in a home in the community, during the final year of her A levels. I believe Auntie did this for two reasons: the "zoobotchem" combination of subjects required long and demanding laboratory time, in addition to the rigourous preparation required to pass A level subjects. This investment paid off because Sonia passed her A level subjects and qualified for university entrance. Ultimately, I do not think that Sonia would have suffered in silence as I did—she had a way of getting what she thought she deserved. For this quality, I admired and envied her. Either I was too intimidated or I was more fearful of the consequence of openly defying authority figures when I was a child. I now believe in my heart that I had been subconsciously aware of my precarious existence without my mother to protect and defend me. It has taken me a lifetime of trial and error to understand my basic entitlements as a human being and to find my voice to speak up and out. When I became a mother, I was transformed into a fearless advocate for my children and learned to make legitimate demands assertively. My sister's attributes remain an inspiration in many ways besides this one.

I do not know what Uncle Harry told Auntie when she came home, but she too got into a foul mood. On the Sunday following, they had a row behind closed doors. I was anxious to hear what they were arguing about so I put my ears to the keyhole. I heard Uncle Harry shouting that he was tired of her family of parasites. He was particularly livid about my father and his two brothers who he said "came off to nothing." At the time, one of my father's brothers was living rent-free on a property that Auntie and Uncle Harry owned in Chudleigh, Christiana, which was my grandfather's constituency and hometown. I do not recall what I heard Auntie say in defence of her family. Given what I have learned about the family dynamics, during the course of this research, Auntie may have reminded him of all of the material benefits he had derived from Maas Charlie when he was a young poor man trying to make a living selling life insurance. Uncle Harry and Aunt Joyce provoked me into understanding how important it was for me to obtain a good education.

My strong desire for education overcame both the melancholy and the hardships under which I had to go to high school and study. I was so grateful to be attending high school that I did not care what it took to be there in order to study for my exams. Doing well at my high school was my way out of servitude and into economic independence and a life of dignity and respectability. I had to find ways to study in spite of these hardships, and I did. These were the burdens and challenges that weighed on my body and mind on that first morning.

When the bell rang, Sonia took me to form 5B where I joined my other classmates, lining up in front of our form for the march to the wide concrete corridors of the of the original classroom building. There, the whole student body would assemble in resolute military fashion, supervised by the prefects who would take their place at either end of the boys' and girls' lines. The head boy and head girl who supervised and inspected the line formations took their place last. To me, the head girl was a goddess, her posture erect, her head held high, her shoulders held back, and her smile composed. Her stiffly starched, white cotton blouse and light blue tunic topped with her navy-blue beret pinned ever so delicately atop her freshly pressed and curled hair told us girls what the standard of dress and deportment would be. Her pleats were starched and pressed razor sharp. They billowed like an accordion in the wind as she swung her hips from side to side. She walked to the beat of the music in her head. It could have been the rhythms of the cha-cha, the twist, the mashed potato, or all three, tempered with the melodies of the "soft tunes." She exhibited the sensuous pleasures of her lithe body. She was the personification of poise and congeniality, tinged with a dollop of English snobbery. The head boy was a perfect portrait of colonial man, young, handsome, athletic, suave, and courtly. Both represented the finest models of the civilizing mission of the Presbyterian and Congregation Union.

The aims of cultivating our minds with the King James Bible, the patriotic hymns of the British empire, the English language and literature, the history of the British empire, and the ideals of British public schooling were as lofty as the hills upon which Clarendon College perched. All of this grooming gave us an image of the cultivated people we were to become. We believed every word of it. We were to become a social breed that was apart from the masses of poor black people and to consider that we were their betters. High school had a sorting effect where only "the cream of the crop" could go. There is much here to explain and understand.

When the marching footsteps had stopped and there was absolute silence, out came the crew of well-dressed white, brown, and black teachers. In time, I learned about this strange collection of people. The white teachers hailed from various destinations of the British empire and beyond: England, Scotland, Wales, Spain, Sweden, and the United States. There were no Canadians that I can remember. Among these individuals were the British volunteers and the American Peace Corp. These bodies were definitely out of place.

The brown and black teachers came from two sources. First, there were the young graduates of the thirteen-year-old University College of the West Indies, which was a sub-branch of the University of London. As undergraduate students they went to formal dinner, Monday to Friday, dressed in long red robes over their shirt and ties. They mimicked what they thought the University of London students were like. In so doing, they plastered over their peasant stock with airs and manners of speech. Their "speaky-spokey" was a constant source of comedy for us students—the patois was always slipping out to blow their cover. They were a new breed of homegrown Caribbean literati.

Then there were those Jamaican teachers who had gone to England to study as young colonials. They were bright enough to earn island scholarships or their families had sacrificed by selling a piece of land or a few heads of cows to send them away to study so that they could join the ranks of the respectable black people. They mimicked the English just like the graduates of the University College of the West Indies, but they were very good at it.

A constant source of humour was the distinction in fashion between the European and the Caribbean teachers. Just to give a few examples, there was a Swede who walked around in her black Oxfords, thick woollen black stockings under her green plaid wool kilt, and turtleneck sweater. She topped it off with her headscarf tied in a knot under her chin. Then there was the English music teacher who could not stand the heat and wore no underwear under her sleeveless moo-moo dresses. The boys in 5B were always late for their agricultural science class because they had to pass by the music room to see her spread her legs and fan her crotch before she positioned the cello and began to play. The teacher thought that the crowd at her doors meant they just loved her cello playing. But the most comical turn for me was given by the English reverend, who taught us bible knowledge—the books that comprised the Pentateuch were required for our Cambridge exams. So were the books of Kings and Samuels. His dress was anything but reverent in the eyes of Jamaicans. No self-respecting Jamaican reverend would ever go without his collar, and he would definitely not wear brown leather sandals, short khaki pants, and short sleeve white shirts. When he came to class, after the exchange of greetings, he would put his bottom on the side of the chair long enough to swing around and hoist his legs upon the desk. We only saw his head between his up-sticking legs as he read the Bible for the whole fifty minutes. He read well. I was entranced by his booming radio voice and how he used it to convey the poetic cadences in the archaic language of the Old Testament. We looked forward to his reading of Second Samuels, chapter 13—Amnon's abuse of Tamar. This chapter was the juiciest of all the readings, and the girls especially wanted to see how he would read this story. He never did. In rereading this chapter about the rape of Tamar and the revenge that followed, I think this story has much to teach young women about the realities of sexual assault in families. There are many lessons young women could learn about protecting themselves from such entrapment. He asked no questions during or after reading, and he did not notice what we were doing while he read. When the bell rang, he would pivot on his bottom, stand up, and walk out. One day, out of boredom, a boy stood up to stretch, peeked over at the reverend's desk, and started the rumour that the reverend wore no underpants. Needless to say, after this, there were many stretchers throughout the class period. The reverend was oblivious to the antics of those little sinners he was teaching.

To return to the assembly on my first day, the teachers filed out of the overcrowded staff room and stood together at the top end of the sloping corridor. A white man marched out last, briskly, and stepped up to the open side of the middle of the three or four classrooms that were located opposite the wide corridor. This position acted as a platform. He stood at attention and craned his neck to survey the formation. While he was so doing, I studied his appearance. His crewcut looked like a toupee of straight pins on the top of his head. His round white face had very finely chiselled features, a straight nose, thin lips, and blue eyes. He was dressed in stiffly starched and ironed khaki short pants, a crisp cotton, short sleeve white shirt, and brown laced-up brogues. His long beige socks were folded over just below his kneecap and held in place with a green tassel, which swung with every firm step that he took to the rhythm of heels in, toes out; heels in, toes out. He almost had knock knees. He walked up to the microphone and said: "Good morning, boys and girls. Welcome to Clarendon College. We shall begin the morning's worship." His Adam's apple moved up and down as he belted out the sounds from his mouth. He paused, changed his tone, and began a short recitation, trilling every "r" and emphasizing every "t" and "d," as if to let us know that we would have to stop the habit of discarding these letters when we spoke in our patois. He recited: "Every good gift, and every perfect gift cometh from the father of light, in whom there is no variableness." After this recitation, he paused for effect and announced the opening hymn. On the first morning of every school year, it was always "Lord Behold us with thy blessing." The rustle of the hymn book pages broke the stillness. We had to purchase our school hymnals just as we purchased our textbooks. The prefects monitored our having our hymnal for morning and afternoon worship. Mr. Hayden Middleton, the deputy headmaster from Wales, as we would come to know him, sang the first stanza, *a cappella.*

Lord behold us with thy blessing
Once again assembled here;
Onward be our footsteps pressing,
In thy love and faith and fear
Still protect us, by thy presence ever near.

Then Mr. Middleton announced that after the count of three, we would begin to sing. He waved his hand to the beat one, two, three, and the whole school sang in unison, while Mr. Middleton conducted and sang above our voices to keep the tempo. We sang all four stanzas. Oh, it was glorious to hear hundreds of children singing their youthful hearts out. The bass and baritone of the boys' section was sonorous with ripening manhood. The alto and soprano voices of the girls' section soared to the highest heaven from the hill. Singing this hymn lifted my spirits. We ended with the Lord's Prayer.

It was the headmaster's turn. Mr. Clevens Levi Stuart, headmaster, whose reputation preceded him as the dearly beloved Pops, stepped up to the microphone. I remember him as stocky, if a little rotund, with a copper-coloured complexion, receding hairline, and a fixed, grave, toothless smile. This is not to say that he did not have his teeth but to say that he did not show them when he smiled. He was formally dressed in a brown suit and tie with matching brown shoes, which were so shiny that they glistened in the sun. He may have been wearing the light blue shirt that I came to associate with him. He walked with the stealth of a spy who habitually showed up unexpectedly to startle hot and bothered teenagers necking and petting in musky hideaways. He paused, raised his chin, grabbed his tie, and straightened it. Then he lowered his chin slightly as he peered out over his spectacles at the new student body. He was a rather soft-spoken man. After welcoming us warmly, he gave us a brief history of the founding of the school in 1945 by the late Reverend Lester Davy of the Congregation Union, who he said obtained support from the Colonial Missionary Society. A house was named for him, and those who belonged to that house were reminded of their responsibility of carrying the torch of the founder. He spoke of the Reverend Frank Nichol's effort to relocate the school on the present premises. I belonged to Nichol House. Every Founder's Day, the whole student body assembled at the original spot of the first school buildings, which was about a mile away down the hill, to mark the occasion. Mr. Stuart reminded us of the tremendous privilege that we had in receiving a secondary education. We were expected to wear the school uniform proudly and to uphold the good reputation of the school. He wished us a good school year and exhorted us to do our parents and guardians proud. In spite of the burdens that I carried, I was bursting with joy and anticipation of good learning times ahead. We were dismissed to walk together loosely back to our form rooms. There we would get our timetables and meet our classmates and form teacher who would take the attendance. Teachers came to our classroom for the various subjects, except in the case of agricultural science for the boys, which was held outside, and housecraft and sewing for the girls, which was held in the housecraft centre.

At the end of the day, we reassembled to pray and sing a hymn such as "Now the Day is over the night is drawing nigh, shadows of the evening steal across the sky." Notices were read out and mail was distributed before we were dismissed. The mail was mostly for the boarders. The rich students got the most mail and packages from home. One could tell how rich their parents were from how much money they spent in the tuck shop the following day. We poor day students would write letters to each other and mail them to the college so that we could have our names read out from time to time. Some of us girls got love letters from our secret admirers. Yet, this formal opening ceremony gave us a clear signal that we were in a special place with many high expectations.

It gives me great pleasure to revisit my high school curriculum, although I still have regrets about not finishing my Cambridge A levels. It was the combination of subjects, the teachers who taught them, my classmates who shared the learning experiences, and the classroom and school settings that made for very pleasant recollections. My O level school certificate is my prompt.

English language was my favourite subject. As a young child coming to awareness, I remember being fascinated with how I was able to put my thoughts into speech. I lived a lot in my head through words and my imagination. In infant school, every new word I learned created magical thinking. I am still fascinated by the brainpower of thought and speech. I simply loved words and the power of words to express sophisticated and complex thoughts. I loved best to mystify and insult my classmates with Latinate words, the bigger the better. With this disposition, I found it difficult to abide by the recommendation to refrain from using these words in my writing. After all, a facility with words is the hallmark of a higher education. The first time that I heard the minister of my church read from the Gospel of St. John, "In the beginning was the Word, and the Word was God, and the Word was made flesh and dwelt among us," I knew for sure that words have sacred power.

Even when I was at May Pen Comprehensive School, I had admired Mr. Lampart's and Miss Broomfield's ways with words. Mr. Lampart was a model public speaker who sometimes preached sermons at St. Gabriel's Anglican Church in May Pen. I have already talked about his homilies around the thought for the day and how they enthralled and inspired me. Miss Broomfield deserves a tribute for widening my world to include an appreciation for brilliant speeches. The context was the talks surrounding the short-lived West Indies Federation, which occurred between 1958 and 1962. As part of general knowledge, Miss Broomfield would bring in the *Daily Gleaner*, which published the full texts of all of the Caribbean leaders debating the merits and demerits of the Federation. I remember a heated debate as to whether the capital of the Federation should be located in Jamaica, or in Trinidad. Freedom of movement among the islands and how this would affect the islands with greater physical resources was quite contentious. The small islands resented Jamaica for what they saw as its excessive demands as the largest of the British West Indian Islands. Miss Broomfield read the speeches aloud to us and thus helped us to appreciate the structure of arguments and the effect of oratory and grandiloquence. She boasted of how those leaders could wield the Queen's English. The speeches of Grantley Adams of Barbados, Prime Minister of the Federation, were particularly impressive.

These were the heady years of the anti-colonial and independence movements all over Africa and the Caribbean. The world was opened up to us in words and pictures. The *Daily Gleaner* carried speeches and pictures of Africans of newly independent nations speaking at the United Nations in New York. Miss Broomfield would also read us those speeches and talked about the pride that Jamaicans felt in seeing African leaders—Kwame Nkrumah of Ghana, Nnamdi Azikiwe of Nigeria, Kenneth Kaunda of Zambia, Julius Nyrere of Tanzania, Jomo Kenyatta of Kenya—and their diplomatic corps dressed in their national regalia. So impressionable were our minds that a big boy came to school one day dressed as Kwame Nkrumah, complete with the staff and flywhisk. He told us all how Nkrumah formed his "cabinet." I puzzled over his use of this word because at that point in my learning of the English language, the only cabinet that I knew was the china cabinet. This was a profound lesson for me in the multiple meanings of words.

Those were also times of great public distress following the assassination of Patrice Lumumba of the Belgian Congo. These anti-colonial conflicts generated much talk among the adults everywhere—in the press, at home, in the rum shops, under the mango trees, in the yards, on the verandas, from the pulpits, and in the marketplaces. Jamaican children were getting an image of Africans that hitherto they had not had. The Garveyites and the Rastafarians found reason to celebrate the dress and eloquent speeches of the African representatives at the United Nations. The pan-Africanists also found reason to feel good in solidarity. Adults at home and in the streets talked and argued about politics and religion constantly. Some arguments lasted for weeks. Oh, these were heady times. We were a colony of talkers. Words were our amusement and our weapons— English competed with the Jamaican patois for dramatic expression.

At Clarendon College, English, and Spanish classes built on the strong foundation that I received at the May Pen Comprehensive School where I studied Latin, Spanish, and English simultaneously. I kept a vocabulary book for each language into which I added new words, their meanings, and usage. In studying these languages, we needed a big vocabulary to do the translation exercises well in the idiom of the languages. At Clarendon College, I remember Mr. Blair, who taught us the English poetry of Blake, Conrad, Browning, Gray, and the sonnets of Shakespeare. We analyzed these poems for metre, rhyme scheme, imagery, and diction. Mr. Blair was so earnest and gentle in his manner of teaching that poems from Blake's *Songs of Innocence and of Experience* and Gray's *Elegy Written in a Country Church Yard* will always seem to be associated warmly with him. I remember Mr. Blair trying to teach us to appreciate *The Last Duchess* for the Cambridge exam. I did not like this poem, nor did I understand its significance.

Mr. Robert Fianda, a Peace Corp volunteer, taught us Shakespeare. Through his voice and eccentricity, we memorized all of *Henry V,* which was the play assigned for the Cambridge examination that year. Mr. Fianda was said to have fallen for rum and black women. I certainly remember that he had a red nose and a wobbly gait. We gossiped over whether his nose was red from the sun or from the rum. He would sometimes miss classes. When he came to the classroom door, he would make a run for the desk and jump on top, open the play, and just read with his perfect radio voice. When the bell rang, he would shut the book, jump off the desk, and leave the room. He cared nothing for the "Good afternoon, sir" or "Good afternoon, miss" routine, which was our standard response to a teacher's greeting. We were so thoroughly charmed by his voice, and we loved the language and the drama so much that we would gather in groups and try to mimic his reading. While writing this section of this book, I have been reciting the prologue to *Henry V.*

The other subjects I took at O level were Bible Knowledge, Spanish, Biology, Needlework / Dressmaking, and General Housecraft. General Housecraft was the most ridiculous subject. Imagine that we girls had to prepare to darn woollen socks over a light bulb, set a tray for tea, and prepare a "convalescent meal" for the examinations. I hated this subject. I needed no more "domestication," since I had had quite enough in all of the households in which I lived.

While I waited for the results of the O levels to come in that New Year, I started A levels. During the Easter term, I took English literature, economics, and history and, in the summer term after receiving the exam results, I changed to "zoobotchem" to be just like my sister. This was a time of great confusion for me. My sister had got a teaching job at Titchfield High School in Port Antonio, which was on the far eastern end of the island. With her leaving, I saw very little reason to stay in school. I could not see myself trying to do A levels under the work regime that Uncle Harry insisted upon. More than ever, I desperately wanted to be like all of my friends who were indulged as children and whose adolescence was ushered in with pride and celebration.

My sister promised that as soon as she got her feet on the ground, she would send me money so that I could be a boarder. She could never afford to do this, but my sister had a way of seeing possibilities where I could not. She was a dreamer. I believed in her promise and because of this I pressed on, but my heart was not in it. My report card for Easter and the summer terms of that year showed the poor results.

In spite of this distress and confusion, I was drawn into the extracurricular life of the school. I was elected to be the captain of the 4-H Club team that competed in the Denbigh Agricultural Show, and the team returned with many prizes, including the coveted prize for cattle judging. I won a prize for being the best cook of chicken fricassee. I became a member of the debating team that Mr. Gunter, our flamboyant science master, took to the prestigious Munro College for Boys in St. Elizabeth. Munro College represented a different world of schooling. We arrived just before suppertime and were warmly and formally greeted before being taken on a brief tour of the college. Then we dined with some prefects, I believe. I could not take my eyes off these black and brown boys behaving like little "English gentlemen" and talking as if they had hot potatoes in their mouths. The big boys bossed the little boys mercilessly. I felt so sorry for them. Clarendon College debated hard. I do not remember what the motion was, but we beat the much-esteemed Munro team on their own turf and qualified to go to the island finals. We were applauded loudly when Mr. Stuart proudly announced our victory at the morning devotion.

We were heroes for beating Munro. In the hierarchy of high schools, Munro, which was built in 1797, had a tradition of being one of the first secondary schools to educate the elite in St. Elizabeth, a parish that had many white settlers, including a significant Jewish population that survived the Spanish Inquisition and lived in relative safety in Jamaica from the time of the Spanish settlement (Brown 1979, 91). The other group of white people in the area were descendants of the German farmers and artisans who had been invited by independent entrepreneurs and the Jamaican House of Assembly in waves after emancipation to give the Negroes an example of European industry and skills (Senior 2003, 211). By comparison, Clarendon

College was a young secondary school, founded only in 1945, which catered to the children of peasant farmers, shopkeepers, teachers, maids, and seamstresses in central and northern Clarendon. It surprises me now to realize that Clarendon, the most productive sugar parish—second only to Westmoreland—had no secondary school until the Presbyterian and Congregation Union established Clarendon College. I speculate that the planters and estate owners of the parish, which included such notable absentee owners as the historian Edward Long and Sir Henry Morgan (of buccaneer fame and the former lieutenant governor of Jamaica), among others, remained true to the colonial ideology that said that education spoils labour. Since most were absentee owners, perhaps they saw no need for secondary schools for their own children. Their resident attorneys and overseers would have sent their children to boarding schools in Kingston or to Munro and Hampton in St. Elizabeth. The peasant parents sacrificed to send their children to school as soon as the opportunity became available to them. Clarendon College was therefore regarded as a cut below Munro. Our debating victory was sweet indeed. We eventually placed in the Island competition—I believe in fourth place.

I also joined the drama club and loved it. Unfortunately, as a day student, I could not be around at nights for rehearsals. At the closing ceremonies for the summer term, I was invested as a prefect. But, as things turned out, I did not stay around long enough to enact this leadership role. I have kept my report cards, and it is interesting to note the three dimensions along which Clarendon College prepared us—as persons, citizens, and workers.

We were groomed to be citizens and workers of the United Kingdom and Colonies. These three dimensions are part of the blueprint that has determined who I have become. I have always been attentive to the presentation of self and to the congruence of character and moral values. I have exercised my civic responsibilities, and I have tried to be a conscientious, hard working person who goes the extra mile. The same pattern of socialization followed into teachers' college.

My sister and I got together with much rejoicing when she came home for Easter holidays in 1961. By this time, we had the results of our Cambridge exams, and we had both been successful. We made Auntie proud. She was so happy. Uncle Harry gave his luke-warm congratulations. He had always told me that he thought the best future for me was to work in a shop. Of course, I could not openly tell him what I thought of that idea. As with the situation at Aunt Joyce's house, I just kept quiet and worked to undo his plans for me.

Besides sharing our happiness about our exams and the doors that our high school education could open for us, we sisters talked at length about our future. Sonia was going to be a doctor, and I was going to be a teacher. We had a conversation about how we imagined our marriages would go, our children, and what kind of aunties we would be to them, and then we talked about death. We marvelled that no one ever came back and told people what life after death was like. We made a solemn promise that whichever one of us died first would make sure to come back and tell the other. Little did we know that this conversation was a foreshadowing of what was to come about in only three months' time. My sister died of complicated and mysterious causes in early July 1961. Her death was a big blow to my hopes of doing my A levels. Without her promised financial support and encouragement, I saw no point in staying in school.

My sister's death brought on a crisis for me. I had to make a decision about extricating myself from a dead-end situation in the Black's household. I made the decision, unilaterally, to leave school and get a job. This decision to leave high school before completing my A levels left me wondering how my life course may have been different had I completed them. I have always regretted that I did not stay to proudly wear my prefect's badge or to become a full-time boarder.

After leaving Clarendon College, I applied to Barclays Bank for a job. The boarders that the Blacks had had, over the years, and who had worked at both Barclays and the Bank of Nova Scotia, may have inspired me to apply there. To my surprise, in a few days, I received a letter inviting me for an interview. The sub-manager interviewed me about banking. I must have given him back verbatim all that I had learned about banking in my sixth form economics class. He then gave me sheets of figures to add up and manipulate. The speed and accuracy of addition that I had learned from filling the orders for Uncle Harry's high-class customers came in handy. After checking my answers, the sub-manager then had a discussion with the manager and accountant while I waited. He offered me a job on the spot as a filing clerk and told me to report for work on the following Monday. I could not believe my lucky stars.

I remember making the announcement that I was going to work at Barclays Bank over supper to both Auntie and Uncle Harry. They were taken aback, as if they were caught unaware. They did not even compliment me but proceeded to tell me that the only reason I got the job was because I lived in their household. I resented this comment and believe, to this day, that I was the one who had applied for the job without their knowledge or reference; that I was the one who had to perform at the interview; and that I did not just walk in to pick up a job that had been obtained for me by the pulling of strings. What they were really saying, I now realize, is that, at that time, the norm was that in order to obtain a job in the bank one had to have important social connections and be sponsored. Their claim did not make sense then and only now does it make any sense in an unsatisfactory sort of way. In the social and economic scheme in May Pen, the Black's had, in my opinion, relatively little socio-economic influence. Uncle Harry ran a grocery shop that catered to the market people and a few high-class families. Their patronage disappeared as soon as the supermarket came. Auntie Black was a civil servant. She had better standing in the community than her husband. Furthermore, they did not even bank with Barclays Bank but with the Bank of Nova Scotia. They must have been referring to the residual influence of their colour. Times were changing from a patronage-based selection based on skin colour and family connections towards a merit-based selection for jobs. The increase in educational opportunities for the majority black and brown population meant that more of them acquired the secondary schooling that was necessary to qualify for those jobs that were previously reserved for white-skinned people. They were stuck in the old colonial system of patronage, which had been under attack and had come to a head in the labour riots of the 1930s. I guess Uncle Harry could not really believe that I would not be his servant for life.

When I got my first paycheque, which was deposited in my own bank account, of which I was so proud, Uncle Harry demanded that I write a cheque handing over the full amount to him. I was so irate that I talked back and said that I would do no such thing. I told him that if he wished to charge me for room and board that I was agreeable, but under no account was I going to give him my paycheque. He became so angry shouting at me that his false teeth fell out and broke. He and Auntie had their closed-door conference, and the sum that I should pay for room and board was decided upon. Auntie insisted that if I was to pay room and board that I would be treated like their other boarders with my own room, my meals prepared, and my laundry done.

These conditions did not sit well with Uncle Harry. He retaliated by starting to object to things like my going to the movies with my work friends or going to Kingston on a Saturday after work. He still expected me to come and work in his shop on Saturdays after work. I detested this man's ways so much and resented his business practices. I could not stand to watch him cheat the poor market people in weight and measure for sugar, flour, codfish, and kerosene oil. He expected me to do the same things. I did quite the opposite by giving the people more than they were due when he was not looking. I would also purposely give some of them extra change. When eventually he became aware of my deceit, he would keep me from the tills and began to watch every customer interaction like a hawk. If he caught me he would get so furious and give me some diatribe about how to do business, telling me that I did not know "a dagone thing" about business. I had to suppress the urge I had to call him a thief, a liar, and a hypocrite.

Eventually, this man's ways became so obnoxious to me that one Saturday after coming home from the bank I packed my clothes and left to board with the family of my best girlfriend. Auntie seemed upset, but, as always, she was caught between her loyalty to her husband and to her family. She always kept in touch with me and invited me to come to visit from time to time. I have come to really appreciate Auntie's quiet strength and family diplomacy. Life must have been very difficult for her. I often wished that I had my mother at these times.

What's a mother? This is the first significant question that I asked when I was about four or five years old. The precise occasion occurred during my effort to bond with Miss Eu's niece, and Miss Eu remarked: "She thinks you are her mother," to which I perked up and asked: "What's a mother?" The question remained significant throughout my life. The meaning of the question is becoming clear as I write about my peculiar experiences of growing up as a motherless child in Jamaica. In writing this part of my life history, I can see how several attitudes in my family were reverberations of the social and economic practices of slavery days. First, as the child of a black woman, I had the mark of the slave child. In slavery days, the children of black women, regardless of paternity, were automatically slaves. As such, they learned to labour as early as six years old by working in the slave masters' households or with the pickney gangs in the cane fields, in cattle pens, or in the provision grounds. It was the mothers who shielded and protected their children from the excesses of this brutal system. After emancipation when children of six years and older could work with the consent of their mothers, very few mothers permitted their children to work. Without my mother, and at the hands of a father who seemed to think that he had fathered slave children, I was left to be taken advantage of by people who still clung to these racist attitudes. They used their illicit power to take advantage of innocent children. This was evident in my father, Aunt Joyce, and Uncle Harry. Now I understand when the folk who were suffering at the hands of such people would bemoan their vulnerability by saying: "Poor me, dead woman pickney."

I can now answer the question: "What's a mother?" A mother is not only the woman who gives birth to children, but she also loves, respects, and protects them from social and economic predators. Auntie Black was a mother, Mrs. Martin, my teacher in May Pen All-Age School, was a mother. I am ambivalent about this status for Miss Eu and Aunt Joyce.

The second practice that harkens back to slavery days was the practice of hiring out slaves to increase the income of the slave master. In those days, whatever the slave earned was handed directly to the master and not to the slave who had earned it. Uncle Harry's claim to being entitled to my paycheque from Barclays Bank was a continuing practice of this tradition. So was his practice of cheating his maids and yardboys out of their fair wages.

A third practice involved the colonial attitude towards the education of brown and black children who were automatically considered slaves in slavery days. This ideology, which was maintained by the state legislature, the planter, and the merchant classes, asserted that education spoiled labour, and, therefore, the only kind of education suitable for these children was schooling that was sufficient to make them literate labourers. This was the kind of education that the state would accede to after emancipation. The Mango Walk All-Age School, the Carron Hall All-Age School, the Domestic Science Training Centre for girls, and the Dairy Farm Training Centre for boys were examples of these kinds of schools. I consider that Aunt Joyce and Uncle Harry were acting out of this impulse, as was, to some extent, my father. I do not think that he had any vision for us beyond the all-age schools that the law compelled the masses to attend by the 1940s and 1950s. The limited state-sponsored educational opportunities resulted in the churches intervening to provide secondary education to those who could afford to pay fees.

My subsequent employment at the bank seems to have flown in the face of the retrogressive attitudes that surrounded me. I had graduated from domestic labour and was out of the control of people who thought they had a permanent control over my life chances. Uncle Harry and Aunt Joyce were looking to make me a servant for life—a euphemism for slave status after emancipation.

During the year that I worked at the bank, I was able to decipher the sociogram of all of the employees of the bank at the time. I could discern how the racial hierarchy matched the positions they held and mirrored the class and colour hierarchy that existed on the island at that time. The manager, sub-manager, and accountant were all white and came from the head office in England. The two cashiers were Chinese—a male and a female. When the female left to get married, I was taken from the filing room and placed on the savings ledgers, and a near-white woman was taken off savings and put on the cash wicket. When the Chinese man was away a few times, I was put on his wicket to do his cash by default. By the social mores of the time, only people who looked to be almost white were put in front of the public to present the face of the bank. Interestingly, *The Encyclopedia of Jamaican Heritage* by Olive Senior reports that the Chinese broke the colour bar of the white English and Canadian banking systems in colonial Jamaica during the 1950s.

I did so well at both customer service on savings and cash that I was sent to be the cashier at the Chapelton and Old Harbour sub-branches all by myself, with a bodyguard and a driver of course. I also did well in this position and was appointed as a cashier in the May Pen branch for the last six months of my stay. Since I had responsibility for the cash, I got to have the keys for the money vault while I was at work. I was entrusted to take in lodgings and to figure the payroll for some of the big sugar companies. I remember processing the payroll cheques for cane workers on one of the large estates. A worker's fortnightly wage on that estate was one pound, one shilling—a "guinea." The ledgers were a challenge to balance, having to deal manually with such large payrolls. Another big job was manually processing the month-end lodgements (deposits) from several sugar estates. I remember the lodgements arriving in huge metal trunks, containing both paper and coins. The paper money was sorted into denominations of 5 pound, 1 pound, 10 shillings, and 5 shillings, with the portrait of the Queen uppermost. The silver and copper coins were weighed out in bags of similar denominations and stacked in order. The accountant and the sub-manger liked me and valued how reliable I was in balancing the ledgers, especially during the busy fortnightly and monthly periods. We could not go home until all of the ledgers were balanced to the penny. I can now see that all of my mathematical learning in school as well as my grooming to be a reliable, honest, and dependable individual worked both in my favour and in my employer's favour.

Without understanding its full significance then, I was the darkest employee in the May Pen branch of the bank at that time. I was aware of the social pecking order along colour, race, class, and gender lines from the moment I started, but I did not know or understand the historical and economic bases of the phenomenon that I was both observing and experiencing.

I became aware of the meaning of the public political debates and protests about colour prejudice in government jobs and in the banks that were occurring at the time. About this time, there were also fierce debates about expanding enrolment in the prestigious secondary schools, which formerly had served only the white and coloured sectors of the population, to include black and working-class children who passed their common entrance examinations at the appropriate level. There were letters to the editor of the *Daily Gleaner*, written by middle- and upper-class coloured and white people bemoaning the fact that their children could be sitting beside the children of their maids and yardboys.

I felt socially inadequate, but I believed strongly in my ability to learn the job and do it well. In spite of proving myself adequate for the job, I could not prove myself socially. Neither my family nor I possessed the requisite social and economic capital that counted. First of all, I had not attended one of the prestigious girls' schools such as Saint Andrew's or Immaculate Conception. I did not play tennis. I did not swim or frequent the beaches on the north coast. I could not drive a car, and I did not belong to a well-known family that would allow me to boast any great family wealth and lore. In fact, I wanted to disown my family. I did not shop at Nathan's or Is-sas's stores in Kingston, which carried the ready-made clothes that I could not afford. My family did not have a cottage on the north coast to offer free weekends to friends and acquaintances in exchange for other privileges. I could not give a garden party. I had nothing to exchange but my intelligence and my labour.

I observed the same socioeconomic pecking order at the Trade Board, which had recently been turned into the Ministry of Trade and Industry, when my Auntie Black got me a job one summer when I was in college. During that time, I came to observe what I would now characterize as a hierarchy of deference along colour lines. It seemed to me that my Auntie Black worked very hard to pass for white in order to hold a high place in the pecking order. She did so by the way she straightened her hair, though she had relatively "good hair," the way she dressed, by her manner of speech, and in her etiquette. She was not putting on airs because she was a circumspect woman with a pleasant disposition most of the time. Aunt Joyce, by contrast, changed speech registers depending on to whom she was speaking. She changed her speech in a like manner as she changed from her drudging clothes to her dress-up clothes. She was always more at ease in the patois and working-class ways of being.

The politics of skin colour were so confusing and full of contradictions. There were three crude categories of skin colour: white, coloured, and black. Sometimes the classification was white, brown, and black. Within the coloured category, skin tones ranged from brown, yellow, and near white, all having various subtle distinctions depending on the eye of the discriminating. The closer the skin tone to white, the better socially—the closer to black, the fewer advantages were accorded in society at the time. Skin colour denoted social prestige and status, which, in turn, involved an irrational interplay of family connections, gradation of skin colour, ethnicity, wealth, and education.

I now wonder what social cachet I may have had, had I known, and could have sung, the praises of my late maternal grandfather, the Honorable Charles Archibald Reid, who was a member of the Legislative Council and the first Negro to be awarded an Order of the British Empire. Charles Reid's biography in *Who's Who and Why in Jamaica, 1939–40* (1939–40, 152) records that he was born in Christiana in January 1887, had a primary school education, learned the shoemaking trade, entered a grocery business in 1919, and became a planter in 1929. He owned citrus and banana plantations in Christiana and, as a literate property owner of independent means, could stand for election to the Legislative Council of the Crown Colony. He was first elected on 30 January 1931 and served on many government boards, including the Civil Service Selection Committee. The *London Gazette* of 17 February 1942 records in a bulletin from Downing Street that the king had been pleased to appoint Charles Archibald Reid, Esq., OBE, as a member of the Privy Council of the Island of Jamaica.

I am now puzzled why only the poor black folk talked to me about him when they found out that I was his granddaughter and why my father's family kept quiet. Any family would surely have been proud to boast of this accomplished person in their family. Adding to this

My grandfather, the Hon. Charles Archibald Reid.

mystery is the fact that, in telling the story of Jamaica, only coloured and white men are shown as actors, even though there were many notable black men in the struggle for personhood. The women's contributions, of course, went unrecorded, except in folklore.

I may have had some social capital to trade on if my maternal grandfather were white or brown and equally accomplished. I would have known about him if he were white. In the cultural world of the Jamaican colony, black skin signified inferiority and exclusion from high society. Wealthy black people who had a certain type of education could push the colour bar slightly. However, there were always the gatekeepers who were ready to remind such black people that they had limited membership and could be slighted without provocation. If you were black or brown and attended one of the prestigious high schools, there was some cachet in being there; and yet, there were powerful social forces to keep people with black complexion, such as my grandfather, out. White skin without money still commanded respect, deference, and unearned privileges. White or near-white complexion could garner respect and regard long after those people lost power and prestige. I guess this is why my father always strutted around and beat his chest when he was drunk, reminding himself and all those around him of his genealogy. Maybe he drowned his shame of falling from landed gentry into near poverty by drinking rum and womanizing.

Women were always kept in a waiting pattern in the bank. It was assumed that they were waiting to get married. They were seldom promoted. Marriage, or the prospect of it, was the central criterion that determined the temporary and transient status of women workers in the bank. No matter how many years a woman had worked in the bank, as soon as she got married she was demoted to temporary staff. I had an aversion to marriage. I saw no good in it from observing the lives of married women around me and by counting the options that were closed to them. I wanted autonomy, self-reliance, and adventure more than anything else. Marriage was antithetical to my ambitions. I also wanted to get away from May Pen and from my aunts and the devouring demands of their egocentric husbands. In keenly observing how much their husbands controlled their lives and killed their spirit of freedom and adventure, I was determined that marriage was not one of my desired goals. In a few years' time, however, I was to learn how religious and cultural imperatives ensnare and trap young women into the "holy estate of matrimony." The catch was that although I did not want marriage, I knew I wanted children. Having children out of wedlock was literally inconceivable for young women striving towards respectability. For many young ambitious women contemplating motherhood and companionship on their own terms, marriage was often a very high price to pay for their respectability and compromised autonomy.

After working for nine months with Barclays Bank, Dominion, Colonial, and Overseas, I began to feel that I needed to leave that place. I could not see a future with the bank, although I loved the work. I looked around, evaluated the status of each woman, and knew why. There was one older woman who was the white wife of an official at Monymusk Sugar Company and who was working for pin money. She talked incessantly about her children who were at boarding school in England. The near-white wife of a Methodist minister made it clear that she was just working until her respectable Barbadian husband was transferred to another district. Then there was a near-white spinster who had roots in one of the sugar plantations but who never revealed her future aspirations. There was another near-white, single, marriageable female who had too many drops of black blood to catch one of the white men in this branch or from the Kingston head office. The men often talked about her being on the shelf behind her back. The East Indian secretary was just waiting to marry one of the black sons of a rich factory owner. The brown man from Barbados could not keep his hands and lips off her body in the lunchroom. A flighty, white Jamaican young woman was at the bank and actively seeking to catch a white man but had plans to go to England if she proved unable to hook the white Jamaican son of the rope factory owner. The near-white secretary to the absent-minded white accountant was just biding her time to emigrate to Canada and to marry her high school sweetheart, who was then studying in the United States. The Syrian young woman of ample means talked constantly of her amorous desire for a white man. The day she heard that a single man from head office in London was coming to join the staff was the day that she made arrangements for plastic surgery on her nose and to buy some new fashionable clothes. She would come to the file room to read the correspondence to obtain all of his particulars. She even planned a welcome itinerary with her family to take place very soon after the bank's formalities. Unfortunately, she was the figurative ugly duckling. She walked like a duck and looked like a duck. After the surgery, she was transformed into a princess waiting for her prince.

The tragedy was that when the gentleman arrived, I thought he was the most boring and unattractive white man I had ever met. On his first weekend, all of the white folk in the bank took him to the high-class country club in Kingston for a proper colonial welcome. At that time, these country clubs were exclusively for Jamaican white folk and their white expatriate friends. Late at night when they were returning to May Pen, the car in which he was riding ran smack into the back of a parked truck. He was killed and so was the accountant's young wife, leaving behind three very young children. The interesting thing to me was that, within a week, funeral arrangements were made for him to be buried at St. Luke's Anglican Church in one of the choicest lots. The Church of England put on the most formal funeral service befitting an Englishman who had died unexpectedly in the colony.

Looking back now, I see why I was a social misfit. There I was, the red Ibo girl, as my schoolmates called me, the one with the brown skin and the "bad hair," who could not pass for white under any disguise. I loved the work and did it well to the satisfaction of my bosses, but I did not fit into the class and colour hierarchy. As a filing clerk, I had the opportunity to read every single piece of correspondence during the time I was left in the vault to file. The vault for the files was next to the cash vault and safety deposit boxes. I do not remember the details of any of the letters and invoices that I read before filing, but I picked up the bureaucratic language of authority and entitlements to land, labour, and capital. Furthermore, I saw and heard the names of those who could ask for, and obtain large loans without collateral or a guarantor and those who could not. I also learned of those who created "bad and doubtful debts" that the bank wrote off. Moreover, I learned about international banking networks that existed among the Bank of London, the Bank of London and Montreal, the Royal Bank of Canada, the Canadian Imperial Bank of Commerce, and the Bank of Nova Scotia. We cleared cheques drawn on any of these banks, and they did the same for Barclays Bank. Each of these banks had a column in the ledgers, which recorded daily transactions.

The turning point at the bank came when I encouraged a male schoolmate to join the branch with me, about ten months after I had joined. He was paid a higher salary than I was. To add insult to injury, I was assigned to be his mentor and to teach him the ledger system. I could not live with this unfair situation, and I could do nothing about it. These were the gender norms of the time. I had to walk away if I did not like it.

— Chapter Five —

Becoming a Teacher: Mico College, 1962–65

When we go forth from the walls of the Mico,
Forth to lead others as we have been led,
See that we hold to ideals that are lofty,
Emulate Mico's illustrious dead.
(College song, stanza 3)

SO IF I COULD NOT CONTINUE at the bank, then where would I go? I considered nursing or secretarial work, but they were not for me. In high school, I had failed miserably at shorthand and typing. I still cannot type. Subservience to a boss was in any event no escape from the stifling male dominion at the bank. The only profession within my reach was teaching. I had a large number of role models throughout my schooling, and I saw a range of ways that I could join the profession of women teachers. The most admirable women, in my opinion, were single, middle-aged female teachers. Most of them were childless or had one child in or out of wedlock. These women were self-confident, joyous, intelligent, ambitious, adventurous, and generous. They dressed well and carried themselves with a self-assurance that said: "I am contented and in control of my life. I do not need a man to make me whole." I observed, listened, and pondered hard on the complexities of real marriages, as opposed to the Christian ideal that was preached.

Most distressing to me, then and now, was the disproportionate amount of work that married women did. Their bodies withstood the wear and tear of pregnancy, childbirth, and lactation. After the birth of their children, they did mother work in addition to housework, wife work, and outside work all at once. Even when these women had maids, they still had to manage household operations and take over when the maids did not show up for work. Often their husbands behaved like potentates, expecting to be waited on hand and foot. Some wives complained bitterly to their female confidants of the audacity of husbands who came home, ate the meal their wives had carefully prepared, and then soon after got dressed and went out with younger women in the clothes that she herself had laundered. Many wives found it hard to admit to the physical abuse that their protests often brought on. Black-and-blue skin and black eyes were carefully explained away in an effort to hide embarrassing facts that everyone could figure out. There was no room in these women's lives for themselves. They personified self-sacrifice.

Some were happy in this state, while others were bitter and controlling of their children and husbands. I often overheard maids discussing the merits and demerits of middle-class marriages by comparing those of their employers. Invariably, the concluding statement would run something like this: "Lawd, missis, me no wah feh married nobady. Me no wa feh mash up like Mistress *So and So*. Me no wah no husban feh tun crasses pan me, yah."

A most interesting revelation came to me upon reading Philip Curtain's *Two Jamaicas: The Role of Ideas in a Tropical Colony 1830–1865* (1958, 25). According to Curtain, when, after emancipation,

Negro women were offered Christian marriage, they refused. They saw Christian marriage as a mark of subordination and slavery to the male. Most chose to stick with common-law relationships and strove to retain their status as income generators from their food-growing responsibilities.

My observation was that the most miserable women teachers were the wives who tolerated the provocation of philandering husbands. On behalf of these husbands, they would keep up appearances of being happy couples in wonderful marriages. Yet society blamed them for their husbands' infidelities. I was definitely not going to be one of those wives. I had no intention of walking in the footsteps of those wives who willingly or unwillingly carried the burden of blame for the wilful actions and choices that their husbands made against their vows of fidelity.

At nineteen years of age, I had important decisions to make about my life as a woman and about my self-sufficiency. I sent for the prospectuses from Shortwood Teachers' College for women and Mico Teachers' College, a coeducational institution. I opted for Mico College because I liked the fact that the institution had trained a long list of prominent leaders on the island and beyond. Although most of the graduates were men, that did not faze me because we had been told in school that "man" and "mankind" included women—and I believed it did. I saw myself as an equal and, at times, as being plainly intellectually superior to my male colleagues. I often out-performed them, especially in both verbal combat and in academic subjects.

I filled out the application and sent it in. I remember vividly the question that asked for religious affiliation. I thought of Auntie Black's insistence on my confirmation and regular attendance at St. Gabriel's Anglican Church in May Pen. I had the distinct feeling that membership in the Anglican Church was beneficial. I had seen the influence of testimonials written by the rector. I also predicted that my attendance at high school, even though I had not completed my A levels, would work in my favour—most applications to Mico College in those days came from those students who had been successful in the Third Jamaica Local examinations. In my mother's day, this exam had permitted candidates to study to be a teacher on the job and to take what was called the pupil-teachers' examination to be certified to teach in elementary schools.

Shortly afterwards, I received an invitation to write the entrance examination. The opportunity came earlier than I expected. My plan was to work for another year at the bank and save up enough money to pay my way through college. I did not expect that I would pass the examination on the first try, so I was planning on trying it a second time. I nonetheless decided to write the examination, and, in fact, it was not the kind of examination for which you could prepare.

One Saturday in April or May 1962, I took time off from work and went to Mico College in Kingston, which was thirty-six miles away, to write the entrance examination. I estimate that some two or three hundred of us sat on that occasion. I came out feeling pleased with my performance, and it was justified. About two months later, I was both pleased and anxious to receive the announcement that I had passed the written examination and should report for an oral examination in July 1962. The anxiety that I felt was because I was not yet financially ready to go to college. However, I put these worries aside and, otherwise, remember feeling no nervousness. I only remember exuberance and pride at making another big decision about my life, independently of my aunts and their husbands. My faith was very strong that I would be successful, and so I was.

Just as the country was busy preparing for its independence celebration, which was to be held on 6 August 1962, I was preparing for my own independent career that was to begin at Mico College in September 1962. I was among the independence batch of one hundred and fifty students—one hundred men and fifty women. We were hailed with great fanfare as the biggest batch to be admitted to date. Moreover, this batch included the largest number of young women.

Prior to this year, the college had struggled resolutely to maintain its all-male membership and, when forced to admit women, had admitted only married or older women, who would presumably be of no sexual interest to the men.

In my year, many single, young women were finally admitted. There were also several more profound changes, which had resulted from student demonstrations of the previous year. At the time, a food strike by the students had hit the news. A colleague from Mico College who was part of the protests has helped me recall several of the grievances. Some students alleged that they were served corn beef on dry bread for breakfast seven days per week. Seniors accused the principal of intimidation and discriminatory tactics that were similar to those of the British colonizers. Some were bitter about what they perceived as a poor quality curriculum. The style of American psychology that was then taught was particularly loathsome. My friend recalled with some bitterness having to learn what Shockley and Jensen had advanced concerning the so-called "inferior intelligence" of black children. Such vocabulary as "disadvantaged" and "culturally deprived" did nothing to raise them up or to give them a sense of agency in building a new Jamaica. Tutors also came in for criticism for allegedly treating students as children.

Another colleague who was part of the protest recalls sexual repressiveness. He particularly resented one tutor of a certain faith who taught "Christian ethics." This tutor also owned a locksmith business. He was legendary, even in my time, for being able to sniff out fornication in whichever room it was occurring and to use his skills to break in on the unhappy malefactors. He was known as the "sex police." My colleague also recalls the repressive measures that were taken to regulate relationships between men and women students. Besides attempting to regulate male–female interactions, there were rumours that the college was trying to expose and root out homosexuality that was alleged to be occurring among and between some students and tutors. Matters around sexuality were so complex and fraught with Victorian Christian morality that dealing with them was said to have caused a big rift among the tutors and an exodus of some excellent ones.

By September 1962, the college had begun reforms that continued during my three years and beyond. One reform that affected my batch was the change of the beginning of our school year from January to September, necessitating two weeks of orientation rather than one.

Women were to report to the women's hostel at Trevennion Road, where we were met in the main building by two of the senior women. This building was an abandoned private woman's hospital, with a large room upstairs that would have been the public ward. It had now been furnished with three bunk beds, making for crowded quarters for six of us. This room was nicknamed "room elastic." In addition, there were a series of private rooms along an L-shaped hallway, each of which was furnished with a bunk bed and a small closet. Also upstairs was the suite of Mrs. Mills, our much-loved housemother. Downstairs was the reception area, with a settee and chair to receive guests. Under the stairs was a large desk and telephone. Receiving telephone calls generally attracted a lot of attention and eavesdropping. On either side of this area were small rooms that held one or two bunk beds, depending on the size.

There was another small house to the east of this building in which a female tutor lived. Farther to the east was a fair-sized two-story house in which another female tutor lived with her English husband and their baby. It was while babysitting for them on one occasion that I was introduced to blue cheese. I could not wait to go and tell my friends that these people ate cheese with "junjo" (mould) in it. The only other cheese I knew at this time was the soft cheddar imported from New Zealand.

In an adjoining property to the west of this main building, there was Hostel B, which housed fewer women but which also had similar furnishings of single beds and bunk beds. A female tutor was resident also in her own private suite. Accommodations were modest but clean and well maintained. The place smelled of floor wax from the regular maintenance of the wood floors. We had all of our laundry done for us, except for our underwear, while the men enjoyed full laundry services, including their underpants. Our suppers were delivered daily to the hostel. We had evening house devotions at nine o'clock and lights out at ten o'clock. We could study in the dining room after ten if we had to. Creature comforts were good.

I would not have been able to afford further education without the generous government subsidy that covered room and board. Mico College was often called the poor man's university. All we had to provide were our textbooks, transportation, and pocket money. When my small savings ran out, I turned to sewing to earn my pocket and textbook money. Auntie Black often gave me gifts of new shoes and fabrics to make new clothes. She was good at tracking down sales in quality merchandise at Nathan's and Issas's stores. I particularly remember my first pair of pearlized grey Bally pointed-toe, spiked-heel shoes, which she gave me. I felt so rich when I dressed up in them.

Orientation began on Sunday morning in the hostel with a certain senior lady waking us all up at five o'clock and having us do laps around the grounds at the big hostel. I resented this activity so much, especially as I deemed that she needed the workout far more that I did. She had us do this exercise every morning throughout orientation. I cannot remember now if we had to find our way to our respective churches that first Sunday. More than likely, we all had to report for chapel service on Sunday afternoon. As part of our clothes list, we had to have two white dresses and a pair of white shoes for chapel services. I have not worn a white dress since college, and I detest white shoes for the constant whitening that they needed to keep them looking clean. We also had to wear a kind of uniform to classes, which comprised dark-coloured skirts and pastel blouses in coordinated colour schemes. The senior ladies and female tutors policed our necklines and hemlines. In the age of the thigh-high micro-mini and the body-hugging hobble skirts, it proved much more difficult to police the skirts than the blouses. The fashionable Peter Pan and rever collars and the jewel necklines concealed just enough neck and chest to be acceptable. There was so much useless fuss made about the shade of skirts that we might as well have been asked to wear uniforms. I did not mind so much because in complying with these rules I limited the "free show" for leering and lecherous eyes.

On the Monday of the first week of orientation, we had to report to the college campus, about a mile away, for breakfast at 7:30. After breakfast, we had sessions on college rules, regulations, and deportment. The senior men and women forewarned us of the initiation—when we would be given our status of "grubs" and "grubbesses"—when the fearsome second-year men arrived two weeks later. We were told to go along with the "ragging" because it was meant to be fun. It was the tradition for the second-year men to do the "initiating." A few of my mischievous batch-mates had had an early taste of this initiation in the first week for being "fat"—that is, being impertinent to our seniors. This part of orientation was the equivalent of boot camp.

The highlight of the week was the social, which occurred either on Friday or Saturday night, for which we dressed in our party best. By this time, crinolines were out, and the hobble skirt was in. I did not care for this style either, but I loved the A-line skirts and the "princess line" dresses that were becoming fashionable. I was happy not to be as self- consciousness as I was in high school. I dressed to "puss back foot" as we used to say and went to the social to see and be seen. No more the bobbing mushroom of high school days, I thought I was petite and rather stylish in my pink and white eyelash-cotton dress and white shoes. In those days, I wore no jewellery or makeup, except lipstick. The really sharp dressers among the men wore bolero jackets and continental pants, which were short enough to show their white socks. The twist and mashed potato dances were on their way out. On the way in were the local sounds of Bob Marley and the Wailers who gave us the ska and watusi dances. The local popular music was growing, with the encouragement of the young Honourable Edward Seaga, the Harvard anthropology graduate who started the annual festival of arts and music.

The soundmen set up on the platform in Classroom B. Among them, I noticed a rather handsome young man operating a reel-to-reel Grundig tape recorder, which played several tunes in a row so we could dance several tunes non-stop. I felt free, lovely, and sexy and chose to dance with this young man. Contrary to what Mrs. Harvey taught me in deportment classes at Clarendon College about waiting for the boy to ask me to dance, I went straight up and asked him to dance. I heard the voice of Sam Cooke singing in my head: "Cupid, draw back your bow / And let your arrow go / Straight to my lover's heart for me." I did not even wait for Cupid either. We danced the night away and like a perfect gentleman he walked me home to Trevennion Road after the party, just in time for nine o'clock devotions and ten o'clock bedtime. (If we ever came in from a party after ten o'clock, we had to sign a book and indicate the time we arrived home.) During the second week of orientation, the second-year students joined us. It was their job to "rag" us and to reduce us to the slimy grubs and grubbesses that, as lowly first-year men and women, we should properly understand ourselves to be. I had never seen such two-legged barbarians in my life. Commands issued by the men included the following:

"Grubbess, get over here and butter the senior man's toast."
"Don't you hear the senior man's orders?"
"Grubbess, get down and polish my shoes."
"Who do you think you are, grubbess?"
"You are nothing but a slimy little paramecium."
"You were nothing but a little monkey in the zoo with the senior man" (this, referring to a date at the Hope Botanical Gardens that I had had with a senior man whom I knew before entering college).

I would have none of their boorishness, and I disobeyed every command. These second-year men chose every opportunity to torment me and to try to cut me down to size. I was provoked at breakfast time at the Mills Hall dining table, at mid-morning teatime, at lunch hour, at afternoon tea break, and after classes. I would not give an inch. Their objective was to humiliate and intimidate me until I broke down and cried. By the conventions of ragging, it was supposed to end at the end of orientation. The intention was that by this time we timid newcomers would have been broken and made docile. Some of the men were alleged to be identifying their female love interest through this process. If they were trying to impress me as he-men, they could not have been more mistaken—I thought of them only with contempt. The word went out that they were going to "swing" this grubbess from the Buxton Tower. To be swung was to be publicly humiliated as in the spectacle of the public hangings during slavery days. Buxton Tower was the highest point on the campus. Swing me they did.

The bullying clowns kept up this ragging for six whole weeks, culminating in a show-down one Friday afternoon when some twenty or thirty second-year men swarmed me in front of Mills Hall and the Science Block as I was on my way home. Those third-year men, who were not yet weaned off this animal-like behaviour but who would not openly indulge in ragging, took up positions as spectators on the second floor balcony of the Science Block to watch the swinging. These two-legged animals made a circle around me and started hurling commands and insults at me. When I refused to answer them and attempted to walk out of the circle, two men criss-crossed their legs and tried to have me step over. Of course, I would not attempt to do that because they would not have hesitated to trip me and to have my skirt above my head. Men were shouting commands from all directions of the circle: "Grubbess! Don't turn your back on the senior man." "Grubbess! I am talking to you, look at me." Their anger and frustration at my obstinacy boiled to a menacing chant: "Cry, grubbess, cry. Cry, grubbess, cry." Like hell! I was not going to give such cowardly creatures the satisfaction of seeing me cry in front of them.

At the moment when I was uncertain as to how all of this was going to end, a senior gentleman, Mr. Fairweather, walked up to the circle of angry men and attempted to lead me out of the circle. By the rules of deference to the senior man, they should have stopped, stepped aside, and permitted us safe passage, so to speak. Instead, a few true wooligans kept on shouting insults at me. Two of the men again crossed their legs, trying to trip me. Mr. Fairweather stood firm, stared them down, and they retreated reluctantly. I was both scared and angry. If I had the physical prowess, I would have thrown feminine modesty and respectability to the wind and vanquished each one with my bare hands and the fire in my rage. Writing this now, I can discern echoes from slavery days. Was this a re-enactment of the public humiliation of the rebel woman?

Mr. Fairweather and I walked in dead silence to Trevennion Road. I was so full of tears, I could not open my mouth to thank him. I would not have him see me cry for all his gallantry and compassion. I just bowed low and shook his hand. I have remained grateful to this day for Mr. Fairweather's chivalry. I went straight to my bed and cried in my pillow for hours. I fell asleep, resolved to pack my suitcase and leave the next day. But where, oh where, would I go? I weighed the future possibilities of staying at Mico as against going away to nowhere. I stayed.

I vowed I would never participate in the ragging of first-year students nor would I condone such behaviours from senior students when I witnessed them. I kept my promise and engendered strong resentment from many of my batch-mates when I was a senior lady and a member of the hostel committee. I ruled against one of my senior ladies at the women's hostel for commanding a first-year student to bow down and polish her shoes. When the first-year woman refused, the student alleged that my batch-mate slapped her on the cheek and accused her of insubordination. The committee met to hear the student's complaint, and I was expected to condone the act and be complicit in a barbaric practice that bred nothing but disrespect and hate. I had nothing good to say to the perpetrators. I am still enraged. I can only liken the practice of ragging to slavery days when Africans were brought to Jamaica as the first stop after the Middle Passage and left to undergo "seasoning" as their initiation into their new status as slaves (Higman 1995). After "seasoning," they were deemed to be docile and were ready to be distributed to the plantations on the other islands as well as on the mainland plantations of British North America. Those who refused to be rendered servile were banished to the harshest conditions.

During my college years, I had my struggles and challenges. I had to struggle against the underlying chronic melancholy and pain of my earlier years, which at times threatened to plunge me into deep depression. The loneliness that I felt for my mother and my need to find out who she was continued to plague my soul. I was unable to unravel the mystery that seemed to surround her and her family among members of my father's family. With my sister's recent death and my estrangement from my two aunts who had helped to raise me, I felt lonely, abandoned, and mournful. I was bereft of any family feeling. I could not suppress the impulse to begin the search for my mother.

"Who was my mother? I had to find out seriously. So one day during my first year at Mico, I decided to show up at the Cross Roads post office to introduce myself to Miss Muriel Reid, who was the head postmistress and who, I had learned from snatches of overheard conversation, was my mother's only sibling. I wanted to see if I might get a glimpse of what my mother might have looked like. In addition, I had hoped that she would have been glad to see me and to tell me why she, my mother's sister, had not taken an interest in me, who was just a baby, when she died. My expectation was based on the custom that the mother's family rallied around her when her marriage was in trouble. Furthermore, the custom was that, should the mother die and leave any infants, it was usually her family that took care of the infant children. I wanted to understand why this custom had been broken.

When summoned, she came to the counter, looked at me with the face of a dead stranger, and asked me who I was. When I introduced myself as her niece, she grimaced derisively, made a sharp about-turn, and marched back to her office. Luckily, I was by myself and there was no one to see my shame and devastation. I stood on the steps of the Cross Roads post office and wept. Trying to find out who my mother was has proven to be the most difficult quest for me.

I could not go to my Auntie Black, whose office at the Ministry of Trade and Industry was in fact close by, to tell her of this incident. I was deterred by the memory of her forbidding my sister Sonia from meeting again with a Mr. Goodwin, whom she had met once and who said he was related to my mother on her mother's side. My brother Trevor was my only confidante, but we lived in different worlds by now. Months later when I visited my brother, I told him of the incident. He smiled a painful knowing smile and told me of his recollection of a day, shortly after the death of my mother's father, the Honourable Charles Archibald Reid, when Muriel and her lawyer came to Toll Gate where they were living and ordered our mother off the property. Trevor started to cry and said that he remembered our mother asking Muriel to wait until she had finished making her Sunday dinner and feeding her family. My brother said that Muriel and her lawyer refused. If this were true, then, this incident would have occurred sometime in 1944 or 1945. Her father died in September 1944.

The opportunity to continue the search came some time in 1964 around the end of my second year in teacher's college. I went to visit Aunt Joyce. This time, when she insisted that I accompany her to visit her brother, I was agreeable, not for the reasons that she thought but, rather, because I saw an opportunity to be able to see the grey tin case again. I had disowned my father since I was fourteen, so I was not at all interested in seeing him. I would, however, be required to fake daughterly affection and deference. When we arrived at my father's house somewhere in Old Harbour, Aunt Joyce knocked on the little wrought iron gate. The maid came to greet us. Aunt Joyce inquired if Mr. Shorter was at home. She replied: "Missa Shaata nat home. You fambilly?"

"Yes, I am his sister, Joyce Hylton." Pointing to me, she said: "This is his daughter, Yvonne." While the introductions were going on, I was busy peering in the door from outside. The familiar Simmons bed had a cover that hung too short. I saw the familiar grey tin case under the bed. The maid invited us in and offered us a drink of water. During the awkward small talk that followed between Aunt Joyce and her inferior, I moved to the bedroom and pulled out the case like an old friend.

I opened it. To my very pleasant surprise, the contents were as I remembered, only dog-eared and dirty from my play when we lived in Louisiana, years before. I saw something I had not noticed before: a teacher's certificate with the name Lucy May Reid written on it. It was the name of my mother. I took it out and showed it to Aunt Joyce who looked singularly unimpressed. I was impressed because this was the first revelation that my mother was more than a dressmaker. It also gave me a hint of the deep resentment that Aunt Joyce had towards my mother. My mother had had more education than Aunt Joyce. By the racial social conventions of the times, a black woman should not have had a higher level of education than a so-called white woman. I now understood what Aunt Joyce meant when she would say to my sister Sonia when she talked back to Aunt Joyce fearlessly: "Just like yuh black mumma who thought she was better than me."

I kept the certificate, put it away carefully, and after a while forgot all about it. I did not even discuss my finding with anyone in my family or with my friends. It was not until 1990, after I had moved to Canada, that I would look at it again. The circumstances were rather sentimental and somewhat melodramatic. I was at home recovering from a hysterectomy and meditating on how my womb had been so violently excised from my body and disposed of in the hospital incinerator. I began to mourn for this—literally—vital organ, one that had given life to three healthy human beings, but which I had never seen.

I started thinking about the meaning of giving birth and of motherhood. Once again, I broke out in sorrowful tears over the fact that I did not know my mother and that I had no trace of her. Unconsciously, I got up and went to a trunk that had all of my important papers and keepsakes. I had not looked at these for some twenty-five years.

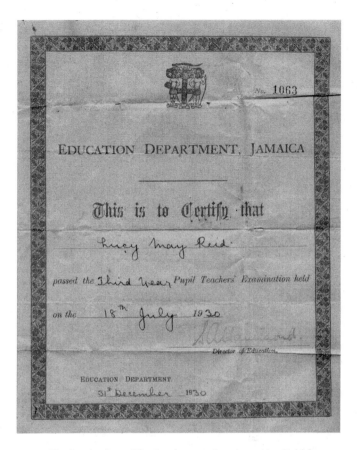

The teacher's certificate of my mother, Lucy May Reid.

I did not know what I was looking for. I opened a case containing old letters and there among them was my mother's certificate, neatly folded. She had been awarded this certificate in 1930, exactly sixty years earlier. S.A. Hammond, Director of Education, had signed the certificate. Coincidentally, I later found some articles written by Hammond in the *Journal of Negro Education*, while I was searching for information on education in Jamaica of the 1930s and 1940s.

This certificate remains my only material link to my mother. I have no recollection of my mother's face, her scent, her body, or her love. My life has been about mother lust. It is consoling to know that I followed her footsteps to become a teacher and, in a twist of irony, a seamstress. Women who knew that I was Lucy May Reid's daughter would tell me what a very fine seamstress she was. Her acts of kindness and generosity were repeated to me often. I feel so deprived for not having known her.

Putting together pieces of hearsay and information that I have received recently from Auntie Black, it was around 1945 when my mother lost her mind and was admitted to Bellevue Asylum, where she later died. I have not yet been able to ascertain the exact date of her death. She was buried in an unmarked grave. I cannot even find the place where her bones rest so that I may go and pay my respects. My mother is lost to me without a trace except for the clouded silhouette appearing in the newspaper clipping of her father's state funeral procession. I do not even know which of her genetic features I carry. The sadness I feel about the loss of my mother will never leave me.

In writing these stories and researching the answers to the important questions that have arisen during the course of writing them, I have learned that my mother was the "outside daughter." The bastardy laws of the time meant that she could not be fully and equally recognized in law and in life as her father's child, even though he gave her his name. The law allowed the father's name to be given to a child out of wedlock only if the father consented in writing to have his name added to the child's birth certificate. The fact that my mother carried her father's surname must have meant that he claimed his paternity—a honourable thing to do at the time when it was so easy for men to walk away. Auntie Black has pointed out that, according to the prejudices of the times, it was difficult for her father, who became a prominent politician, to "own" her publicly. His wife and his lawful children would have probably hated and resented the outside child and its mother, even without the added "insult" of having to share the father's name with her. The outside child usually would have carried the mother's name and would have been stigmatized to live in the shadows of lawful children.

When I compare the different life chances that were given to these two sisters, it reveals much of the family and the legal battles that may have been fought to distinguish lawful, from unlawful, progeny. Muriel Reid was sent to Saint Andrew's Girls School and later became the head postmistress of a very large post office. Saint Andrew's Girls School was the school for wealthy white and coloured people as well as a few children of so-called respectable black people. When I asked myself why there would have been different kinds of schooling for two sisters who carried the same father's name, I have come to learn that the grammar schools of the day refused to admit illegitimate children (Senior 1991, 23). This might explain why my mother got the best that "private lessons" in the all-age schools could offer. These schools were designed in the nineteenth century for the children of former slaves. Since she could not go to secondary school, the next best thing was that she should learn a trade. With a grammar school education from one of the finest girls' schools on the island, Muriel must have been regarded as the child of a respectable black man who had been voted to the legislature, mostly by the white people of northern Manchester. My Auntie Black likes to remind me of this fact when she breaks her silence briefly enough to answer my probing questions.

Lucy Reid was allowed to remain in the all-age schools of the time, which were meant to prepare literate labourers. She was allowed to rise beyond this level by being given private lessons in order to pass her pupil-teacher examination so that she could teach in the elementary schools. My aunt has insisted that my mother wanted to be a seamstress rather than a teacher, and therefore her father sent her to a renowned seamstress in Kingston to learn her trade. My mother may have chosen to be a seamstress out of practical economic necessity of being my father's wife and, no doubt, of having to shoulder the full responsibility of raising her children. In those days, to be a seamstress was a perfectly respectable trade. Seamstresses were able to earn a very good living before the advent of ready-made clothes.

The shunning of the "outside child" was demonstrated clearly when I obtained and read the report of her father's state funeral in the *Daily Gleaner*. Although my mother was included in the photographs and named as Mrs. Lucy Shorter, she was never recognized as his daughter. Only Muriel, his lawful daughter, was so recognized. I can only imagine how this must have hurt my mother, especially after I learned, during the course of this research, that my mother was her father's right hand during his political campaigning and electoral victories.

According to the articles of the inheritance laws, illegitimate children had no rights of inheritance. Muriel, being the lawful daughter, could have disinherited my mother with impunity. It seems that Muriel disinherited more than just my mother. During one of my visits to Christiana to find people who might remember my mother and her famous father, a nephew said: "That Muriel, she is an awful woman." He revealed that the family feuds that followed Maas Charlie's death were so nasty that some family members have not spoken to her since her father's death.

The surviving members of my mother's family, on her mother's side, refused to speak to Trevor and me. I can only speculate that dreadful things must have happened to cause such irretrievable damage in the families. I have never learned where my father was in this entire crisis or where my mother's people were. Was she so totally and utterly alone in the world? The more I came to know of my mother's existence, the sadder and more depressed I became—now as then. I kept these revelations to myself, for the most part, to spare my brother painful remembrances. My brother is seven years older than I am, and he witnessed much. To his death, he carried the burden of the family atrocities that he witnessed.

At Mico, my challenge was to shake chronic depression and bouts of melancholy, which I had to keep to myself. I plunged into my studies in the hope that they would help me rise above the pain and enable

Me at Mico College, 1963.

me to live a better life in the future. I knew full well the importance of this educational opportunity. In order to do my best, I developed a steely determination to suppress these memories and to get on with life. My brain was ravenous for knowledge, and my soul was hungry for adventure—to study, to travel, to work abroad, and to travel around the world. In fact, the urge to travel was so great that I planned to take a trip while I was in college on the *Federal Palm* or the *Federal Maple*, two boats that Canada had given to the now defunct West Indies Federation to facilitate freedom of movement among all of the British West Indian Islands. Taking this ten-day boat trip was then like the grand tour for the University of the West Indies students. Regrettably, I never did take the trip because I simply did not have the money.

However, my spirit was in flight. The conditions at Mico were just right for me to devote all of my time to study. I did not live in the oppressive households of my aunts, and I did not have to do housework or shop work. I was now independent, and I felt both confident and scared at once. I did not have to worry about my material comforts. The government of Jamaica paid tuition and room and board for all students. Moreover, the tutors were very caring and respectful. I got along well with most of my batch-mates, although I was by no means "popular." Some of the wooligan men called me the "arrogant bitch," especially at times when they were talking foolishness, to which I would respond with an authority that they so resented coming from a woman.

I can still remember one idiot who always jumped up like a jack-in-the-box at every student council meeting to interrupt and obstruct the proceedings. The meetings were run according to parliamentary procedures and *Robert's Rules of Order*. The idiot would jump up and shout: "On a pint of aada, Mr. President, a pint of aada." When he proved to himself and the audience that he had no point to make, he would change course and babble just to hear himself speak to an audience. If the president asked him to cease and desist interrupting, he would jump up again and bellow: "On a pint of privilege, Mr. President, a pint of privilege." I would invariably walk out of the meeting to the strong roar of objections by the other fools. Some of the women thought I was "extra" (extravagant or boastful). While this attitude towards me bothered me sometimes, I felt confident, free to grow and to be joyful. Looking back now, I realize that while I attended Mico College, I had the comforts of school and home, all in one. I use my transcript as a guide to revisit my college experiences and to pay tribute to three of the best years of my life.

Education studies included child psychology, school management, principles of education, history of education, and practice teaching. Child psychology redefined childhood for me and, consequently, held endless fascination. We were taught that children were unique and developed according to their own timetable. Play was actually good for children! The role of heredity versus character training began a debate that ran through all three years of college. I had to work to overcome a mindset that believed strongly that children were born to be who they were and no amount of training would change that. The folk, in their frustration with obstinate child behaviour, would say, for example: "Ah jus so im baan. Yuh cyant do nuttin bout it."

The most important influence of psychology throughout my three years in college was that it offered me the opportunity to think about others and myself in positive, non-judgmental ways. The one thing that I did not endorse then, and I still do not, was the way in which teachers were encouraged to bring up specific family practices into teacher talk as a way of explaining and excusing some child behaviour and performance. I do agree that home life affects children's learning readiness and ability to sustain learning, but I believe that far too much emphasis is placed there. Teachers forget sometimes that school can be, and often is, the refuge and stimulating learning environment for many children. School has the power to make up for some socioeconomic deprivations. The schools such as Carron Hall Infant School, May Pen All-Age School, and Clarendon College, which I wrote of earlier, were learning havens for me, and gave me a better sense of who I could become. My home conditions more often than not worked against my learning and personal uplift. Good schools with kind and caring teachers can and do counteract the negative influences of home. In the society in which I grew up, poverty and illiteracy were very prevalent. Schooling offered children alternative visions of a brighter future for themselves. Most parents and guardians wanted their children to "take book learning." It was a source of pride for parents—and grandmothers especially—to say of their son or daughter: "Him have brain fe tek book learning."

We had little curriculum covering school management, as such, but we did look at the principles of education. This subject offered so many ways of teaching that I could not wait to get out on my practicum to try them out. The idea of teaching all subjects from a centre of interest immersed my pupils and me in many creative opportunities for inquiry and critical thinking. To this day, the project method and "centre of interest" remain sound principles of my teaching. I have used them in my teaching from the elementary through to the university level. Another sound principle of education that has stayed with me is teaching to develop citizens who will live and work in a democratic society. My understanding of the child-centred classroom, which can provide multi-sensory active experiences, stood me well in my practicum.

The history of education in our first and second years was mostly derived from the history of education in Europe. Such names as Pestalozzi, Comenius, Montessori, and Froebel stand out. The folk schools of Scandinavia and the progressive education movement in England and the United States fascinated me. Through learning about educational philosophies and the work of these educators, I travelled imaginatively to Poland, Norway, Germany, Italy, and the United States. In our third year, we learned about the history of education in Jamaica and the British West Indies, from emancipation to the present. What a stark contrast it was to be learning about the ideal learning conditions of a German kindergarten and an Italian Montessori classroom, with all of their learning toys and learning centres, compared to teaching in overcrowded classrooms with chalk and talk. This contrast inspired imaginative ways of inventing toys and teaching aids to get children excited about learning and exploring.

Practice teaching was my greatest love. It was a bit like the serious imaginative play of my childhood, full of invention and acting. We had two practice teaching periods per year—a short one, followed by an extended one. In first year, we studied psychology, methodology, and practice teaching for the elementary curriculum. In second year, we did the same thing for junior grades of secondary and comprehensive school. In third year, we chose to specialize in either elementary or secondary teaching. I chose to concentrate on secondary teaching.

During my training, I loved the elementary children. They were full of curiosity and good humour, and we enjoyed our exciting adventures in story telling and the magic of science. It was sheer joy to hold a class of over forty Grade seven boys and girls spellbound with my story telling and drama. Science experiments on air pressure, pumps and hydraulic systems, plant transpiration, photosynthesis, and the study of plant and animal habitats pulled the children into hours and days of conversations about their physical universe. I was one with them in their wonder.

My approach to teaching crystallized around my understanding of the child-centred classroom, as expounded by Mr. R.A. Shirley in his course at Mico on the principles of education. Mr. Shirley's mantra was: "Children learn by doing." As a result, he took the trouble to demonstrate as many strategies as possible, by which we could teach children to be independent learners. I understood my role to be the magician who charmed the children with multi-sensory activities in all of their subjects. Mrs. Ivy Williams, who was the psychology tutor in my second year, emphasized the multi-sensory nature of learning—the greater number of senses we engage in teaching the more likely the children will remember the materials taught and the more they will be likely to make connections and ask probing questions. I designed learning activities to lead the children to generate their own questions and to engage in speculation, inference making, debates, and questioning. I enthused the children in language arts and general science, which were my passions. Mrs. Merton Wright, our first-year language arts tutor, did an excellent job of teaching language arts and reading readiness. By using dioramas, flannel boards, cardboard televisions, puppet theatre, and drama improvisations, I could hold a class of forty to fifty children spellbound in the storytelling experience.

The patois was generally forbidden in the classroom. In those days, it had no legitimacy since it was regarded as the language of the illiterate and a sign of retardation. I permitted children to speak it because, in the patois, the children could demonstrate superb comprehension and joy. Joy and laughter were important elements of my classes—they still are. In their writing exercises, I would help children translate the patois into Standard English. Many years later when I studied sociolinguistics, I learned that what I was doing was called code switching or learning when to use different registers.

General science offered the children and myself endless opportunities to be curious about phenomena in the world of plants and animals; the quality of soils for planting; weather patterns as manifested in the wind and rain; habitats, and the life cycles of the flora and fauna they supported. Looking back now, I can see that I was building upon the interest ignited by my Carron Hall Infant School nature walks. The *UNESCO Sourcebook of Science Teaching* (1963), to which Mr. Hutchison, our science tutor, introduced us, provided numerous examples of simple science experiments and projects grounded in children's everyday experiences. The most exciting thing for me, then, was that I did not need a laboratory in order to teach kids science. A science corner in the classroom with a balanced aquarium, among other projects, kept the children enchanted and engaged. Nature walks with simple hand lenses introduced children to microscopic life forms and structures. I complemented these sources with issues of *Scientific American* magazine that I myself bought at the F.W. Woolworth store located in Cross Roads, which was close to Mico. The illustrations and explanations were so good that they were another source of my own science continuing education. Student teachers could also go to the United States Information

Services (USIS) to obtain free science textbooks. Though most of the examples in the science texts were about conditions and examples of the temperate zones, there was much that I could adapt to the local environment. Although I was generally weak in mathematics, I expended great effort in understanding and translating the concepts into practice and applying them to concrete situations. By doing this, I overlearned the concepts so that I could overcome my insecurity about teaching the subject.

My final teaching practice remains a high point in my maturity. The classroom at Greenwich Town All-Age School was one of those two-walls-and-a-roof buildings with long benches and desks anchored in the concrete floor. I applied the best of the principles of teaching and learning that appealed to my intellect and personality in order to create exciting learning. The teachers in the school were fascinated by how this four-foot-eleven-inch tall young woman, weighing just ninety-five pounds, could get the children to "eat out of her hands." I made a point of sitting with the children whenever they were doing group work or seatwork. Since the children and I were about the same size, the headteacher, Mr. Blair, got confused the first time he came to my class. It took him quite some time to identify me among the children.

It was the custom that selected classrooms of outstanding student teachers might have a surprise visit by a team of three examiners. One day, the examining team, comprising Mr. Glen Owen, the principal; Mr. D.R.B. Grant, a renowned teacher educator; and Mr. L.H. Facey, my economics tutor, arrived to observe. Happily, the children were engaged in one of those absorbing, blissful moments of peace and quiet as they worked away. This quiet was a significant contrast to most of the classrooms at the time, which were characterized by a din over and through which some teachers chose to lecture. Sitting there among the children, I did not get up immediately to greet the visitors. We had been advised to continue with our teaching when the examiners arrived. However, these three examiners walked around the class, looked at the children's work, and then stood looking quizzically around the room. The children looked from them to me until a boy blurted out: "Lawd Gad, teacha so sumall dat dem no see har." The class burst out laughing, and I stood up. "There you are!" exclaimed Mr. Owen.

While the children settled down and continued their work, the examiners looked over my lesson plans, teaching aids, and engaged me in an intense conversation about my philosophy of teaching and evaluation of learning. The examiners were impressed. I was elated that the approach to teaching that I was developing was seen as having great merit. I earned a distinction for my practicum, and at graduation I was awarded the teaching prize. The realization that I could teach without the aid of straps, whips, and intimidation was a spiritual triumph. A good curriculum and a high positive regard for children's integrity have served me well as the schoolteacher I became.

Academic studies provided me with a broad liberal curriculum in the first two years. The menu of courses comprised English composition and grammar, English literature, mathematics, general science, history, geography, economics, religious knowledge, music theory and practice, art, crafts, physical education, Spanish, and home economics. However, I found the load of thirteen subjects in my first year, and twelve in my second, to be too many.

There were four of these subjects that caused me distress—mathematics, music theory and practice, art, and physical education. Of the four, mathematics gave me the greatest frustration. I was put in remedial mathematics perhaps after my first term. In my second year, I remember Mrs. Ballentyne, who was hired to help students such as myself, working until she sweated to get me to learn a language that I seemed incapable of comprehending. In going through my college keepsakes, I came across some examination problems of my second year. Now as then, I cannot reason these problems out.

Here is an example of a problem: "A person due south of a lighthouse observes that his shadow east at the top is 24 feet long. On walking 100 yards due east he finds his shadow to be 30 feet. Supposing him to be 6 feet high, find the height of the light." I earned a "D" in mathematics in both years. I have not improved since that time.

The language of music was not much better. The concepts of scales, intervals, sharps, flats, and chords of music theory make no sense to me. Such concepts as pitch, timbre, melody, and harmony stayed with me just long enough for the examinations. The definitions of fugues, oratorios, symphonies, and arias were a little easier, because I could listen and appreciate these forms, now as then. In fact, the college had very brilliant musicians and music educators who trained melodious choirs with piano, violin, and recorder accompaniment. Many of my batch-mates excelled in music. For me, however, it was at the edge of my abilities. My efforts to learn the recorder were a most humiliating experience. This instrument was required in order to teach music and to help "solfa" sheet music notation. When I was in my second year, it somehow came about that I needed to teach Brahms's "Lullaby" using the recorder. For all of the practising that I had done, I could get neither the tune nor the timing right. The children were unable to recognize the tune, and so was I. I gave up and have never attempted to teach music again.

During my time at Mico, we had the best music educators on the island. Miss Olive Lewin was the respected and multitalented music director. She instituted and led the most comprehensive music curriculum for Mico. Besides music theory, she provided opportunities for talented students to learn to play various instruments—recorder, melodica, violin, and piano. She also nurtured three choirs under the able direction of Mr. Arthur Clarke, Mr. Lloyd Hall, and Mr. Morris. Her classes in classical music appreciation have left me with an enduring appreciation for such music. I caught her enthusiasm for the works of Beethoven, Chopin, Mozart, Schubert, and Schumann, as did many other students who would not otherwise have had this exposure. For many of us, this appreciation for European music developed alongside a blossoming appreciation for the local, nationalistic musical forms. Miss Lewin was to become the foremost musicologist of indigenous Jamaican folk music.

There were numerous accomplished musicians among the students also—many having been members of their church choirs, and some receiving music lessons from the organist and teachers in their villages. The Mico, as we affectionately called our college, was alive with music.

Christmas in 1964 remains etched in my memory. The music tutors and their music specialists wrote and performed a Christmas pageant. They converted the ground corridor and the first floor of the west wing of the Buxton Block into stages. The whole student body sat on chairs arranged under the stairs in front of a large wooden platform. The lighting shifted the scenes from the large stage to the stages set up in the corridors. It was a perfect setting for the choir to perform: "Oh holy night, the stars are brightly shining. It was the night of the dear Saviour's birth." The unpretentious magnificence of that performance came as close, in my imagination, as anything could to recreating the solemnity of the nativity. At that same concert, I heard for the first time the Caribbean carol:

The virgin Mary had a baby boy,
The virgin Mary had a baby boy,
The virgin Mary had a baby boy,
And they say that his name was Jesus.
(Refrain)
He come from the glory,
He come from the glorious kingdom.
He come from the glory,
He come from the glorious kingdom.
Oh, yes! believer! Oh, yes! believer!

He come from the glory,
He come from the glorious kingdom.
The angels sang when the baby was born,
The angels sang when the baby was born,
The angels sang when the baby was born,
And they say that his name is Jesus.
(Refrain)

The bass section of this choir was heard with all of the masculine pride and power of which the bass voice is capable. Mrs. Merton Wright, our Girl Guide sponsor, had the Girl Guides rehearse and perform "The Little Drummer Boy." As I write about this place that contributed so much to my maturity and independence, the melodies flood back in medleys. I pause and give thanks.

Mr. Claude Case, a Peace Corps volunteer, taught drawing. He was a good artist and a good teacher, but his efforts were somewhat wasted on me. I remember well the exercise of using charcoal to draw faces in order to show different expressions. A batch-mate pointed at one of my studies and declared with a mocking giggle that the face had "liquid eyes." Crafts were akin to art, and I did little better there. Pottery and ceramics, with Mrs. Berry, left the most lasting impression.

Although Mr. Freddie Green and Mrs. Edith Allen provided a fine physical education program, athletics and sports were for me not so much instructive as downright painful. I hated the uniform, which consisted of ridiculous little short white bloomers and pleated skirts, that we had to wear for our classes. While our games were sex-segregated, the wooligan men attended our netball games with the expressed purpose of leering at our bosoms, crotches, and legs. Their sideline comments were full of embarrassing sexual innuendos, which made it difficult to concentrate on the game. For example, when the ball was in play they would repeat: "On your balls, girls, on your balls." Then there would be some loud comment about so-and-so knowing how to handle her balls. When a woman jumped to intercept the ball, the men would shout: "Grab your ball, girl, grab your ball." And how I loathed the house competitions. Out of house loyalty, one had to compete in every sports event so as not to let your house down. My poor performances would garner much teasing about my size, height, and less-than-skilled performance. I would endure teasing about how good I was at carrying the bucket, meaning to come last, which is what I did in every race. I had to endure subsequent greetings of "Bucket!" from some of my colleagues, mostly the notorious second-year men.

My final year in college was the most enjoyable. I worked very hard. In addition to two education courses and practice teaching, we had to choose two academic subjects and one practical subject in which to specialize, in addition to the compulsory English composition and grammar. My two academic subjects were biology and chemistry, while my practical subject was home economics. This was quite a change as I was carrying three courses rather than the thirteen in my first year and the twelve in my second year.

Mr. Henry Hutchinson who taught both biology and chemistry knew his subjects well and was also an excellent role model as a teacher. He had been recruited to Mico College following the dismissal of a science tutor whose doctoral qualifications were found to be fraudulent upon a formal investigation prompted by student complaints.

The evolutionary biology approach, which Mr. Hutchinson adopted, gave me a good sense of order and progression. We were especially interested in the study of vertebrates. Through dissection of specimens, some of which were preserved in formaldehyde, we studied the anatomy and basic physiology of the following systems: circulatory system, reproductive system, endocrine system, nervous system, and the renal system. When we came to the mammals, we dissected the guinea pig and were informed that the systems in the guinea pig were similar to those of humans. Similarities were carefully noted. As we were studying the reproductive system for its likeness to humans, I could see no accounting for female menstruation. I put my hand up and asked: "Mr. Hutchinson, when does the guinea pig menstruate?" I was earnest and serious in asking and meant no mischief. My classmates, however, ever ready to tease and jeer, burst out laughing. Mr. Hutchinson's blush was hard to detect under his ebony skin. Stuttering to find his composure, he gave me the serious and respectful answer that I deserved, and his attitude vindicated me before my classmates.

Mr. Hutchinson made biology interesting, even for those who did not specialize in this subject, by providing ever-changing displays in and outside of the science labs. He created a balanced aquarium in an old bathtub, which provided a source of fascination and discussion about the gas exchanges and food chains and the life cycles of both aquatic plants and animals. When I had my own elementary classroom, I recreated a balanced aquarium with my pupils and also enjoyed with them the enchantment and mysteries of the life cycle: birth, growth, reproduction, and death.

Chemistry was more challenging for me than biology. I found organic chemistry very difficult and frustrating. However, the magic of atomic and molecular combinations hooked me so firmly that I studied chemistry night and day. I saw the evidence of chemistry in the commonplace of the home, such as in the process of food preparation or in the working of detergents. Hydrogenation explained how margarine was made; fermentation explained the production of alcohol and the leavening of bread yeasts; emulsification was evident in the production of mayonnaise; and so on. I was so impressed with the application of biology and chemistry to everyday life that my graduating project for home economics was titled Science and Home. I turned my pure biology and chemistry into applied food and textile sciences. Many of my tutors who viewed the graduating displays complimented me on their originality. Going into my final exam in chemistry, I worked very hard to improve my "D" grade and earned an "A." A number of us who were weak in chemistry were given considerable help in a study group led by my batch-mate Neville Robinson who was the most able chemistry and mathematics student in our class.

I had two great composition and grammar teachers in my second and third years. Mrs. Thomas, an Englishwoman, came from Titchfield High School in Port Antonio to teach at Mico College in my second year. She took my class through the rudiments of composition in the most learned and erudite manner. She was teaching us her mother tongue, which we used only formally. Our everyday speech was the unwritten and expressive patois. This lady brought us to attention, so to speak, and taught and demanded expression in the Queen's English. In my final year, I had Miss Dora Edwards, a Jamaican who had earned her Master of Arts in Edinburgh, Scotland, and her Diploma in Education in London, England. By the time she came to teach us, we knew that she had gone to the mother country. She had erased every bit of her patois and Jamaican accent and now spoke with the accent of the British literati, and she taught us as such. English tenses were her forté, and she drilled us in their usage. She introduced peer editing to our writing. Miss Edwards taught me that writing could be published. It was a revolutionary notion that we, as humble colonized people, could actually write for publication. Although she did not push us to publish any of our writing, she planted the seeds of possibility and showed us a process.

Mrs. Thomas had equal commitment to teach us good writing and accurate grammar. Writing précis of numerous texts forced us to be precise in word usage and to develop a sizeable English vocabulary. I have often been complimented on the precise English of my speech. English language and composition was one of the distinctions that I achieved in my final examination. I write of these teachers' work in order to pay tribute to their fine teaching.

Mico College, which I had the privilege of attending from September 1962 to July 1965, has left indelible influences on my character as a teacher. After entering at the age of nineteen, I spent the best three years of my youth there. I have talked about the curriculum and the pedagogical practices of my tutors. I would now like to look at how the institution was organized into a total educational institution.

All but a handful of students were boarders. As such, our waking and sleeping hours were organized and controlled. I have already described the women's hostel. The men lived in Mills Hall and other adjoining male hostels located on the campus.

As boarders, our nutrition and health were fully taken care of. We were fed breakfast, lunch, and dinner and had a mid-morning snack with a sugary, pink beverage we called "pug" and afternoon tea. The lunch queue that spanned the length of the lounge in the Mills Hall block was a place "to see and be seen." To one end of the large dining room was a section where the tutors dined. Animated conversations and laughter echoed throughout meal times. Mills Hall was also the place where one could see and enjoy the jokes of the anonymous cartoonists who captured the social activities in our college life. My notorious romance caught the attention of the satirists. After one Saturday-night social, a brilliant cartoon appeared that was entitled: "The sergeant major and his lady." The "sergeant major" was my date, who was in the army cadets—his drills were evidently legendary.

Mr. Glen Owen, the principal at the time, wore a dignified persona that earned him the nickname the "Keps," which was derived from combining the sounds of the Latin and French words for principal. In my eyes, he was both the principal and a man of principles. Obviously, many of the young men thought so too because several of them imitated his manner of speech, gestures, and chivalry. There was a certain batch-mate who was dubbed "likkle Keps" (little Keps) because he imitated the principal so closely, which I found attractive. Some others who tried to imitate these standards of conduct earned themselves the nickname "crowd ass" because they simply could not carry them off. Looking back, I see that the imitation of these English gentlemanly behaviours among some of my male counterparts—

standing when a woman enters a room, holding the door so that a woman enters first, walking on the sidewalk so that the man is next to the traffic—constituted dramaturgy without substance. Men and women in the college practised the social roles and behaviours assigned to the masculine and feminine gender of a colonial society that was striving to adopt the manners of the British upper class. Some were more successful than others in holding on to these codes of conduct.

Mr. Owen and his staff set the tone, which emphasized personal dignity, moral character, and scholarly leadership. In addition to the formal curriculum, the administration had a comprehensive plan for our social organization within the college and engaged us in the leadership of various youth organizations. We were expected to be able to lead Girl Guides, Boy Scouts, Cadets, and other extra-curricular activities after graduation. The plan included religious socialization, athletics and games, music and culture, secular youth organization, the house system, inter-house competitions, and the student of the year competition.

Although the college was founded on non-denominational principles, it demonstrated a commitment to Christian moral socialization. All students were required to have a denominational affiliation and to attend this church on Sundays, except for the Seventh Day Adventists who attended on Saturdays. Furthermore, the whole student body was expected to attend the college's chapel service, I believe once per month, on a Sunday afternoon. There was usually a special preacher, and a choir sang.

Morning worship occurred after the first two class periods. We worshipped in a variety of places. First, there was the house worship when we gathered with first-, second-, and third-year students belonging to the same house under the leadership of the housemaster. The pattern of house worship occurred in three parts. First, the student leader would call the worship to begin with the announcement of the hymn. The hymn was sung *a cappella* or accompanied by a pianist or a few recorder players. Then another student would read a passage from the Old or New Testament. Finally, we would recite the Lord's Prayer. House announcements were made at this time. The housemaster took the opportunity to praise us for house loyalty and to celebrate any victories that had been made to honour the house. He would never fail to remind the Buxtonites that we were the best. We belonged to the house named for the great emancipator, Thomas Fowell Buxton, who was one of the founding trustees of the Lady Mico Trust, from which the college was originally funded. The Buxton Tower was built and named in his honour in 1896. Thus, he shone the light of education as the great emancipator from class and race oppression. Did not white men such as Buxton see through the great social evils of their day and had they not done something about them?

Wednesday mornings were reserved for general assembly when the whole student body worshipped together, just before a public lecture on current events was delivered by a variety of speakers—some dull, but most engaging, many brilliant, and a few memorable. I always looked forward to them. The whole college assembled, seated on chairs arranged in the open air under the ackee shade trees in front of the west wing of Buxton hall. The long corridors or veranda served as the platform for the tutors and guests. The assemblies were meant as sessions to groom us in public speaking and to give the seniors an opportunity to read the Bible passages with perfect cadence, intonation, and pitch. My batch-mate R.T. Campbell was the best at this when he became a senior. He read the Bible as if he were reading poetry with his radio voice. Senior students were also given the opportunity to compose and deliver votes of thanks. The best part for me was question time. I took great pleasure in finding the holes in the speaker's arguments and exposing them.

There was this one memorable general assembly that occurred in my final year. The guest speaker was none other than the Honorable Edward Seaga, Minister of Development and Welfare, in the first

Parliament of independent Jamaica. Mr. Seaga had recently returned from Harvard University where he acquired his degree in anthropology. He had written a thesis on the slums of West Kingston, which was the district that became his constituency. He was young, handsome, and brilliant. He described a well-conceived plan for community development and economic self-reliance for the peasants in the country parts of the island. However, in my view it had a big flaw.

I rose at question time to pose my question, prompting an uproarious teasing with the men shouting "Stand up, senior lady, stand up" in obvious reference to my height. It took a while for Mr. Owen, the principal, to settle things down enough for me to ask my question. But as soon as I began, the shouting started again: "Speak up, senior lady, we can't hear you." At which point, Mr. Seaga took the microphone and said: "Come up here, young miss, and ask your question." I went up to the microphone, but since my head was barely above the lectern this was again a reason for more teasing. When the microphone was adjusted, and I could at last speak, I boldly praised Mr. Seaga for his brilliant plan but said: "Sir, I do not see how your plan for the people to set up small businesses on their own will work, without start up capital. How do you propose to make capital available for starting up such businesses of which you so eloquently spoke?" At this, the audience burst out cheering, clapping, and whistling and shouting. "Point well taken." Mr. Seaga had no choice but to concede the point. I have often wondered what became of those community development plans that lacked the available start up capital.

One or two mornings were devoted to worshipping with our batch-mates. It was on these mornings that issues concerning the batch were discussed after the worship. Batch socials, disciplinary matters, and graduation plans were made after we worshipped together. Thursday afternoons were reserved for the whole student body to meet in religious fraternities. These were presided over by a chaplain or other official representative. I belonged to the Anglican fraternity. Here, we would discuss church doctrines as they pertained to the holy sacraments. The marriage sacrament generated many lengthy and animated discourses around celibacy versus pre-marital sex. Most of us were young and single and expected to enter into Christian marriages at some point in the future. Catechism was also conducted for those interested in joining the Anglican Church. I enjoyed these fraternity meetings, especially when Reverend Weevil Gordon, from the Allman Town Anglican Church nearby, was in attendance. In his company, I felt the same fellowship that I enjoyed with the Reverend Neville De Souza in the Anglican Young Peoples Association (AYPA) at St. Gabriel's Anglican Church in May Pen. Young Reverend De Souza, who later became the Anglican bishop of Jamaica, introduced us to the new ideas in theological thinking. I learned the word "existentialism" from him in those AYPA sessions. Both men took us on theological excursions that went refreshingly beyond the boundaries of the Biblical text.

In writing and thinking about my religious upbringing, and the Biblical instruction I received throughout my formal schooling, I pause to articulate the influences that these have had on my ethical thinking. Although I have fallen out of the habit of church attendance, religious and Bible lessons have remained indelibly embedded in my psyche and continue to inform my ethical thought and behaviour. At the simplest level, I can appreciate Biblical allusions and themes that infuse the poetry, novels, and dramas of Western literature. Biblical texts exposed me to a variety of literary forms: parables, sermons, epistles, letters, jeremiads, books, psalms, gospels, and songs. More deeply, my personal ethics and world-view are guided by Judeo-Christian principles of unconditional love, justice, truth, redemption, deliverance, and faith. Virtues were instilled in us.

Closely allied to the system of religious fraternities was the tutorial system whereby each tutor was assigned to meet a group of about ten to twelve students of all years, once per week. This group was like a group counselling session on academic development, social belonging, and moral and spiritual well being. In my first year, I was in Miss E.M. Duncan's tutorial. She was of the Pentacostal denomination and, to my way of thinking, a little too concerned about our salvation. I had a batch-mate of a rather mature age, named McBean, who shared Miss Duncan's enthusiasm. He testified in the tutorial that when he accepted Jesus as his personal saviour, it felt like eating a cool cucumber. I thought they were all a bunch of cool cucumbers and skipped the very next meeting. Since she lived at the hostel, she made a point of finding me and upbraiding me the same evening. I felt like such a sinner that I went sheepishly back to the meeting the next week. Such was the social control of the college—if one did not arrive where one was supposed to be, someone in authority would hold you to account and demand to know where you had been. At least so it was for the women.

Athletics and games had an annual cycle. Cricket, netball, and track and field each had their season. Cricket was for the men and netball for the women. The women also played rounders, a female version of baseball. Some people pursued these sports informally. But we prepared for track and field events very seriously, with the goal of preparing the talented athletes to compete in the annual inter-college championship held at the national stadium. This was another occasion where the spectators paraded in the latest casual dress. Looking back now, I can see that this event was an opportunity to show off our differences in material status. On other occasions, more uniform dress prevailed.

In addition to the inter-college championship, we had inter-house competition. Every single student had to participate. On the one hand, this competition was a great way to get all of us involved in physical activities outside our compulsory physical education classes. In this case, the races were both for the swift and for those that endured to the end. However, on the other hand, for non-athletes such as myself these occasions were times of intensely negative self-consciousness. I recall learning to throw the shotput. When I threw that heavy metal ball, it just pulled me along with it. I inadvertently provided entertainment in the long and high jumps. I would have done anything to stay out of the celebratory parade of the houses. On the whole, it must be said, the games and the athletic program contributed much to our character building. Vinton Powell, a batchmate, came into his own as a runner during his Mico College years. He went on to become an international track star and athletic coach.

Participation in musical and other cultural activities such as drama and dance was encouraged and expected. I had no musical talent or skills to join any of the choirs or to be a soloist or part of the duets, trios, and sextets. Worse yet, I could not play any of the musical instruments—I tried, but I learned quickly that I had no aptitude. Had I been lucky to have been given piano or violin lessons at a young age, perhaps I would not have had the inhibitions at this late stage. This is a regret, as I would have loved to be able to lose myself in playing the piano or the violin. I learned enough music theory to be able to attend the symphony and understand a performance, and I am grateful for this exposure. Classical music is good for the soul and lifts the spirit.

Drama came more naturally, and I remember enjoyable drama productions, which a group of us put on for the whole college, during my first or second year. Mrs. Edith Allen choreographed a few dances in which I performed with some enjoyment.

Club days were set aside for two kinds of clubs—academic and uniformed. The academic clubs comprised the drama, music, parliamentary, Spanish, and camera clubs. I do not remember these being strictly enforced. I was part of the drama and parliamentary clubs, which met in the evenings. The parliamentary club took on debating many current political affairs. I loved the verbal jousting and acrobatics in the parliamentary club. One high point was the debate in which I participated concerning the United States's power in the Panama Canal zone. I took the side of Panamanian independence and self-reliance. My side won the debate. My collegial esteem went up notches. In preparing for this debate, I had my first intellectual excursion beyond the history of the British empire.

Students in the camera club chronicled special events in the college. We were able to purchase prints of special occasions from club members.

The uniformed clubs included scouting, guiding, the boys' brigade, and army cadets. As graduates, we were expected to sponsor a youth club in our community. I opted for supporting the Girl Guides. Mrs. Merton Wright and Mrs. Edith Allen were our sponsors. I appreciated their dedication and enthusiasm. Through their efforts, I was able to experience Girl Guide camps in partnership with the Shortwood Teachers' College Guide Company. In the summer of 1963 or 1964, they took us to camp in Mandeville where we had the opportunity to explore the private botanical gardens of a doctor whose name I do not remember. It was a cultivated and cultured landscape in the island that I would not otherwise have seen. Miss Hoylett, the Girl Guide mistress from Shortwood College, designed the most impressive activities to get us to explore the physical features of the garden landscape. I believe the doctor's gardener, or perhaps the doctor himself, gave us a botanical description of specially imported plants and flowering trees. It may have been a reproduction of the English country gardens in the tropics.

In February 1965, we camped at Pax Acres Guide Camp. Miss Hoylett was present again, and this time she taught us mountain climbing and stargazing. I was quartermaster at this camp. My leadership and organizational abilities really surprised me. I received high praise for my accomplishments. That same year, the college company hosted several guide companies during Guiding Week. I learned very valuable organizational and management skills. The discipline and decisiveness of being a patrol leader toughened me up. It took quite some courage to give commands on a parade and to prepare a company for inspections. The threefold promise was to do my duty to God, Queen and country, to help others, and to keep the Girl Guide Law. The three-fingered salute and the three-leafed clover (trefoil) engraved on our belt buckles symbolized our pledge and promise. We made this salute as we repeated our promise at every meeting. Between the motto—"Be prepared"—and the ten-article Guide Law, I learned to be alert, adaptable, and giving. I did have difficulty with Article 6—a guide is obedient. Unconditional obedience was, and still is not, what I am inclined to give.

Though I can now look back and criticize the quasi-military nature of Girl Guiding, and can see how it was a socializing organ of empire, I have to say it worked well as a sorority of empire. When I moved to teach in rural British Columbia in 1969, I had instant membership in a familiar organization. The next year, I assisted with commanding the South Slocan Guide Company when Princess Anne visited Castlegar, British Columbia, in 1970. I have my guide belt, whistle, and penknife still, and the guide song means much to me. Howard Arnold Walter, a congregational pastor and missionary, wrote the song as his creed in 1906. "I would be true for there are those who trust me," sung to the tune of "Londonderry Air," refreshes all my youthful idealism. Through this song, I have been inspired throughout my life to be courageous in the face of adversity and suffering. They are my guiding ethical values:

I would be true for there are those who trust me;
I would be pure, for there are those who care;
I would be strong, for there is much to suffer;
I would be brave, for there is much to dare.
I would be friend of all, the foe, the friendless;
I would be giving, and forget the gift.
I would be humble, for I know my weakness;
I would look up, and laugh, and love and lift.

The house system was very familiar. I had belonged to Sharp House when I attended May Pen All-Age School and to Nichol House when I was at Clarendon College. At Mico College, there were five houses named mostly for English men who had done outstanding service in the college as advocates, trustees, and principals. The names of the houses during my time were Arthur Grant, Bishop, Buxton, Lushington, and Rodgers. Thomas Fowell Buxton, an abolitionist, and Dr. Stephen Lushington, who were among the original trustees of the Lady Mico Charity, were appointed in 1834 by Sir John Leach, Master of the Rolls, to establish schools in the West Indies for the Africans released from slavery into apprenticeship. Four years later, in 1838, these apprentices were fully emancipated.

I belonged to Buxton House for whom the original building on the present site is named. The Buxton Hall was built in 1894 when Buxton was chairman of the board. He also donated the clock tower—the Buxton Tower. Who would have thought that I would have come to know Thomas Fowel Buxton in this personal way by being a member of a house named for him? Mr. R.A. Shirley was my housemaster. As in his teaching, he encouraged us to reach for greater heights and to be the best that we could be in everything.

I have mentioned house worship and inter-house sports competition earlier. Inter-house competition included academics, community service, and the personal deportment of its members. The house system brought together students of all ages, classes, and interests to foster friendly competition and camaraderie. We fostered house spirit by identifying and valuing the talents in each other. Our house gathering brought us closer to being peers and role models. We learned to value and compliment each other with genuine affection and admiration. I certainly benefitted from the esteem showed me by the tutors and students in Buxton House. It seemed that there was a place for everyone in the house system.

I think the college tried hard to regulate male–female relationships. Young women were strictly controlled in the hours they were allowed to be away from the hostels. The nine o'clock devotion was roll call before bedtime. There was an eleven o'clock curfew on Saturday nights. I always felt that I was being watched and monitored. I did not resent this control because I believed that my tutors cared deeply about me and I knew many had high ambitions for me.

Heterosexual tensions among young men and women were ever present and evident. Less evident to me was the tension that must have existed between homosexuals—males and females. I was aware of the rumoured male homosexual relationships but was totally unaware of the lesbian relationships that must have also existed. The relative awareness may have come from the fact that there were religious sanctions against male homosexuality, while it seemed that no one cared about the level of intimacy between and among women. I was immersed in heterosexual tensions both within myself and in my relationship with my male colleagues.

The greatest challenge in college was how to suppress and mask my desires to explore heterosexual relationships in a context that was both sexually repressive and aggressive. The repression came from the advice of our tutors, chaplains, and religious leaders, who admonished us to preserve our virginity until marriage to the "right" Christian man. Waiting for marriage before exploring our female sexuality was deemed to be a measure of a decent and respectable woman. To have sex before marriage was tantamount to sacrilege. In a secular sense, abstention had the practical value of saving one from sexually transmitted diseases and from pregnancy out of wedlock. To catch sexually transmitted diseases was cause for utter shame and disgrace, never mind the wrath of one's family if they found out.

I dreaded becoming pregnant for two reasons. First, it was a matter of honour for me that no man should be able to say to me:

"I married you to give your child a name and to save you from disgrace." The second reason for my fear of becoming prematurely pregnant had to do with my observation of the large number of young women whose future was ruined because of pregnancy. I also heard the stories of regrets from women who had to marry before they were ready, or even against their better judgment, because of an unwanted pregnancy. Abortions were regarded as one of the greatest sins that a woman could commit. I knew of abortions that caused medical complications for some young women and in a few cases took lives. I still feel sorrow for school friends who met their untimely death because of septic abortions.

The sexually aggressive aspect of Mico College was manifested in male sexual behaviour towards the females. Both sexes had three categories for each other. The men categorized the women as the "lady," the "platonic friend," or the "streggay" (equivalent to whore). The "lady" combined the Jamaican sense of beauty at that time and something called "lady-like behaviour." This category of woman was both desirable and aloof. She was placed on a pedestal. She was treated with all of the outward trappings of chivalry and deference. Some men behaved chivalrously towards her out of genuine admiration and affection, while others masked lechery and lust with gallantry in a bid to undermine her persona.

The "platonic friend" was almost the man's equal, like his sister, and was his confidante. This relationship was characterized with less sexual tension, even if it sometimes became intimate. Those women who were regarded as the "streggay" were treated with the utmost disrespect, as if they had no human feelings. Some men would circulate "lie and story" about some alleged sexual aberration on the woman's part. They never, of course, implicated themselves as the villains in these stories.

The women's categories comprised the exact counterparts: the "gentleman," the "platonic friend," and the "dog." The "gentleman" was the opposite of the lady, and every heterosexual woman desired such a man for a husband. It was rare to find such a one. The "platonic" boyfriend was like a brother—he could be trusted and respected, and it could be a relationship having real bonds of affection. The "dog" was the man who undressed you with his eyes and was largely incapable of any conversation beyond smut. The "dog" took pleasure in attacking female sexuality and in slandering any female who dated two men of which he was not one, especially if she had refused his overtures. Interestingly, a person could be in at least two categories at the same time, depending on the eye of the potential mate.

Another aspect of aggression came from the fact that there were fewer females than males. Thus, the so-called "sexually appealing" females found themselves in the company of several eligible males engaged in aggressive sexual competition. When I would look back on the various approaches, even then, I would have flashbacks to the sexual behaviours that I had observed on my early nature walks and on the farm. It seems crude, but I could not help recalling the lizards, the roosters, the drakes, the ram goats, the donkeys, the bulldogs, and the bulls. In the local parlance, they would be known as the "bull cows" or the "cock chickens." On the one hand, what should have been natural and beautiful romantic play often was interpreted by some as an opportunity to "score." Some males, on the other hand, would pursue females in a manner that said: "I would very much like to 'score,' but even if I don't, I still like you."

Given the lessons that I had learned about sexual treachery in the lives of women and men I had known and observed, I was determined to be cautious and careful. My firm resolve was never to let a man distract me from my fervent desire to excel in college and to strive to be a scholar and to be economically independent. I excelled in college in order to become an able teacher and scholar. I felt beautiful, ambitious, and strong.

It was through the house system that the annual "Student of the Year Contest" was organized. The purpose of the contest is explained in the following quotation from a June 1965 concert program, which

I found among my college memorabilia: "Mico College Student of the Year contest began four years ago to provide an additional incentive for our students who are preparing themselves to guide our country's youth." Only students in their final year were eligible for the award. The criteria on which students were assessed included integrity, courtesy, speech intelligence, deportment, initiative, and service to the Mico and the community.

Each of the five houses mentioned earlier nominated its most outstanding male and female students. I was the female nominee for Buxton House. I was described as courteous, alert, trustworthy, mature in outlook, and a very promising teacher. Once I was nominated, I took the competition very seriously. I dismissed predictions that certain men were surefire winners. Past experience showed that all winners to date had been men and that they had been either student council presidents or outstanding athletes. I was none of these. My attitude was that once we were nominated we were equal competitors and would be judged on our performance in the competition. I set about finding out how the competition was conducted and speculated on the sorts of questions that we were likely to be asked. I also thought hard about ways to appear knowledgeable on all of the possible subjects on which we could be interviewed. We were judged at two levels of competition. At the first level, a college panel that included the principal, vice principal, the sports mistress and the sports master, and the principal's wife interviewed us. Mrs. Gloria Owen, the principal's wife, was very active on three fronts: in the organization of the competition, in acquiring prizes, and in mobilizing influential friends of the college. She made the student of the year competition a highly talked-about event in and outside of the college.

Six finalists were selected and sent forward to the second level of competition. I was among these students. I remember pointedly thinking about, and preparing myself to answer, the questions about Washington, DC, the official destination for the winner and chaperone. I went to the *Encyclopedia Britannica* and to the USIS, which is a place I frequented to obtain curricular materials. I also thought about the very important persons who comprised the panel and tried to second-guess what these people might ask a young teacher-to-be. By the time this round of the competition arrived, I was ready for anything. I remember two of the questions. The first was a question about hobbies. My childhood experiences did not allow for hobbies or leisure activities. I made up some answer about my hobbies being reading and sewing. I felt pretty silly after giving that answer. However, I bounced back in top form when I was asked about the city that the winner would be visiting. Later, I learned that the panel asked all of the competitors that question and that I was the only one who had been prepared with the answer. This panel ranked the six finalists in order of merit based on their performance in the interview. The top male and top female student would be announced, and one of them would be declared student of the year.

On a Monday night, 7 June 1965, the Mico College student of the year concert was held at the Little Theatre in Kingston under the distinguished patronage of His Excellency, the Governor General, Sir Clifford Campbell. Sir Clifford was a graduate of Mico College and our nation's first governor general after independence. The college and the young nation were so proud of him. The evening was full of pomp and ceremony as befitted the celebration of the independence batch. During our three years, we were told repeatedly that we were among the leaders of tomorrow. As the first post-independence graduating class, we were exhorted to "go forth from the hallowed halls of The Mico" and help build the new nation. Oh, the expectations were high indeed. (As I am writing and reliving the time, I realize how far I have fallen short of these expectations by leaving the island after only four years of teaching.) Miss Olive Lewin and Mr. Arthur Clarke, our music tutors, planned the program, which featured some of the best musical and dramatic artists of the island. The result was an evening of top-notch cultural performances that included clarinet, violin, and piano solos of European and American composers.

AUGUST 27, 1965

THE GOVERNOR-GENERAL
Sir Clifford Campbell talks
with Miss Yvonne Shorter,
Mico College's "Student of
the Year" (centre) when
she visited the Governor-
General yesterday morning at
King's House. Accompany-
ing her were Mrs. Edith
Allen, chaperone (left) and
Mr. G. H. Owen, Princi-
pal of Mico College at right.

The Governor-General, Sir Clifford Campbell (left, back to photo)
congratulates me on being named Mico College's Student of the Year.
Second from left is chaperone Edith Allen, and at right is Glen Owen,
principal of Mico College. (*Jamaica Daily Gleaner*, August 27, 1965)

The Mico College choir and soloists were at their best. The performances were interrupted at three different points in order to present
the competitors.

First, the six finalists were presented. The top male student was
Ivor Wilson and the top female student was Yvonne Shorter. The
air was charged until finally the announcement was made: "The
Student of the Year for 1965 is Miss Yvonne Shorter." I cannot say
the choice pleased everyone because there was a noticeable booing
coming from the back of the theatre. Still, I walked up proudly to be
honoured as the first female student of the year in the college's history. What an honour! Of course, I thought "if only my mother were
here." No family member was present to witness this moment—in
the midst of this joy I was overcome with loneliness.

Mrs. Edith Allen, the sports mistress, was my chaperone on my
official visit to Washington, DC, which took place in July after final

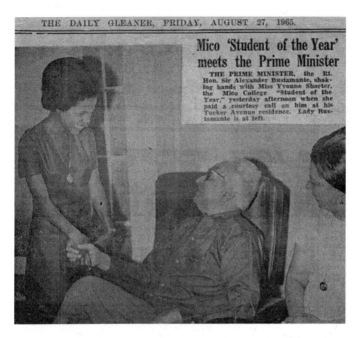

Mico 'Student of the Year' meets the Prime Minister

THE PRIME MINISTER, the Rt. Hon. Sir Alexander Bustamante, shaking hands with Miss Yvonne Shorter, the Mico College "Student of the Year," yesterday afternoon when she paid a courtesy call on him at his Tucker Avenue residence. Lady Bustamante is at left.

The Prime Minister, Sir. Alexander Bustamante, and I at Jamiaca House, the prime minister's residence. Right: Lady Gladys Bustamante. (*Jamaica Daily Gleaner,* August 27, 1965)

exams were over. While we were there, we had official visits with the Jamaican Embassy, the US Department of Health, Education and Welfare, and the National Education Association (where I was given a mountain of curricular materials). Of course, our program also included visits to the Smithsonian Institution, the Space Center, the Washington and Lincoln Monuments, and much more. We also went shopping. I was truly overwhelmed. All of the festivities and preparations for my final examinations had kept the depression at bay.

When I returned from my prize trip, the Owens prepared the finest program of official activities to fête the Student of the Year. By so doing, they also promoted the Mico College as a significant institution in the life of Jamaica. In addition to making an official call on the governor general at his King's House residence, we also called on the prime minister, the Right Honourable Alexander Bustamante, at Jamaica House. I was interviewed by the Jamaica Broadcasting Corporation Radio and Television and featured in the *Daily Gleaner*.

I pause once again to thank the late principal, Mr. Glen Owen, and his wife, Mrs. Gloria Owen, as well as the tutors and staff at Mico College, 1962–65, for giving me the sense of self that I have tried to live up to and that has sustained me in the teaching profession and in all aspects of my life.

The Student of the Year competition was not the event that marked my graduation from Mico. The final examinations and the preparation of the "matter book" of teaching and learning resources, which Mr. Shirley insisted we produce before we graduated, were yet to be done. He had difficulty ensuring compliance and resorted to staring at those of us who had not handed them in, as we walked up the aisle of, I believe, the Kingston Parish Church, where our graduation ceremonies were held. (This was more like a college-leaving ceremony since we would not have the results of our final examination until August.) Mr. Shirley's actions were well meant, born of his appreciation of the desperate need for good teaching and learning resources in the resource-poor environment of the island. I was among the guilty ones. As I write, I smile about the good humour and affection that Mr. Shirley shared with the independence batch of graduates. There was just so much to be done that it was extremely difficult to put in the labour required to produce this book. I believe we appreciated only superficially then what Mr. Shirley fully understood as the urgency and enormous responsibility that we were taking on to educate the large population of school-age children and to raise the standards of education in the new nation.

We graduated from Mico College in July 1965 and had to await the results of our final examination, which would determine our certification and ability to find a job. It was a nail-biting time for me. I had separation anxiety from leaving Mico and its security. The results of the examination would be published in the *Jamaica Gazette*, along with the results of the five other teachers' colleges— Bethlehem, Moneague, Saint Joseph's, Shortwood, and West Indies College. In writing about this time of my life, I had to go back and check the *Jamaica Gazette* for August 1965 to verify my recollection that I had passed my examinations and placed in the Honours Division with distinctions in English language and composition, chemistry, and practice teaching. I gained more distinctions than any other student in any of the colleges. I look back with great pride to this period of my life.

In late August, I received an appointment at the May Pen Junior Secondary School, which was modelled after the May Pen Comprehensive School experiment that I had attended from January 1957 to December1959. Although I returned to the city of my childhood and was hailed with great honour, I knew in my heart that I did not want to return to that scene. Some of the old ghosts had begun to haunt me. For example, Uncle Harry seriously expected me to come back to help him in his shop, and Auntie wanted me to be her household helper again, although she at least was subtler in her approach. Echoes from a past in slavery!

December rolled around, and it was time to return to the college for the presentation of our teaching certificates and prizes and to see our tutors and batch-mates again. Looking over the program helps me to make meaning of that very special occasion. This ceremony had a big surprise in store for me. I believe the ceremony was held at the amphitheatre where that special Christmas concert that I wrote about earlier was held. Although we were no longer a Crown colony, it was too soon to switch cultural allegiance away from the empire. After all, the Queen was still our Head of State. The hymn chosen for the occasion was the hymn that I learned for the coronation of Queen Elizabeth II in 1953: "I vow to thee my country." I now wonder if we had consciously changed from thinking of ourselves as subjects of the British empire when we sang that hymn that night. Once again, we had the company of our native Governor General Sir Clifford Campbell and Lady Campbell. He gave the formal address, and she handed out the certificates. At this ceremony, many prizes and cups were handed out for both academics and service. I received the Glen Owen Cup for education, the Doris Morant Cup for home economics, and the Duff Memorial Prize for the most outstanding student in the final year. At that time, the Duff Memorial Prize was one of the most prestigious prizes. I am proud to say that I was the first female recipient of this award. Mr. John Hartley Duff was the first Jamaican to become principal of Mico College, his tenure lasting from 1920 until 1923. Once again, I am proud to record that I walked off with the most prizes.

When I came to the bottom of the steps after receiving my certificate, a very tall well-dressed black woman greeted me warmly and hugged me. She said: "My child you do not know me. I was your mother's best friend. I left for England for three years and when I came back she was gone. I have been looking for you for nearly twenty years. You were the baby. I have always wondered what happened to you." I must have looked at this lady like a ghost, transfixed. I cannot remember for sure, but I believe she said her name was Mrs. Smith. She said she had been following the television and radio appearances and the news items about me and became convinced that I must be the child for whom she had been looking. She gave me her address and asked that my brother and I visit her. When we did, my brother remembered her, and they began to talk about the misery that our mother suffered at our father's hands. My brother cried so hard that I had to ask her to stop talking. I have always had a soft heart for my brother's suffering—to the very end, indeed, when in 2000 I sat at his bedside and watched him die of cancer.

Not appreciating her importance, I never went to see this lady again. I forgot even her name and wish now that I could remember it because I would surely love to attempt to find and talk to her. Yet she appeared on my path. The folk might say my mother was up in heaven observing the ceremony and that she had sent her friend to represent her.

My graduation from Mico College in 1965 marked the beginning of another stage of restlessness and yearning for a family, of my own making, and for a new life in a new place. I would have to come to terms with marriage, work, children, travel, and emigration. It has been forty-five years since my graduation from teachers' college, and, in that time, I have fulfilled many of my dreams and achieved most of the major goals I set for myself. Earning a doctorate was the last of these. My dream to become a university professor will likely go unfulfilled. I survived and lived, to write the life stories that I always promised myself I would.

EPILOGUE

COMING TO THE END of researching and writing this memoir, I am forced to reflect upon the overwhelming dominance, wealth, and power of the British empire of my youth on the one hand. While, on the other hand, I consider the existence of the stark contrast of the psychological, social, and economic deprivations and suffering unleashed upon the majority African population by centuries of the Atlantic slave trade, plantation slavery, and emancipation without reparations from enslavement. Before I began writing these stories, I had perceived, fuzzily, a link between the inferior status that the British had assigned to Africa and African-descended people in Jamaica and the inferior status that my father's family had accorded to my mother. As counterpart to this inferior status was the pervasively lofty presence of the British empire in the culture of my schooling and in the political economy of the island.

Once in Canada, I saw that the knowledge regimes of the British empire under which I was schooled were as tenacious here as there. It amazes me still to recall how well equipped I was, educationally, to teach home economics and English when I immigrated to Canada some forty years ago. I was licensed to teach, based on my teacher education in Jamaica. I had known the curricula before I arrived. My teacher's college curricula were based on those of the English normal school. Those who are familiar with curricula extant today in schools and universities will perhaps have discerned the similarity of the curricula of my schooling and teacher education that I have recalled in some detail.

The cultural "civilizing" mission of the European empires, including the British, and the imperial knowledge regimes that they inaugurated over the last five hundred years, form the matrices of contemporary discourses on post-colonialism, neo-colonialism, anti-racism, multi-culturalism, and globalization of labour and capital. And yet, how often still do these discourses exclude the scholarly voices of the formerly enslaved and colonized and further repress and subjugate the histories of Africa and its place in world civilization. The suppression of these histories is foundational to the genesis and maintenance of European hegemonic structures.

In classrooms and in the workplaces of Jamaica and Canada, I have often felt like a ghost made flesh, who had come to stalk the halls and classrooms of the academy to remind my classmates and peers about these repressed histories of Africa and their embodied presences. Like the African ancestral dead who has not been properly buried, my restless spirit roamed the halls and classrooms searching for those bodies of knowledge that would speak truth to me of Mother Africa and her motherless offspring scattered in the Atlantic diasporas. These repressions sometimes burst forth from me, as from the bastard sitting at the dinner table who, provoked by the untruths and hypocrisies, interrupts the upright family conversation by blurting out the carnal transgressions of the father, in respectable company, causing embarrassment and subsequent punishment.

I found myself working within the knowledge regimes and institutional structures of the academy, listening to and observing proponents of contemporary globalization behave as though globalization had no antecedents. This represents a colossal forgetting. This memoir is in part a reminder that all of the components of globalization have had their antecedents in land appropriations and the extermination of indigenous peoples, the slave trade in African bodies, mercantilism, colonization, and empire building. In the contemporary discourses on globalization, Africa is assigned an inferior status or else excluded entirely. And, yet, its minerals and oil factor in the global economy in both white and black markets. Things have not changed for Africa in the so-called "new world order."

It may be considered that these assessments are partisan, self-serving, and unduly harsh. However, let us consider the following. In 1969, I left the island of Jamaica for the then Dominion of Canada. I was a resident of British Columbia for thirty-nine years, becoming a Canadian citizen in 1976. I learned that the founding of the colony of the province of British Columbia formed a keystone in the extraordinary reach of the British empire. The provincial flag still bears the device of the sun in glory, just like when the British dominion was established on the west coast of the Americas and the empire girdled the globe. It was an empire on which the sun literally did not set. The brutal consequences of imperialist territorial ambitions are with us today, celebrated by the descendants of the founding fathers of empire but cursed by the descendants of the enslaved and colonized.

In inquiring into certain haunting memories of family, education, and scenes of people and landscapes of parts of Jamaica, I was able to analyze and comprehend the historical bases for my experiences and perceptions about my own status and the status of Africa and Africans, in Jamaica and in the world. This has given me a much more rooted understanding of the pervasive repression and omission of the exploitation of African human and physical resources in the development of the British, French, Dutch, Spanish, and Portuguese empires.

I attribute the want of proper acknowledgment of the centrality of Africa to the economic and cultural history of the world to a collective desire—conscious and unconscious—to conceal a very shameful and horrific past. To acknowledge the past would necessarily be to acknowledge the injustices of the present, and the so-called civilized world is largely incapable of this recognition. Even if we concede that the beginnings of the slave trade were acts of mischief by a few loutish fifteenth-century mariners, nevertheless they turned into a five-hundred-year nightmare for millions of captive Africans and their descendants in the Atlantic diaspora, as well as enormous profits for merchant capital and a rise in consumer commodities.

To acknowledge culpability in the historical and contemporary abuse of Africa and its peoples would force a revision of all righteous claims of the European "civilizing mission," modernity, enlightenment, and white moral supremacy. Notions of aid and development would have to be reframed as acts of reparation and restitution for the plunder of gold, uranium, diamonds, cocoa, rubber, coffee, copper, and people. And so the dark secrets of empire must be repressed, just as the dark secrets of my family were repressed.

I say a silent requiem for my mother, Lucy May Reid, and for all those who perished in the cross-Atlantic trade in African bodies.

FAMILY TREES

— for Shorter, Reid, Goodwin —

Descendants of
JOHN THOMAS SHORTER

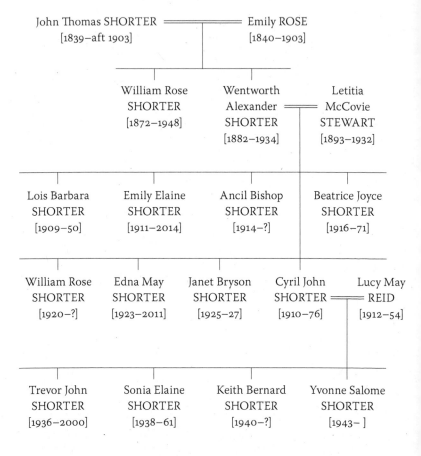

John Thomas SHORTER ═══════ Emily ROSE
[1839–aft 1903]   [1840–1903]

William Rose   Wentworth   Letitia
SHORTER   Alexander ═══════ McCovie
[1872–1948]   SHORTER   STEWART
                              [1882–1934]   [1893–1932]

Lois Barbara   Emily Elaine   Ancil Bishop   Beatrice Joyce
SHORTER   SHORTER   SHORTER   SHORTER
[1909–50]   [1911–2014]   [1914–?]   [1916–71]

William Rose   Edna May   Janet Bryson   Cyril John   Lucy May
SHORTER   SHORTER   SHORTER   SHORTER ═══════ REID
[1920–?]   [1923–2011]   [1925–27]   [1910–76]   [1912–54]

Trevor John   Sonia Elaine   Keith Bernard   Yvonne Salome
SHORTER   SHORTER   SHORTER   SHORTER
[1936–2000]   [1938–61]   [1940–?]   [1943–]

NOTE: double lines between two people indicate that they were legally married;
dotted lines indicate that the two people were unmarried.

Descendants of
THOMAS REID

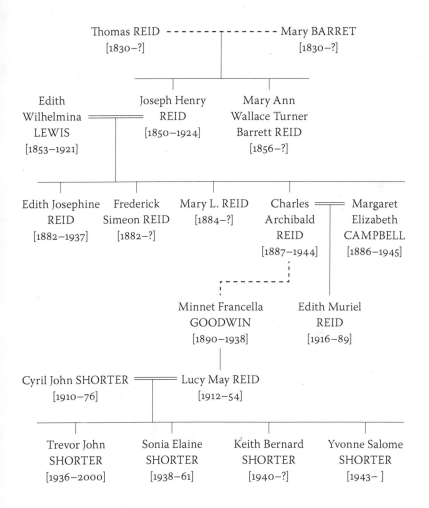

Thomas REID - - - - - - - - - - - - - - Mary BARRET
[1830–?]   [1830–?]

Edith   Joseph Henry   Mary Ann
Wilhelmina ═══════ REID   Wallace Turner
LEWIS   [1850–1924]   Barrett REID
[1853–1921]   [1856–?]

Edith Josephine   Frederick   Mary L. REID   Charles ═══ Margaret
REID   Simeon REID   [1884–?]   Archibald   Elizabeth
[1882–1937]   [1882–?]   REID   CAMPBELL
                                                    [1887–1944]   [1886–1945]

                        Minnet Francella   Edith Muriel
                        GOODWIN   REID
                        [1890–1938]   [1916–89]

Cyril John SHORTER ═══════ Lucy May REID
[1910–76]   [1912–54]

Trevor John   Sonia Elaine   Keith Bernard   Yvonne Salome
SHORTER   SHORTER   SHORTER   SHORTER
[1936–2000]   [1938–61]   [1940–?]   [1943–]

Descendants of
EDWARD GOODWIN

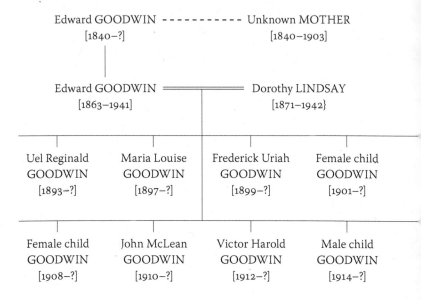

Edward GOODWIN - - - - - - - - - - Unknown MOTHER
[1840–?]   [1840–1903]

Edward GOODWIN ═══════ Dorothy LINDSAY
[1863–1941]   [1871–1942}

| Uel Reginald GOODWIN [1893–?] | Maria Louise GOODWIN [1897–?] | Frederick Uriah GOODWIN [1899–?] | Female child GOODWIN [1901–?] |

| Female child GOODWIN [1908–?] | John McLean GOODWIN [1910–?] | Victor Harold GOODWIN [1912–?] | Male child GOODWIN [1914–?] |

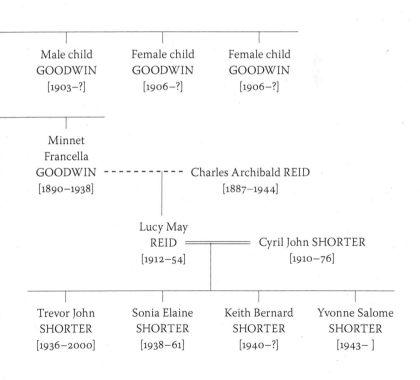

Male child
GOODWIN
[1903–?]

Female child
GOODWIN
[1906–?]

Female child
GOODWIN
[1906–?]

Minnet
Francella
GOODWIN
[1890–1938] --------- Charles Archibald REID
[1887–1944]

Lucy May
REID ========= Cyril John SHORTER
[1912–54]   [1910–76]

Trevor John
SHORTER
[1936–2000]

Sonia Elaine
SHORTER
[1938–61]

Keith Bernard
SHORTER
[1940–?]

Yvonne Salome
SHORTER
[1943–]

CODA TO THE
SECOND EDITION

— *Finding Mother* —

THE SEARCH FOR MY MOTHER, Lucy May Reid, is more than a search for the person that she was. The quest is bound up with my own search for understanding how bearing and raising my own three children have irrevocably transformed my youthful personality and as importantly, influenced my way of being in the world. Without having my mother's presence in my life to share our profound experiences of childbearing and child-rearing, furthermore, finding out that many mothers are reluctant to step outside of the Christian patriarchal edicts of the self-sacrificing, all-giving mother, I began to ask blasphemous questions in writing my journal regarding the negative portrayals of women in the Bible and in the Christian sermons and sacraments about the gift of life and the passive position expected of mothers. I yearned for the divine mother, the giver of life, God the Mother! Each Christmas, when the organ strikes up the opening chords to the hymn *Joy to the World,* I imagine that to be the moment when Mary gives the final push to deliver the Christ child. On Christmas Day 1990, for example, after participating in yet another story of the virgin birth of Christ, I went to my journal and poured out my thoughts. My journal entry of 25 December 1990 shows examples of these kinds of questions:

> *I have been reflecting on the passive nature of Mary's role in giving birth to the Christ child, and wonder how women would write the drama of the birth as the real birth. I imagine it would have the rhythms and movements of contractions; the sounds of moaning and groaning, deep and shallow breathing as she works with the essential pain and the fluids of life-giving blood, sweat, and tears. This is something for me to perhaps make a project of and use it as a means of getting in touch with the birth process, which I entered into totally ignorant and alienated from. How do I make sense of the serving of the body and blood of Christ during Holy Communion? Whose body was broken? Whose blood was shed in giving birth to new life? How do I make sense of the liturgical invocation: In him we live move and have our being? Has there ever been a time when men were pregnant with a living being moving in their body? Whenever I hear these words, my internal voice repeats to myself: God the Mother, God the Father, God the Son, and God the Daughter.*

From that psychological quandary, I have sought to find out if God was ever portrayed as mother. To do so, I turned to Christian feminist writers to find fuller meanings of motherhood. During the decades of the 1980s and 1990s, by reading intensively and reflecting on the scholarship of several feminist writers and scholars on the subject, I explored motherhood in myth, antiquity, theology, spirituality, psychology, sociology, history, anthropology, and art. (See Sources for the Coda, page 297, for a sample list of readings). Through these readings, along with African and diaspora fiction and the writings in my journals, I have come to the startling revelation of what I characterize as the deliberate theft of the primordial "mother right" by dominant, patriarchal institutions! The most blaring example of this theft of mother right occurred during the transatlantic slave trade and plantation slavery. For over three hundred years in the Caribbean where my ancestors lived, moved, and had their being, enslaved African women's bodies were turned into both labourers and reproducers of future human units of labour. Slave mothers had no mother right to the children they bore. The children they birthed, whether sired by their own men, or by the slave master, belonged, like livestock, to the master's inventory of his property. There were extremely few church or civil marriages permitted under enslavement, but enslaved Africans invented their own means of partnering, nurturing, and remembering kin and kindred when they could.

The legacy of the language of animal breeding can still be heard among some sectors of the Caribbean society. So, too, is the practice of some men of conceiving children with multiple women as was practised during the post-slave trade period, between 1807 and 1838, when enslavers increased and replaced their stock of labourers by setting up breeding programmes. The enslaved men at that time were not expected to step up and claim their biological paternity along with their cultural, religious, and economic responsibilities. Instead, they were also treated with the same practice of animal husbandry. Men during this period gained a reputation for virility based on how many women they could impregnate—the stereotype of the "stud" is borrowed from descriptions of a virile horse. Their enslavers appropriated their children as just more alienated labour. Today, some men still brag about how many women they have impregnated. Some fathers, as allowed during slavery, have denied paternity, failed to take on fatherly responsibility, or both. The phenomenon of the outside child and the bastard child, which by law becomes the total responsibility of the unwed mother, usually brings shame to Christian, respectable families and financial hardship to poor women. I grew up unfortunately, knowing the social stigma attached to such children and the traumas that many suffered. I have come to discover that my own mother suffered the same stigma.

As I tell the story of each family with whom I share blood relations, I hope the reader will see how history's legacies of race, class, and colour are alive in the official Jamaican birth, marriage, and death records. This historical background provides the foundation for family intrigues, lies, and secrets, too. The historical period I have chosen as the backdrop to my perspectives on the good, the bad, the ugly, and the beauty of my family's heritage is the post-emancipation period, 1839–1965, namely, the year after the Emancipation Proclamation in 1838, declaring "full freedom" to enslaved Africans who were serving a transitional period of apprenticeship, (between 1834 – to 1838). This period of apprenticeship was supposed to give planters and enslaved labourers a period of adjustment but was just as exacting, if not more so, than the actual slavery as practiced up to this date. These dates encompass the birth date of the oldest patriarch of the three families in my personal history. Most importantly, the second date, 1965, is when I concluded the first edition of *Dead Woman Pickney*. I will leave this sketch of my struggles with the definition and understanding of mother and motherhood in slavery and in my own experience, to delve a little deeper into major internal and external events over which the inhabitants had no control but nonetheless, determined the kind of society that was possible to create after the qualified freedom and not the full freedom that the enslaved people were expecting. The imperial government granted no land, no provision for education, no alternative to estate housing of slavery days, and no ability to bargain for their terms of employment. I have prepared a timeline to show major events that complements the narrative that follows.

The Historical Setting for My Post-Emancipation Descendants

With the help of genealogist Ann Marie Lazarus Grant, we have found birth, marriage, and death records that have been of immense value in finding the identity of my mother. In Jamaica, my mother's identity is embedded in the larger history of class, colour, colonial, and imperial politics, and Christianity, which evolved from African enslavement and plantation aribusiness in sugar cane, coffee, and later, banana. My mother's life story is enmeshed in the rise and fall of different classes and colours as they struggled for survival and power under the terms of the Emancipation Proclamation. Jamaica's total population at the time of emancipation was 371,000 people, which shows a statistical colour and class stratification as follows: Whites 15,000; Free Blacks 5,000; Coloured or Free People of Colour 40,000; Blacks 311,000. This last group would become the labouring class. As per the Emancipation Proclamation, the responsibility for constructing the new society was delegated to the following: former slave owners who remained in the island, the representatives of the churches and their handmaidens in the church schools, the laws of the local assembly of merchants, planters, and to men in general. Following conventional practices in England, at that time, women and their children were to become wards of men, removed from the workforce, and exiled in their homes. Yet, only White women and some Brown women were afforded this full-time housewife status. Black women continued to labour in the cane fields and banana plantations side by side with their men. Not surprisingly, Black women were paid half the wage that men were paid for the same jobs.

Eighteen thirty-eight marked two important transitions for Jamaica and Jamaicans: The first was that Queen Victoria ascended the British throne the year before, at nineteen years of age; the second was that the British parliament officially abolished slavery in its overseas colonies, including Jamaica. Historians declare the long reign of Victoria (1837–1901) as the Victorian Age of British Prosperity for good reason. First, the British capitalists and parliamentarians redesigned the terms of their colonial trade preference for goods produced in their colonies in favour of a free trade policy of market competition among slave-produced sugar from Cuba, Puerto Rico, Haiti, and with their former Southern United States colonies. Consequently, by 1846, eight years after emancipation, Britain introduced the Sugar Duties Act that ended the preferential trade in sugar with their colonies. The results were disastrous: a drastic drop in sugar prices, low island exports of agricultural commodities, lower wages, and high unemployment. After the non-compensatory terms of freedom, the Sugar Duties Act was the first of many more economic blows that led to deadly upheavals and local conflicts such as the 1865 Morant Bay Rebellion and the 1938 Rebellion against the colonial governor, and the establishment of many Royal Commissions of Inquiry.

The second major transition followed from new economic and imperial priorities. As mentioned above, British politicians and capitalists were anxious to rid themselves of the preferential trade deals that they had made with their overseas sugar-producing colonies and wanted to turn to free trade with Europe and the former American colonies. They decided that they would abolish slavery on their own terms by using the language of British justice and benevolence. When one reads the terms of the Abolition Proclamation, the terms were anything but noble and benevolent. All constituents knew it too. The large landowners who owned thousands of acres of hereditary land, which was for the most part free land granted as a reward for settling Jamaica in the seventeenth century, following the Barbados model, were allowed to keep their thousands of acres of land, as well as given compensation, per head for their enslaved Black and Brown people. With these lucrative compensation packages, the landowners could move on to avail themselves of new economic opportunities and statuses within the newly expanded colonial service, from which governors, military commanders, colonial secretaries, attorneys and solicitors general, and heads of departments were recruited. Thus, even after the legal abolition of slavery, these same actors continued to exploit the post-slavery economies, because the land and income taxes, and import-export earnings on agricultural commodities had to pay the salaries and underwrite the cost of the ceremonial duties of British colonial officials where ever they were posted. Thus, the political and economic power remained in the hands and pockets of the colonizers and ex-slave owners and local oligarchs, thereby increasing their power over the ex-slaves' futures and their continuing dispossession. These were mainly English, Scottish, and Irish capitalist and absentee owners, some of whom were Members of Parliament and the local Assembly. Some were also leaders in the Sugar Lobby in London that bargained for advantages during the heyday of the slave trade and plantation slavery.

There was another group of White people who became worse off in the process. They were mostly of the poor English, Scottish, Irish, and Welsh descent, who were sent out to the colonies as indentured labourers in the beginning of settlement, and later on were the blacksmiths, carpenters, coopers, bricklayers, tailors, attorneys, and overseers who ministered to properties for the absentee sugar barons. They had lower status, smaller parcels of land, and relatively few slaves. At emancipation many went bankrupt because they could not afford the paid labour costs required to keep their relatively small-holdings productive, nor could they obtain loans from the banks to renew their mortgages and pay their land taxes. Most galling for this group was that their former slaves were no longer at their beck and call. They had to negotiate wages, make their peace with Black people whom they considered their inferiors, or else fall into poverty and distress for lack of steady labour and reliable income, but for the whims of the international market. The White and Brown tradesmen and women fared somewhat better since their skills remained in demand.

This fall from White power over Black people's labour power unleashed the Whites' resentment and nightmares, even as it released Black resistance and subversions. This racially charged social predicament foretold that someday, Black people would gain political as well as economic power, over the minority White and Brown sectors of the population. Neither group wished to see the day when Black people ruled. Consequently, the ambitious Brown men sought alliances with the White men in politics and business, when it suited them. They shared the same officious and condescending attitudes towards Black people, in general. Wealth in the form of land ownership, independent employment, and literacy were cleverly manipulated, by law and political chicanery, to restrict or delay the franchise for Black people. The Black Intelligentsia and some non-conformist church leaders found ways, over time, to acquire the legal requirements to be elected; first, to the parochial boards, and eventually to gain the majority in the Legislative Council. By 1935 Black men achieved their goal of political dominance in the Legislative Council, with Charles Archibald Reid among them. My research into my father's family, the Shorter side of my ancestral heritage, leads me to conclude that they belonged to this category of the poorer, White to near-White class of Jamaicans. John Thomas Shorter was born in 1839, a year after Emancipation. He was a member of the Clarendon Parish Council in 1865, the time of the Morant Bay Rebellion, and subsequent massacre of several hundred Black people by the English Governor. Interestingly enough, the Shorters of my father's generation lied or exaggerated about their ancestral heritage when they wanted me to believe that they were descended from large landowners and not from the poorer Whites. The story of each family that I construct from the public records and discuss in the following sections, however, reveals a very complicated mix of racialized liaisons and political and economic alliances and interdependencies. Before I move on to construct each family history, I want to say more about the Brown people.

There was a second group of people named in the Emancipation Proclamation: the Brown people. These were the offspring of British fathers and African mothers – the slave master and the enslaved female and Black or Brown housekeepers. If their White fathers manumitted them before slavery was abolished, they were termed Free People of Colour or Coloured. They were a relatively privileged group based on the status of their white fathers. They asserted their privileged status and obtained their right to vote on the same terms of the White men in 1831, when the majority Black population had to wait until Universal Adult Suffrage in 1944. The People of Colour also considered themselves in a better class than the group from which their Black mothers came. It was especially so if their Black grandmothers and mothers earned their living as field labourers, higglers, cooks, washerwoman, domestic servants or housekeepers. Here, I will assert that most families in Jamaica have a Black Grandmother who was the breadwinner who earned the stable income to pay for generations to climb to middle class status. Powerful individuals from this group both rivaled the White group and or joined their political projects to promote their own advantage. This group became the buffer between the white and the black strata of the post-slavery Jamaican society. The Whites did not consider the Brown people as their equals and did what they could to keep them from gaining political and economic power. For the most part, the Brown people, with few exceptions did not see any advantage of making alliances with the black people. The Black people for their part returned the sentiment. Each group devised a repertoire of curse words to express their resentment and mistrust of each other. The people of colour strove to gain and hold political power to even replace the White ruling class. They also endeavoured mightily, to exploit the Black people of their mothers' roots. These are the roots of Brown and Black politics which emerged and took hold in the society in the 1920s and thereafter.

The third group named in the Emancipation Proclamation is the African or the Black majority. The formerly enslaved majority of the population was and still are oppressed and exploited in every way, by both the White and Brown people. Black people saw very clearly the deceitful language of the Emancipation Proclamation. The historian Thomas Holt, for example, quoted one person as saying wryly: "What kind of free this? This the free them gee we? This free worst than slave, a man can't put up with it." Among this group were Black people who bought their freedom (free Blacks) or were manumitted by their masters as a reward for faithful service. During slavery, they had to carry around their "freedom papers" to show their free status, or else they could be considered as run-away, enslaved persons, and returned into slavery. Black skin had become the body badge of enslavement and servitude. From the ambitions and resourceful-ness of this group, arose the relatively small group of black Jamaican writers, thinkers, clergy, politicians, and educators, which the histo-rian Patrick Bryan terms the Black Intelligentsia. This was the group that came into prominence as the nascent black nationalists, espe-cially active after the Morant Bay Rebellion of 1865 and the social up-heavals that followed. Some acquired sizable land holdings by which they could meet the land ownership threshold to enter parochial board politics and eventually the colonial legislature. My research shows that the Reid family, to which Lucy May Reid's father belonged was a part of this group. I will elaborate later.

As we can see from the terms of the Emancipation Proclamation, Black people as a group were destined to be the landless proletar-iat. Or worst yet, the idlers and vagrants who would throughout post-emancipation history be apprehended by the Royal Constab-ulary and other Special Constables, and sent into the penal system, to perform another kind of forced labour, and to receive corporal punishment. These were the people who filled the workhouses, the madhouses, and the poorhouses after emancipation. Land was vital for the survival of these people, as for all people, but the terms of the Proclamation turned them away from whatever precarious hold they had had on their living quarters and their kitchen gardens on the plantations, unless they agreed to stay and be employed on the terms of their former enslavers. Many people from this group were helped by various Christian missionaries to rise above the grinding poverty through the formation and establishment of Free Villages in rural parts of the country. The Baptists, Moravians, and Presbyterians for example, purchased large tracks of abandoned lands of reasonable sizes. They subdivided and sold in small plots to people of humble means but of steadfast desire to better their lot and raise families. The freeholders constructed the schools, churches and houses in the Free Villages. I have found the least amount of recorded or oral information about the Goodwin family (also, part of my mother's maternal family), but from the evidence I have so far, I believe that they were part of this group of the landless.

To return to the Black Intelligentsia: they were literate, widely read, furthermore, some of them wrote articles and books about their desire for, and the necessity of achieving self-determination. Members of this group made petitions and gave evidence at Royal Commissions of Inquiry into the social, political, and economic conditions in the colony after Emancipation. They made written, legal, and verbal complaints about the severe economic exploitation of their labouring compatriots, and as importantly, concerning the miscarriage of justice that they suffered. Members of this group comprised teachers, clergy, small planters, farmers, dressmakers, shoemakers, tailors, native medical doctors, and clerks of the colonial bureaucracy. They pioneered their own public opinion, and articulated their own ways and means of self-determination and economic advancement. This group included such individuals as Robert Love, a Black medical doctor who launched his own newspaper, the *Jamaica Advocate*, (1894–1904). William Bailey, Joseph Henry Reid, William F. Bailey, Rev. R. Gordon, R. Dingwall, Rev. S. J. Washington were also part of the Black Intelligentsia. Five of these named persons wrote and published a book in 1888 entitled *Jamaica's Jubilee or What We Are and What We Hope To Be by Five of Themselves*. I will show that in my mother's family, Joseph Henry Reid belonged to this group. From this group came the next generation of well-known Black leaders such as Marcus Garvey, Amy Bailey, Victor Bailey, Ethelyn Rodd and many more. On my maternal side, my great-grandfather, Charles Reid's father, was Joseph Henry Reid.

With this broad sketch of the history into which my descendants were born and struggled to survive, I have laid out the terrain along which I will travel to recover my mother's identity. In using this historical approach, my intention is to be able to interpret individual decisions, family tragedies, class cleavages, Victorian cultural socialization into respectability for both men and women, and the desire to have a good reputation among the male population. I hope to temper any harsh judgments I held before I undertook to write this Coda to the first edition of *Dead Woman Pickney*. My perspectives are now grounded in my understanding and appreciation of the historical material conditions that shaped people's personal and social attitudes and behaviour. What I once regarded as hypocritical, fake deference, and dissembling in front of powerful personal and institutional forces, I can now interpret as coping strategies to gain and maintain status within such a caste-like stratification. Members of each group verbally policed the maintenance of the colour class stratification. To this day one can hear the following: You pass yuh place; yuh too even up; me and yuh not from de same class; Yuh outa order. Some of the epithets are unprintable. These expressions, I know sum up the legacies of slavery and post-emancipation in the land where I was born and grew up. I now move to introduce each of the three families: Shorter, Reid, and Goodwin. My mother, Lucy May Reid appears on each family chart, on pages 246–49.

The Post-Emancipation Descendants of John Thomas Shorter

I start by introducing my construction of the history of the Shorter family first. There are several good reasons for doing so. I know more about them than about the Reid and Goodwin families. To begin with, Shorter is my maiden name. Having been raised mostly by my father and two of his Shorter sisters. I observed and experienced first-hand, their cultural legacy, attitudes and behaviours. Best of all, I heard family lore from different members of the family and from acquaintances. I also have had life-long conversations and disagreements with my Auntie Black, my father's elder sister (Elaine Emily, whom I call Auntie or sometimes Auntie Black, her married name). I wrote about her kindness to me as a motherless child in my first edition of *Dead Woman Pickney*. In this Coda, I quote from some of her letters and conversations that I have had with her, throughout my presentation of each family, as I build my argument that it was the entanglement of the Shorter, Reid, and Goodwin families that determined my mother's fate. The dates of births, marriages and deaths, of members of each generation, are shown in each family chart, when I have found the official records. The dates of birth, marriage, and death captured in the records, place each family in the historical timeline. These vital records also provide startling information about the social and economic status of each family member.

The last gentleman in the Shorter family—John Thomas Shorter—was born in 1839, one year after the abolition of slavery my Auntie Black asserted when she was angry and reluctant to tell me about her Shorter ancestors and descendants. I used to be curious about the failings of her three brothers, Cyril, Ancil (Bishop), and William. Auntie was meticulous in describing her English and Scottish forebears. Never, until her very old age, did she mention the name of any African/Black forebears. I will reveal more of the Black part of the family story in a later section. Auntie Black said that her grandfather, John Thomas Shorter, was a vet and owned property in Main Ridge and Mount Regale in northern Clarendon, and further that he was an elected member of the Clarendon Parish Council. I have found corroborating evidence that the planter John Thomas Shorter of said location was indeed a member of the Clarendon Parish Council. As mentioned earlier, he along with the magistrates, clergy, and other inhabitants of the parish signed a letter in support of Governor Eyre's brutal response to the Morant Bay Rebellion that occurred in 1865, in which Governor Eyre declared martial law and carried out revenge killings of hundreds of Black suffering people (many of whom had not been involved in the Uprising). This rebellion occurred twenty-seven years after the Emancipation Proclamation, which as I have argued in the historical background of the Coda, made the majority Black population landless and without the means to build family, community and economy on their own terms.

In 1865, the rebellion of a segment of the population began in St. Thomas in the East and spread across the island. The White and Brown segments of the population feared a rebellion of the scope and devastation as occurred earlier in Haiti. The Black population felt they had no choice since all reasonable efforts to obtain relief failed to deliver them from hunger, landlessness, the droughts and hurricanes that killed their crops and small livestock and rendered many homeless. The Baptist missionary reports of suffering and hardships by such as Bleby and Underhill went unheeded, or else Governor Eyre and his supporters denied the reports that appeared in the British press over years. Furthermore, the people's petitions to the Governor and to Queen Victoria for relief only brought further oppression in rising food prices, land hunger, taxation on their huts and horse kind, higher rents and leases, high unemployment or no employment at all, and lack of political representation. The implications of colour and class cleavages are shown in the following quote from the letter sent from Clarendon "...a most diabolical conspiracy to murder all the White and Coloured inhabitants of the island, and so delivering ourselves and others, from the repetition and horrors enacted in the said parish of St. Thomas in the East." Since the state did not require the registration of births, marriages and deaths until 1877, we turned to church registries to find vital records for people who were born before that date and who belonged to a church denomination. We found that John Thomas Shorter was born in June 1839 in Main Ridge, Clarendon, Jamaica and was baptized three months later. He married Emily Rose, a needlewoman, on 19 January 1870 in the Wesleyan Methodist Church, in Ashley, Chapelton, Clarendon. Auntie Black always talked about her maternal grandfather William Rose as a large landowner and planter in Summerfield, Clarendon. She said he gave his daughter Emily Rose three hundred acres of land.

As you can see from the family tree, John Thomas Shorter and Emily Rose had two sons: William Rose Shorter and Wentworth Alexander Shorter. We are concerned here with the descendants of Wentworth Alexander Shorter and his wife Letitia McCovie Stewart. Auntie would dwell upon the pedigree of her mother, Letitia. She said her mother was an only child and an outside child too and that her mother died young. Her father, Alexander Stewart, she said was a rich landowner and boarded his orphaned daughter with Emily Crosskerry. A Hugh Crosskerry, with the titles J.P. and M.R.S.C. Ireland, signed Letitia's marriage to Wentworth Alexander Shorter. The identity of Letitia's mother remained in the shadows for a very long time. Auntie would describe Letitia as very pretty, with flaxen hair and blue eyes. You would never think she was coloured, Auntie said. She was very kind to her workers. She stressed the McCovie Stewart name to the extent of giving me the correct spelling of Stewart, not to be confused with Stuart.

The story of this Scotsman is confusing. Auntie said Alexander Stewart was a Scotsman who owned and/or was in charge of an estate at Danks in Clarendon. That he was a married man seems to be certain but what was uncertain was whether his wife was left in Scotland, or if she joined him later in Jamaica. One story goes that he was engaged before he left for Jamaica and planned to return to marry and bring his wife back; but that he loved the people so much he stayed. Auntie said that when Letitia became pregnant, she was forced to marry Wentworth Shorter against her father's wishes. Her father washed his hands clean of her but was reconciled later, with the marriage. When he did, he called Wentworth to come and see him, because he was ill but Wentworth never went to his father-in-law. Auntie said Alexander Stewart was never able to leave an inheritance for his only child. She said Alexander Stewart died on his way back to Scotland and never returned to Jamaica. I have not been able to find a death certificate to date. Auntie later told me that Stewart's wife managed the estate pretty well until she sold it and went back to Scotland. So, Stewart's wife must have been in Jamaica for some time, before or after his death. The birth story of Letitia stopped abruptly here, until I picked it up with Auntie in the 2000s. I searched for and found Letitia's birth record. She was born on April 2, 1893 in Summerfield, Clarendon. The name given at birth was Letitia, the female child of Beatrice Howell, a domestic servant, no doubt Black, judging from the skin colour of Letitia's aunt Sylie. The space for name and occupation of father was left blank. This was so because she was an illegitimate child. Beatrice Howell's mother signed the birth registry with an X on May 15, 1893, indicating that she was illiterate. When one considers the terms of the Emancipation, it was certainly not unusual to find Black people who could not read and write. As I wrote in the first edition, the colonial government and the sugar estate capitalists agreed that it was in their interest to keep Black people illiterate; any measure of literacy and numeracy allowed was to make Black people into literate labourers and domestic servants.

The marriage record for Letitia McCovey Stewart and Wentworth Alexander Shorter names Alexander Stewart as her father. They were married in 1909. As head of his family, Wentworth lived through the economic depression of the 1890s and part of the 1930s economic depression. The family chart shows Wentworth and Letitia had seven children, but only six were ever talked about. Lois Barbara was briefly mentioned as a half-sister, and I remember seeing a gravestone for her when Aunt Joyce took me to Main Ridge in the late 1950s. Lois's birth record confirms that indeed she was a half-sister by another mother. Although her father was not named at birth, her marriage record names Wentworth Alexander Shorter as her father. She must have been accepted as part of the family since she carried the name Shorter and she was present at the birth of Janet Bryson Shorter. Janet Bryson was never mentioned but her death record shows that she died in infancy from shock induced by a fracture of the skull and laceration of the brain. Within a day of the child's death, Emily Shorter (Auntie Black), then sixteen years old, took the corpse from Main Ridge to Chapelton (the capital of the parish) for the post-mortem and registration of death of her sister, Janet Bryson Shorter. The coroner wrote that an inquest was not ordered. This is yet another tragic episode in the Shorter family story.

There is more to come: In my retirement after 2008, when I went to spend time with the two remaining sisters: Emily (Auntie Black) and Aunt May, I would make time to spend exclusively with Aunt May, whom I spent relatively little time with as a kid. I told the story in the first edition of her coming to rescue me from eating dirt when my mother was taken away. Aunt May and I would have long conversations, sometimes over cups of tea, poured from her bright red teapot. Over time, she seemed to have looked forward to "have a cup of tea with my niece." Aunt May had a very difficult life, having married young and mothered ten children. I admired her intelligence and hard work to see her children well educated and to give much love and care to the community. I wanted to hear her life struggles. She told me of her childhood at Main Ridge in the big house with lots of help (servants). She described the trauma of seeing her beloved father going crazy and that he terrorized the children. This might explain Janet's death. She said she was eleven years old when the people from the Lunatic Asylum (as it was then called) came for him, put him in a straitjacket, and took him away. This recollection usually chokes her up. She also spoke of the grief of the sudden death of her mother, Letitia, in the Chapelton Hospital from meningitis in 1932, when she was nine years old (Aunt Joyce was sixteen and Auntie Black was twenty-one). Auntie Black being the oldest girl had become the guardian of Aunt May but Aunt Joyce, William, and Bishop gravitated to their grand-aunt, Silly Howell, Letitia's aunt. Two years later, in 1934, Wentworth Alexander, originally a planter and land owner in Main Ridge, died poor in the Lunatic Asylum, and was designated the status of labourer. He died from chronic dysentery. I appreciate even more the characteristically pained look on Auntie's face that she wears when she has to deal with yet another family tragedy. Earlier on I told of her revealing that her father, like my mother, died in the asylum, and that they had been buried there. This might have been so for her father; but I have found my mother's death record, which reveals the truth that she died there; but she was not buried there. I will tell the truth of when my mother died and what happened to her body later, when I sketch out the Goodwin family story. The fact of Wentworth dying in the Asylum and the family leaving him to be buried there remains a shame and embarrassment. The death of the Wentworth and Letitia occurred during the Dirty Thirties. The circumstances of unemployment among the Shorter siblings coupled with the loss of property must have posed grave economic hardship; so grave that, they had to make the very difficult choice to leave their father to be buried by the government. My father, the eldest, has never shown any sense of family responsibility.

I can confirm that the Shorter, Rose, and Alexander families owned land. I found evidence in government land reports, which list the owners of land over fifty acres, that in 1912 Wentworth Shorter owned one-hundred fifty-three and one-half acres of land in Banks, Clarendon, valued at one hundred fifty pounds. It was described as sparsely cultivated. The 1920 report showed that his brother, William Rose Shorter owned another seventy-three acres in small cultivation worth seventy-three pounds. Auntie often told me that there was family land in Banks cultivated in sugar cane, coffee, and other ground provisions. I am not surprised to find that the family land was sparsely cultivated, and lying fallow, because the family lived through two economic depressions: 1890s and 1930s. During these times export prices for coffee, pimento, sugar, and other commodities fell sharply while the price for import staples such as codfish, flour, and rice rose sharply. It becomes apparent that the Shorter family could not afford to pay the cost of labour, and had to work the land to produce these crops. The Shorter sons were not expected to do manual labour on any account, so mobilization of family labour was out of the question. On one occasion when I questioned Auntie Black about what became of the property in Main Ridge, she confessed that her father, Wentworth, turned to gambling and lost their house and land in Main Ridge. William Rose, Emily Rose's father, owned seventy-five acres in Kelletts worth one-hundred and fourteen pounds, cultivated in sugarcanes and provisions, and had tenants, in 1912. The 1920 report showed he had one hundred twenty acres, worth two hundred pounds in Brandon Hill. That land was residential and tenanted. That same report showed another fifty-five acres worth one hundred forty-eight pounds, which he occupied and mainly tenanted in Crawle River, Clarendon.

Alexander Stewart, Letitia's father owned 2,577 acres of land in 1920 valued at 4,200 pounds in Longville, Clarendon. No wonder he did not approve of the match with Wentworth Alexander Shorter. They were clearly not in the same league of property owners and wealth. This is what Auntie told me of the family circumstance: *On the subject of Education, my parents could not afford to give us secondary training and we had to do with the elementary schooling which would fit us for the available jobs such as nursing, police, teaching and the post office. A third-year Jamaica Local [exam] was good enough then. Entry to the Civil Service would require secondary schooling. I left home at sixteen and lived with a wonderful family and was helped by them. They had a daughter my age. We went to a private school and ended up with a commercial course. My adopted family came from Syria and was business people.*

Auntie Black, whom I affectionately call Auntie, has lived through many family tragedies, shame, and of course, celebrations. She lived through the life passages of each of her five siblings and of the children of Cyril, my father, and Aunt May. Only two of the six surviving Shorter siblings of Wentworth and Letitia had children. Auntie lived to see every last one of her siblings pass to the other world. She died at one hundred-and-two years old. Her memory was sharp and she was quick to perceive the ironies of life. I carried her voice throughout my search for my mother, and throughout my archival and historical research. I was able to follow leads I took from our conversations over the years and confirm many historical episodes and political personalities in Jamaica's history. She was especially knowledgeable about the Dirty Thirties, hard economic times in the island and during WW2 in the international arenas. She avidly read all the available newspapers and she followed the career of local politicians, merchants, the Anglican Diocese, and the education system. She was a living reference library on Jamaican history. As I construct the Reid and Goodwin stories next, I bring to the reader, in question-and-answer form, some of the very difficult revelations I have learned about the history of the Shorter family and their relationships with the Reid and Goodwin families.

The Post Emancipation Descendants of Thomas Reid

Thomas Reid and Mary Barrett Reid, parents of Joseph Henry Reid, were born around 1830, roughly eight years before the abolition of slavery. As children they must have experienced the pre-abolition upheaval caused by the implementation of an apprenticeship system, which was touted as a period of gradual emancipation by the end of which the Black population would be ready for the responsibility of free labour. The terms of the apprenticeship exacted over fifty hours per week of free labour for slave owners for a six-year period. At the end of this period the Black people were to be set free. The astute Black people understood the apprenticeship policy as slavery by another name. Of historical significance, Thomas and Mary were born a year before the 1831, Daddy Sharpe Rebellion, which historians believe led to the ending of the apprenticeship after four years rather than the intended six years. This rebellion ultimately hastened the final abolition of slavery in 1838. They had two children: a son, Joseph Henry Reid in 1850 and a daughter, Mary Ann Reid in 1856.

We are here concerned with the offspring of Joseph Henry Reid and his wife Edith Wilhelmina Lewis. Both were teachers, but we do not hear the women's voices, or their activism in the construction of the post-slavery society. As per the Emancipation Proclamation they were playing their role as helpmeet to their husbands at home and at work. They were expected to be wives and mothers and manage the home sphere raising children and taking care of domestic labour. Most worked for wages inside and outside the home. They could not afford economic dependence, even if they wished to. The thrust in the post-emancipation construction of the new society was all about joining the brotherhood of man. As one reads accounts of the period, the vocabulary reflects the masculine orientation in such talk as "the making of men and gentlemen," and the "recovery of Black manhood crushed out by slavery," "the need for the Blackman to have land to earn enough to be the ruler in his family," and so on. Joseph Henry Reid's life is significant in that he left some of his words and deeds on the official record. Those records become part of the Reid family story. He was a schoolmaster and believed to be a graduate of Mico Teachers College, the preeminent institutions for training head masters and lay preachers. (Incidentally, that was the same college from which I graduated in 1965, when the 1890s suspension of the co-educational pillar of the Lady Mico Trust was restored).

The historian, Patrick Bryan quotes several of Joseph Henry Reid's articles that he published in the weekly *Jamaica Advocate* in his historical study of *The Jamaican People 1880–1902: Race, Class and Social Control.* As discussed earlier, the *Jamaica Advocate* was the organ founded by Robert Love and others that publicized the philosophy of what Patrick Bryan called the Black Intelligentsia. Bryan quotes J. H. Reid's articles that he published in the Jamaica Advocate between 1895 and 1897, bearing such titles as "Negro Education," "Educating the Peasantry," "The Negro Slave," "Legality," and "The Bursting of the Clouds." I have had the great privilege of reading and sharing with my adult offspring his chapter in the book *Jamaica's Jubilee: Or What We Are and What We Hope to Be,* entitled "The People of Jamaica Described by J. H. Reid." He also gave evidence at two Royal Commissions established by the imperial government to investigate post-emancipation social and economic conditions in Jamaica: firstly, the Commission appointed to report upon the conditions of the juvenile population of Jamaica, 1879; and secondly, The Royal Commission appointed to investigate and report on the economic conditions throughout the British Caribbean caused by the drastic decline in sugar revenues resulting from British consumers being able to buy cheaper sugar produced in Fiji, Natal, Mauritius, Cuba, Brazil, and Java that flooded the free market. As mentioned earlier, the 1845 Sugar Duties Act had removed the preferential market in Britain for West Indian sugar produced in their colonies. Joseph Henry Reid held several other positions which I will mention as the story of the Reid family continues to unfold. Joseph Henry, who sometimes signed his name Jos H. Reid, held other civic positions. He also owned enough land and income to ensure that he could vote and be elected to the parochial board, in the parish of Manchester. Both Joseph and his wife, Wilhelmina, laid the intellectual, occupational, and economic foundation for their offspring to take advantage of leadership and advancement to a better life, amid the massive economic and social upheavals.

Joseph and Wilhelmina had four children: Edith Josephine, Frederick Simeon, Mary Louise, and Charles Archibald. The children were born to upwardly mobile, middle class parents. They were exposed to rich intellectual conversations among their parent's generation of educated and visionary men and women. They would have heard discourses on such topics as the founding of the Jamaica Union of Teachers, labour advocacy, the importance of land distribution and agricultural development, and Black political participation. There were books, local and international newspapers and the Bible of course, and church news. The minutes of the Legislative Council meetings, I am guessing, would also be among the readings and discussions. Joseph Henry Reid died in 1924: Edith Wilhelmina died earlier in 1921. Joseph Henry left a will that had great significance for the legislative council election of his youngest son, Charles Archibald Reid. In reading the will, I learned that Frederick Simeon Reid had migrated to Boston, USA and Mary Louise Reid had migrated to Detroit, USA. Edith Josephine had married George Ivor Allen and settled in Christiana, in the parish of Manchester where her younger brother Charles Archibald had settled too. Seemingly, Charles Archibald was the only one of the four siblings who might need to use the value of Joseph Henry Reid's legacy in land and money.

Joseph Henry Reid willed to Charles Archibald all his real estate property, house, and personal effects he owned at Wesley Cottage, Browns Town in the parish of St. Ann. Charles Archibald was charged to use his inheritance as he saw fit. I was able to find, in the report of owners of lands over 150 acres, that that land of over

150 acres which Joseph Henry Reid owned at Wesley Cottage in the parish of St. Ann where he retired to, passed to Charles Reid in 1929 when he probated his father's will. It seemed as if Charles Archibald was ready to build on his parochial board experience and run for higher office in the Legislative Council of the colony. He did not probate his father's will until five years after his father's death in 1924. It was just in time to qualify him to run for the election to the Legislative Council in 1931, in a by-election.

At this point, I will focus on Charles Archibald Reid, the last child of Joseph Henry and Edith Wilhelmina. It would appear that Charles was destined to carry on his parents' intellectual and political work to lift the status of Black people. Charles's political contributions through parochial board and legislature to Jamaica's political and economic history from 1920 to 1944 deserves a book by itself, which I am currently researching to write one day soon. Suffice it to say, for the purpose of finding my mother, I want in this second edition, to tell of the part he played in connecting the three families, and in my mother's marriage to Cyril John Shorter.

Charles Archibald Reid's birth record shows that he was born on 11 January 1887, the fiftieth anniversary of Queen Victoria's reign, at Moravia Station, in the parish of Manchester. I note that a Jos H. Reid, Registrar of Births and Deaths registered the baby, the very next day. At the time of registration, the baby had not even been given a name yet. Given what I have come to know of the biography of Jos Henry Reid, his father, I wonder if he saw his legacies being carried on by this lovely little boy. Charles must have been a lovely young man; he was nicknamed Regal Reid in his youth. My nephew, Leopold Shorter is a living replica of Grampa Charlie as I have come to call him at the point when I fell in love with him. It was the day in the National Library of Jamaica where I spent many hours over the last ten years, reading *The Jamaica Hansard Proceedings of Legislative Council of Jamaica*, from 1931, (the year he was first elected, in a by-election to the Legislative Council) to 1944, when he died on the job. His second election was in 1935, and since the general election for 1940 was cancelled owing to the Second World War, he continued serving a third term.

During the Spring Session in 1942—four years after the devastating Labour Riots of 1938, and three years into WW2—when unemployment and prices were high, and children were being kept from school for want of food and clothing, The Honourable Charles Archibald Reid, MLC, brought a very controversial motion to the floor which read in part: *"This Council is of the opinion that, having regard for all the circumstances surrounding the social, economic and health conditions of the country, the time has arrived when Government should consider giving what assistance may be possible to voluntary clinics and Local Health Authorities, who desire to disseminate information and offer other facilities re birth control and who are prepared to establish centres for this purpose."* When I read his motion and his arguments in defence of voluntary birth control for women in 1942, I could tell that he listened to "The Ladies" as he would say and especially to his schoolmate, the teacher Amy Bailey, a tireless women's and children's rights advocate. I was disheartened and continue to be so, when I think of the contents of the rebuttals from the clergy and other sexist men, but I was especially taken aback that the medical doctor, Anderson, saw no medical reason to help women who were having twelve to fifteen children. When I was growing up, the folk would say of a poor woman: she loses a tooth for every baby she carries. That was no joke: some women's enamel even looked almost transparent as a result of nursing so many babies' extracting calcium from malnourished maternal bodies. Although the motion was defeated, eighteen votes against and only five in favour, I was very impressed with the wide knowledge of comparative statistics of infant mortality rates, the Anglican Diocese's positive vote on the matter in England, and the acreage and cost of land it took to sustain a family. I had to conclude that Grampa Charlie knew whereof he spoke; he had first-hand observation of having too many children without the means to support them. When you meet the Goodwin family, whom I will introduce next, you might appreciate why this particular motion among many others advocating on behalf of small farmers, schoolchildren, and women, that he brought to the floor touched me so much.

As a boy child born to married parents who have a high standing in their communities, he would at least carry his father's surname and be known as Jos and Edith Reid's last boy. Charles went to school at New Roads School in Westmoreland where his parents were teachers. So too was Amy Bailey's father, William Bailey. Charles had no secondary schooling but he would have attained the well-regarded Standard 6, the highest form (class) of the All-Age government schools. Only a select few students in his time achieved this grade. Many well-known, articulate Jamaicans had this qualification. He made his home in Christiana, Manchester where he practiced his chosen trade as a shoemaker, for a while. When the mass-produced import of shoes, especially from the Bata Shoe Company, flooded the market, and he could not make an adequate income, he became a grocer. Then came the opportunity to make a better income in the thriving export trade in banana and citrus exports to markets in the United States, United Kingdom and Canada. So he became planter of bananas and citrus in various parts of Manchester. He had acquired land both by his own means and by inheritance from his father.

Charles met Minnet Goodwin, a young higgler who sold garden produce in the Christiana market. As the oldest of twelve children, in a family of modest means, no doubt she had to help with the family's earnings. I am inclined to imagine that they fell in love and had intentions to marry; however, my inclination is tempered by what I know of parental preoccupation with their children marrying into the right class. I do not know if Joseph and Edith accepted Minnet. With Minnet, Charles sired the female child, who would be later known as Lucy May Reid in 1912. He did not eventually marry Minnet; instead, he married Margaret Elizabeth Campbell of no occupation (as per their marriage certificate), with whom he sired another daughter named Edith Muriel Reid in 1916. It would seem that by marrying Margaret Campbell, who was literate and had no skills to work outside the home, Charles could have the ideal respectable family: stay-at-home wife, membership in the Christ Church, Anglican Church, and a lawful daughter, Muriel. He was the unquestioned breadwinner and head of his household. Muriel was a lawful child whereas Lucy was not. This contrast in status would complicate my mother's life as the outside child, as wife, mother, and in her inability to fulfilling her intellectual potential. The differential status between Lucy and Muriel provided part of the family intrigue. Up to a point, the sisters seemed to have gotten along well enough, because Muriel was a witness at Lucy's marriage to Cyril John Shorter in 1935. Muriel and her mother were named at important official functions as the Honourable Charles Archibald Reid's family.

Post-Emancipation Descendants of Edward Goodwin

I began the search for the Goodwin family without even knowing the family name. I dredged up the memory of more than 60 years ago, when Auntie forbad my late sister Sonia to speak of a Mr. Goodwin, whom she had met at the May Pen Railway Station. The Goodwin name was not a name that was called in the Shorter family and I did not know any member of the Reid family to ask. Readers of the first edition, might remember the episode that I recalled in chapter 5 of going to meet my mother's half-sister Muriel Reid, the head postmistress at the Cross Roads Post Office and the humiliating rebuff she gave me? I thought the Shorters and the Reids were hiding secrets. My father never took me to meet any member of my mother's family, nor the Reid's for that matter. When my brother and I went to Christiana in 1998 to find people who could tell us about our mother's people, no one would call her family name. We found Eric Allen, an elderly nephew, born to Charles' elder sister, Edith Josephine Allen. He told me about his Uncle Charlie and the big family row after his uncle's death, when Muriel kicked everyone out the shared family houses in Christiana. He could not tell me much about my mother. I was left to wrestle with my Auntie Black to get clues to the secrets that were being hidden about my mother and her people. Here are samples of the fragments that I had to piece together to tell my mother's story.

Auntie, who was my mother's mother? *Miss Mini!* What was her last name? *Me no remember. But she was a market woman.*

Auntie, could you tell me more about my mother? Do you have a picture of her? I know if you did you would have shown it to me but just in case you do, I would love to have it. She answered my letter as follows:

I cannot tell you much about your mother. We lived in different parishes, miles apart. She elected to do dressmaking after she finished Elementary School and did all the Jamaica Local Exams. Her father sent her to Mrs. Kitchens a leading dressmaker in Kingston where she completed the course. She opened a parlour on King Street in Kingston and I joined her. Being new with limited capital it did not last very long. Besides, all the stores on King Street like Issa's and Hannah's and Jews were selling imported garments. I became ill as a result of a miscarriage, which required major surgery. Harry was transferred to Montego Bay and I had to follow him the moment I was well enough. The parlour had to be closed and she went back to Christiana and got married and started a family.

Muriel, her sister went to St. Andrews High School as a boarder and when she was finished, she entered the Postal Service to be trained as a telegraph clerk. On completion of her training, she served at different post offices in that capacity until she became the postmistress at Cross Roads only after the death of Mr. Reid. He had nothing to do with the appointment there.

I do not know if Lucy was very happy. May be because of your father's heavy drinking habits. She never complained to me when we met which really was not very often because of transportation difficulties and my job was very exacting. Also, we lived very far from each other. She attended her father's funeral and got ill shortly after and was hospitalized. I visited her there and made sure she did not perish in the fire in in 1946. She did not last long. Sorry I have not got a picture of her. In those days not many of bothered taking pictures. Besides being costly, we did not think of posterity. Her relatives in Christiana could perhaps have. You could ask them. There is one thing that stands out in my memory of her, she was very attractive lady and knew how to dress. She was neatly dressed and carried herself very well. You seem to have inherited that.

On another occasion I showed Auntie the clipping from the *Gleaner* of the Honourable Charles Archibald Reid's state funeral and asked her to read it and tell me what she thought. I was curious as to what she would have said about my mother being at the funeral as Mrs. L. Shorter and bearing no relation to her father, while her sister Muriel was acknowledged as his daughter. I learned later that Charles Archibald's wife, Margaret was unable to attend because she was very sick with cancer. This is what she said: *Well done but they goofed in not recognizing his two daughters as such. He would have been disappointed because he made no distinction between them.*

In another conversation I asked: Auntie, when did my mother die?

You were a babe in arms when she died. She got sick because she was not officially accepted at the state funeral. Muriel was not nice to her. Lucy was not mentioned at the time of the nomination because she was illegitimate, conceived at the time when Maas Charlie was sowing his wild oats. After all, you could not have a whoremonger representing the people in the Legislature. A lie is a lie and no matter how you whitewash it, it cannot be true. But if Mr. Reid did not lie about his illegitimate daughter, just think the country would be deprived of a great noble Jamaican. He got a chance to show his potential.

I was shocked and angry to hear my aunt use that word to describe my grandfather, especially considering the number of children her eldest brother, my father, sired with poor Black women, without taking any responsibility for them. Several of these children showed up at her door like strays fleeing neglect. She took several in, including my sister and me. She must have seen the look of anger as I winced when she delivered those words with an air of moral superiority. She changed her tone, smiled with that scornful demeanor that I detested, and started to lecture me on what was required of politicians during my grandfather's time and how the White people respected him. She reminded me that it was mostly the White people of Manchester who had voted for him.

I would have taken this proposition of Black dependency on White patronage as given, had I not had the stories from Black people who knew Mr. Reid. Besides, I witnessed the reverse of White dependency on Black people in the society, generally, when I was growing up, in the Shorter family and in many other situations. It was this sort of inferiorization of my mother's family background that eventually propelled me to commit to research and write Charles Reid's political biography, and to continue the search to find out who my mother's people were. Auntie threw up the comparison between my grandfather and a well-known white man who could not run for office because he was not independently wealthy; he was on someone's payroll. This is the same woman who insisted on telling me that my grandfather was poor and he did not have much, when she thought that my intention was to seek a legacy. She even denied that my mother's half-sister, Muriel Reid disinherited her after her father's death. I have found the proof that she did, in the *Jamaica Gazette* of 22 March 1945, where Edith Muriel Reid applied to the Supreme Court of Jamaica as the sole legitimate heir to all of her father's personal effects, and monies. Charles Reid died in September 30, 1944; her mother died of cancer within six months of her father's death in 26 February 1945. Muriel had already consulted a lawyer, in time to write a Letter of Administration to appear in the government newspaper in March. Several attempts to receive a copy of the details of Charles Archibald Reid's estate have failed, even though the Supreme Court acknowledges that it is indexed.

By my calculation, I would have been one year old when Grampa Charlie died, and when my mother's, half-sister, Muriel turned her off their father's property in Toll Gate, Clarendon, where my mother and her children lived, in a house that her father had given to her. Since the Honourable Charles Archibald Reid allegedly died intestate, her legitimate sister could turn her out with impunity, because the law gave her that right. The Goodwin family chart represents what I was able to find out about the Goodwin family who were indeed my mother's people, who were also from Manchester.

It is evident from the Goodwin family chart how incomplete is the documentary evidence that we were able to collate, after five years searching through the Registrar General Department's records and the Mormon Family Search data base. We found out that Edward Goodwin (1863–1941), a planter, and his wife Dorothy Lindsay (1871–1942), who was a labourer, together had twelve children – six girls and six boys. Only two of the six girls were named on their birth registration records: Minnet Francella Goodwin (1890–1938) and Maria Louise Goodwin (1897–????). We could not find marriage records for them. Four of their brothers were named at birth: Uel Reginald Goodwin (1893–????), Frederick Uriah Goodwin (1899–????), John McLaren Goodwin 1910–????) and Victor Harold Goodwin (1912–????). Again, we were unable to find marriage and death records. Without names we could not track down marriage and death records of most of them. Minnet is the only one of the siblings for whom we were able to find a death record; Lucy May Reid her only daughter registered her death in 1938. We were also able to find the death record for Minnet's mother, Dorothy Lindsay, who died in 1942. I can see the looming abandonment that my mother Lucy may have felt by 1942 with the loss of both her mother and grandmother. By this time Lucy had given birth to three children one of whom she lost. I imagine that she carried a great responsibility for the care of us children in the face of being a Black woman married to an abusive, alcoholic Brown man, with an air of entitlement. By the things my father's sisters have said about my mother over the years, especially Aunt Joyce, I guess that she was not accepted by the Shorter siblings.

Minnet, as the first-born of the Goodwin twelve, seemed to have co-mothered her younger siblings. For example, the birth records show that Minnet registered three of her siblings as follows: A male child born 3 October 1903 in Christiana, Viewfield in Manchester. She was only 13 years old. Minnet again registered a female Goodwin, born 5 April 1908, in Christiana. This time Minnet was eighteen years old. She registered her brother John McLaren Goodwin born 3 January 1910 in Brackley Christiana, Manchester. Minnet was now twenty years old. Two years later, on Christmas Day 1912, Minnet gave birth to a female child, later named Lucy May Reid. Her mother, Dorothy Lindsay, registered the child with an X as her name. Earlier in the same year, 12 April 1912, Dorothy, had given birth to Victor Harold Goodwin. It was not uncommon for a mother of such a large number of children to be pregnant at the same time as one of her older daughters. This is why I surmise that Victor and Lucy grew up together as siblings, though Victor was Lucy's uncle. Seven of the twelve children were born in Chudleigh, a district close to Christiana, the same areas where Charles Reid's home was.

As with the Shorter and Reid family, I looked at the Goodwin family occupations, and land ownership status. Unlike the previous two families, I found no record of landownership of fifty acres or more for Goodwin. Edward Goodwin, recorded as a planter on his children's birth records, may have had the customary size plots that small planters and farmers had — five-, ten-, or twenty-acre lots. These were not reported individually but as statistical aggregates in the government reports on land settlement schemes for the landless of the emancipation. They could be freeholders or leasers of the land. I did not find Edward Goodwin on the voters list either. Given the property requirements to qualify to be on the voters list, suggest that he, perhaps, did not qualify to vote or that he chose not to be enumerated. Women did not have the right to vote at this time. Literacy, land ownership and a minimum level of income of ten shillings were required to be able to vote. Edward was literate but Dorothy was not. This does not mean that Dorothy was unintelligent. The higglers such as I paid tribute to in Chapter 3 of the first edition, are some of the most resourceful people I know. They were and still are the backbone of the post-emancipation economy and in families. They deserve their honorific: Mothers of the Nation. Another consideration I took into account in determining the Goodwin family's socio-economic status was the sheer number of offspring they had to feed, clothe, shelter and educate. This was the situation I had in mind when I earlier referenced the Honourable Charles Archibald Reid's motion that he tabled in the Legislative Council, on the need for voluntary birth control in the island, in 1942.

It was customary for large families such as the Goodwin's for parents and children to work side by side to grow ground provisions and garden vegetables to feed the family and to produce some cash crops for both the domestic and export markets. Small farmers with a large family had to diversify and maximize the production of their relatively small plots in a number of ways. First, to produce enough ground provisions and small livestock (chickens and goats especially) in order to feed the family. Some eggs would be sold in the markets, and the goats were essential for providing milk for the babies. Some might even afford to raise a heifer for milking and send any surplus milk to the condensery. The ground provision would comprise yams, sweet potatoes, dasheen, corn, cow peas, Congo peas, and red peas, and Irish potatoes which thrived in the Manchester soil. For home consumption, the property usually had some perennial food trees such as breadfruit, avocado, ackee, mango, and citrus. Second, a surplus of the ground provisions, and citrus could be sold in the local market. Third, small farmers could participate in the export market if they grew enough good quality bananas to sell to the United Fruit

Company. The Banana Industry Aid Board provided assistance in loans to small Banana Growers. They could also export ginger, logwood chips and arrowroot for income. These agricultural commodities were small enough and sensitive to fluctuation in market prices. Some crops such as some varieties of bananas, and coconuts were wiped out by leaf spot diseases and storms. The small farmers' life was economically very precarious existence.

Parents and older children had to work off the farm as casual labourers and domestic or shop help to augment the family income. Minnet, the oldest daughter would have been an important wage earner for her family, hence her role as a vendor of food produce in the Christiana market. The family stood in some way to benefit from Minnet's liaison with the relatively well-off Reid family. That Lucy was given the best education allowable by the education system for the illegitimate child of a poor mother is significant. She studied for and obtained her Pupil Teacher Certificate issued by the Department of Education in 1930. After that, she undertook formal dress design and apparel construction from an expert dress designer, meant that her father Charles Archibald Reid supported her financially. I speculate that he perhaps contributed more than Lucy's maintenance to the family. Charles Archibald was in a position to extend financial and other assistance to the Goodwin family: he was himself a big planter of the lucrative export banana and citrus crops; he was a landowner, a Justice of the Peace, an Alderman, and eventually a famous Member of the Legislative Council. I will now conclude this Coda by tying up some loose ends by bringing together a few relevant episodes that occurred between Auntie and me over many years, through our conversations and letters. They concern my search to find my mother and her people and in particular the spot of ground where my mother was interred. The episodes are important for what they reveal, and what they hide, just as they have been clues for me to find the answers. I will also reconnect with the mystery woman, Mrs. Smith, who appeared at my graduation from Mico College, and with my godmother's daughter.

Tying Up Loose Ends

Another time in conversation, I asked: *Auntie, could you tell me how my father and mother came to meet each other?* She replied that she did not really know but added that it was certainly not a match made in this family, meaning the Shorter family. I wondered what she really meant but could not bring myself to ask her at the time. In another conversation sometime later, she said that my father, after his marriage to my mother, lived in his father-in-law's home. Mr. Reid had to put him out because he was such a drunkard and so disrespectful. Then she said offhandedly: "He was made promises." Again, the look from her said: do not ask what promises. I took it that she was implying that my father's behaviour was as a result of unfulfilled promises that Mr. Reid made to him. This led me to wonder if my parent's marriage was arranged by my grandfather in order to save his political face. At that time, by the conventional expectations of having a respectable status, a man had to be married with a wife and children, and be the breadwinner for his family, in order to be considered respectable enough, to advance in politics and business. Lucy and Cyril married the August before her father would stand for election to his second term in the Legislative Council, in December 1935. Knowing my father, I suspect that he thought he was entitled to a job with more prestige than the one Mr. Reid facilitated for him with the Public Works Department. Auntie hinted as much.

Since Auntie claimed that she worked for Mr. Reid and knew more about his business than anyone else, I asked her to tell me about working for Mr. Reid. Here is a synopsis of some of what she revealed. During the war years, there were no food imports because several ships were torpedoed. In addition, the British government ordered the colonial government to build an internment camp to house up 9,000 refugees from Gibraltar and Malta and other countries. The refugees were to be fed from local produce. The Honourable Charles Archibald Reid, who had a good reputation as an advocate for small farmers and who knew the officials in the various growers associations (Banana Growers Association, Cane Farmers Association, Coffee Growers Association, Jamaica Agricultural Society, and so on) was appointed to work with Mr. F. E. V. Smith, the Competent Authority, to procure food from farmers around the island. The goal was to supply food to Coronation Market in Kingston and to supply the Gibraltar Camp for the refugees. Food had to be collected and transported. The existing railway lines that served the United Fruit Company to collect bananas for export were used to transport the food. A Marketing Board was set up with offices at main points to handle the receipts and payments to the suppliers. Mr. Reid hired Mrs. Black, (Auntie) to work with the Marketing Board to keep the books. When the war was over the Marketing Board was disbanded. She was unemployed for three years.

She talked about the three years of hardship that she and her husband experienced. She said Mr. Reid promised her a job with the Trade Board that administered the import/export licensing of goods entering and leaving the island. The Trade Board handled an important source of revenue for the colonial government in the collection of important import/export duties. The condition was that she had to first obtain the necessary qualifications. She had no money. She said that Mr. Reid paid for her to go to Durham College, for a three-month course, to qualify to work with the Trade Board. When the Trade Board was made into the Ministry of Trade and Industry, she continued to work until her retirement with a pension in early 1980s. Again, Mr. Reid helped by facilitating a job for her husband, selling third party insurance. She said it was a posh job and in her own words she went from rags to riches.

Auntie said that Mr. Reid, as a member of the Legislative Council, was also in charge of price controls. During that time, she said Mr. Reid would bring bags of food for her from his own farm in Christiana and Toll Gate, when he came back to Kingston for his weekly Legislative Council meetings, which were held from Tuesday to Thursday each week. As she did frequently, she would speak of his kindness. She said that he did this for her as he would for anybody, downplaying her indebtedness to the Black man's patronage. This last statement proved to be true. In my research on Mr. Reid's life and times (1887–1944), that was a consistent commentary regarding his kind, principled and fair character. This came from the people whom he represented, as well as people in distress who asked him for help. His business-like approach to serving "the grassroots," as he would say, earned him the nickname Bishop of Manchester from his elected legislative colleagues. Such comments were consistently stated in the *Gleaner* editorials, and letters to the editor, over the seventeen years he served in electoral politics at the Manchester Parochial Board, in the Legislative Council in the Crown Colony Government, and, finally, during his eulogy at his state funeral.

In 2001, during a visit, Auntie and I had a particularly difficult discussion again about the disappearance of my mother. She did not want to talk. She shed tears as if she was weary of my persistent questioning about my mother. She said this: *Why remember these things to burden yourself. I got involved in the church, joined the choir, and the Women's Auxiliary. I went to work from Monday to half-day on Saturday and found time to go to choir practice and attend church meetings. I also helped in the shop. I lived my life in dignity so that those who come after me can have an example. I don't fret about anything. Fretting don't help. I dressed well and invented my own blouse and skirt uniform. I bought pound cloth and made them myself. Could get two bits of cloth, about two yards for four pence.*

Auntie described her philosophy of life accurately. That is how I knew her to behave in times of family crises and there were many that her siblings created, including my father. She just literally takes a deep breath, and figures out what needs to be done in the situation, and just moves to get things done to fix what she could and leave the rest alone. Discussing feelings and shedding tears were not part of how she dealt with things. Since doing the research on the Shorter side of my family, I have come to realize that Auntie carried a lot of responsibility as the first girl child born to her Anglo-Scottish descended father, William Wentworth Shorter, and his Afro-Scottish descended wife, Letitia McCovey Stewart.

I am happy to report that I found the mystery lady, whom I remembered as Smith who showed up at my graduation from Mico Teacher's College in 1965. My brother connected us. We exchanged letters and I actually met her and spent a weekend with her and her husband in 2000, on the occasion of bidding farewell to my brother when he passed away. I watched him die, as I had watched my sister die some forty years earlier. I am the only one of my mother's four children still alive. Her married name when I reconnected with her was Mrs. Monica Liburd. An excerpt from her letter follows:

My Dear Yvonne,

I received your kind letter two weeks ago. My dear child let me thank God for his loving kindness and protection. I am sure Trevor told you of the reunion. In the year of our Lord 1944–45 I met your mother through a friend from my home country in Trelawny… I was very unhappy and could not have eaten as I wished. I told Evadney and she went and told Lucy Shorter. Evadney came back for me and took me to your mom, at that time her address was 9 South Avenue, Kingston Gardens. She sent a letter to my father by Evadney. I remember Evadney telling everyone how my father cried. At the time they called me Lillian Smith. Your mother was a patriot—she was kind, humble and willing to do anything to help her children. At times she pushed a cart to take the box from the tramcar. The house where we lived was big so it was shared with…. I remember her saying, Lillian I'm obligated to your father and she would do her best to make me happy. By then your dad was a driver with the Corporation [Kingston and St. Andrew Corporation] and for weeks he would be away from home in other parts of the island and she was the one to hug and kiss her children. She would say, Trev, me one little son, Soney and you the baby. She was medium built —your father was brown and short, she was black. At this time, I can't remember what happened why she had to return home to Toll Gate in Clarendon. She wanted was to take me along with her but Mrs.... insisted that I stay with her... How then were you raised? As you said you did not know when she died and where she was buried. The good your mother did will never be in vain. Whenever you come to see Trev, come to see me.

With kind thoughts and best wishes
Sincerely,
Monica Liburd

Another significant contact I made was with Mary Keeling, the daughter of my godmother, Alice Salome Goodgame, or Mrs. Keeling to me, who remembered that Aunt Joyce had taken me as a babe in arms to meet her. Her husband was the butcher whom Auntie used to send me to buy her meat from. I was unable to find Mary for many years because she had married twice and changed her last name. Finally, in 2018, I heard of a big funeral of a past student of mine from May Pen, Jamaica, where I spent part of my childhood in the same school with Mary. I inquired if Mary Keeling was at the funeral, and can you imagine the joy I felt when I got her phone number and called? We have become fast friends. Mary was able to share some of her mother's memories of my mother. They were young women together in Toll Gate when Mrs. Keeling worked for John G. Miller, the very rich landowner who would contest and lose the 1931 legislative bye election to Charles Archibald Reid. Mary said her mother never stopped taking about her friend, Lucy Shorter. Lucy, she said, was very kind; she was a talented dress designer and dressmaker. She made Mary's mother's wedding dress. When I visited Mary in her home in 2019, she showed me the framed and well-preserved picture of her late parents' wedding photograph. Although the black and white photograph was faded, I could see the silhouette. I wept! Lo and behold, my middle name, Salome, I believe was in honour of my mother's dear friend. As I said in Chapter 3, although Mrs. Keeling lived close enough in May Pen, I was never allowed to visit and get to know my mother's close girlfriend.

I have come this far in sharing the circuitous historical and archival journey that I have taken to find out who was my mother and her people. I am now left to give the reader, the definitive answer to when my mother died and what became of her body. I found her death record in 2015, after going through hundreds of names on the Family Search. org site. It was three in the morning. Can you imagine the shock I got to discover that my mother died in June 1954! My mother did not die when I was a babe in arms. She died 8 June 1954. I was eleven years old. The record confirmed that she died in the Mental Hospital in Kingston, that she was married, that she was forty-one years old, that she was a dressmaker, and that she died of pulmonary tuberculosis. An inquest was carried out on 25 August 1954 and death registered 2 September 1954. The law required that the family should be notified of her death. It does not appear that any family member from the Shorter or Goodwin or Reid family claimed her body and gave her a proper burial. Tears of sorrow were not enough! I continued to try to find her resting place in order to pay my respects to her bones. I was going to make a last try.

Since Bellevue Mental Hospital could not give me information where her alleged resting place was, I turned to the next best source for help. I arranged to meet Doctor Frederick Hickling who was once the psychiatrist in charge of Bellevue. He has written several books and articles on the historical trauma of slavery, colonialism and their aftermath in contemporary Jamaican society. He was retired in 2018, when he agreed to meet me, when I was on yet another research trip to the archives. I was confident that I would finally locate my mother's unmarked grave. He gave me an audience in his home office. I presented him with a copy of the first edition of *Dead Woman*

Pickney and a copy of my mother's death certificate. He spent a long time looking at the certificate, as he lowered his head and turned his face away for a while. Then he turned around and faced me with the most merciful look I ever saw. My heart skipped a beat as it registered that Dr Hickling was about to give me bad news. He said, in the quietest voice: I am sorry to tell you that if your mother died in 1954 and no one claimed her body for burial, her body would be have been donated to the University College of the West Indies Medical School to be used as a cadaver. I did investigate how the bodies were disposed of at the end of their usefulness to the medical students. I could only wish that the students who learned medicine using my mother's body were kind and respectful, and that the knowledge they gained made them compassionate doctors. The tears for the sad ending to my mother's life still flow.

As the three family charts show, Lucy's birth and marriage linked the three families in differing relations. Worst of all the intersections of these three families occurring in the post-emancipation period, when race, class, colour and status created so much inequality and prejudices, determined my mother's demise. The line on the family chart connecting Minnet Goodwin and Charles Archibald Reid is broken to indicate that they were not married but were parents of Lucy May Reid. Note also that the line connecting Charles Archibald Reid to Margaret Elizabeth Campbell is a double solid line, indicating that they were married. The Reid family chart is useful in giving a visual presentation of the unequal locations of the two sisters, Lucy and Muriel—as illegitimate child and as legitimate child, respectively. The marriage of Cyril John Shorter and Lucy May Reid, and the birth and deaths of three of their offspring—Trevor John Shorter, Sonia Elaine Shorter, Keith Bernard Shorter are also shown. Understandably, my death date remains blank. I have lived to tell my mother's story.

I can say to the world that I never stopped searching for Lucy May Reid, born to Minnet Francella Goodwin and Charles Archibald Reid, and married to Cyril John Shorter. My consolation is that I have

solved the mystery of her disappearance. I found her in the maelstrom of the socio-political and economic history of post-emancipation Jamaica. All that is left for me to do is to meet her, one day, in
the hereafter.

Greetings Mother! I have come to the end of my life-long journey in
my search to find you. I have learned many painful historical lessons
about the political, social, and economic forces that shaped peoples'
lives, including yours, and mine, in post-emancipation Jamaica along
the way. I conclude that you suffered multiple traumas that made it
extremely difficult for you to have kept your sanity. I will give you the
many reasons that have led me to this conclusion.

   In the first place you were conceived by Minnet Goodwin and
Charles Archibald Reid, who were from opposing classes within the
society. Your mother was a black-skinned humble woman, the oldest
of twelve siblings. Minnet, affectionately called Miss Minnie, worked
very hard as a young woman to make a living as part of a large family
of twelve siblings. She took up the trade of higglering, which was a
legitimate business practice for the women in farm families as the
Goodwin family was. While Minnet's father, Edward Goodwin, was
literate, his wife Dorothy was not. Charles Reid on the other hand was
also black-skinned but he belonged to a proud middle-class family
that boasted parents who were teachers that were politically active
in the early Black conscious group. Charles' father Joseph Henry Reid
was also a published author and counted among the advocates for
the education of the peasantry and for adequate wages for working
class Black people. The Reid parents may have frowned upon their
ambitious son having an intimate relationship with Minnet. In
middle-class circles the match would have been disapproved of.
In their minds their son was marrying down and would spoil their
reputation. It was evident that your father supported you financially
but you carried the status of his outside child when he chose to

marry the fair-skinned Margaret Campbell. Your outside child status became even more exaggerated when Charles and Margaret produced Edith Muriel four years after you. You lived your whole life as Muriel's half-sister and second class. The difference in the type of education each of you received really underscored your inferior status. Muriel turned out to be the wicked half-sister who disinherited you and other competing members of the Reid extended family, immediately upon the death of Charles Archibald Reid. By the time of his death on 30 September 1944 your father had become famous, holding several postnominal titles: Justice of the Peace, Alderman, Member of the Legislative Council, Privy Councilor, and Order of the British Empire for service to his country. Muriel made sure that your relation to your father would go unrecognized at the state funeral. She was named as his only child. I can only imagine your humiliation, when I looked at the photograph of the funeral procession as appeared in the *Daily Gleaner*. You were standing alone. You were simply named as Mrs. L. Shorter, and bearing no relation to your famous father. Muriel took all the reflected glory as his daughter.

The second major trauma really began with the arranged marriage to Cyril John Shorter in 1935, just before your father would make a second bid for the legislative seat. The part that I found most painful about this episode is that you married into a family that perhaps regarded themselves as their British counterpart—the genteel poor—with roots in the slaveholding class. At the emancipation they could not return to England to a country estate and they could not any longer earn enough to pay their mortgage, nor pay for the labour required to continue to work their relatively small land holdings planted in coffee. They had lost their real estate and labour assets but none of the superior attitudes toward the Black people whom they depended on for their survival but without the power over them as their ancestors did during enslavement. As I discovered from the things said and done by your husband and his sisters, they resented the fact that you were better educated than they were and that you dared to behave with character and decorum. Most humiliating for the Shorter siblings, including your husband, is that they depended on the patronage and largesse of your father, the Honourable Charles Archibald Reid no less, for their economic survival. Characteristic of many members of the White and Brown middle classes, the Shorters carried shame, grudges, and envy that a Black man should be so intelligent, educated, and fiercely ambitious and generous towards them. He was one of several Black men whose ancestors had worked hard to gain the political and economic power that would make them the rulers of the colony. That Black men should achieve status and power was the realization of the worst nightmare of the White and Brown middle and upper class Jamaican.

We come to the third major trauma in your life that really began with your outside child status, compounded with your arranged marriage and the coming of children within a sick marriage. Within a year of marrying Cyril John Shorter, you had your first child named Trevor John Shorter, in 1936 at the upscale Mandeville Maternity Hospital, in Manchester where your father was the elected representative in the Legislative Council of Colonial government. Incidentally this was where I gave birth to my first-born too. That is where in the throes of seventy-two hours of labour and abandonment, I heard my fading voice cry out: Mother, My Mother! Two years later, in August 1938 you gave birth to Sonia, your second child, a home birth. In October of the same year, you buried your dear mother Minnet Goodwin. I can only imagine your grief in losing your mother at a time when you needed her support. At this stage, at least you had your grandmother Dorothy Goodwin. In 1940, two years after your mother's death you gave birth to Keith Bernard Shorter, your third child, also a home birth. Keith died in infancy, from what family lore said was kidney failure. I am still trying to find his death record. Two years later your grandmother Dorothy Goodwin died. I ask myself what kind of relationship you may have had with your mother's family, the Lindsay family. I have not found out how they factored in your life. You carried a lot of grief and pain within a few years.

Your father began to hint in the Legislative Council that his health was suffering. He took sick leave in 1943 the same year that you had me at the Victoria Jubilee Lying-In Hospital. I can only surmise that he had begun to suffer from physical and psychological burnout owing to the grueling workload and social justice concerns that he carried for his "grass roots" constituents and for the whole island that he was commended for widely for. His outstanding service earned him the Order of the British Empire upon the recommendation of the Governor and by public opinion. His workload involved driving from Christiana, his home and constituency office, to Kingston to attend weekly, Legislative Council meetings from Tuesday to Thursday at Headquarters House in Kingston for most of the year. In addition to participating in various government committees and agricultural marketing associations, he carried on his pseudo-judicial work in his constituency as a Justice of the Peace and an ex-officio member of the Manchester Parish Council. I understand that you were his right hand in his work and political campaigns, along with a Reid nephew, Victor Allen whom Muriel also evicted with his family. The turbulent labour strikes and riots of 1938 and during ww2 demanded and used his conflict resolution and mediation skills on government committees to bring labour peace.

Throughout your married life you experienced racist and classist rejection from the Shorter family and maltreatment from your husband, who was a drunkard, a gambler, a womanizer, and woman batterer. He appeared to have taken no responsibility as a husband and father. Throughout all the Shorter family crises he and his two brothers were absent or ineffectual in stepping up to carry their share of the burdens. Your father had been your main financial protector, though I am mindful that he may have helped, perhaps inadvertently, to create the terrible matrimonial mess through which you had to navigate to hold up your head. Now that I have studied the matrimonial laws of the time, I can see how you found it very difficult to extricate yourself from an exploitive and brutal situation while at the same time bearing and raising young children. I can imagine the psychological and physical exhaustion that you had experienced carrying the weight of your precarious status in all three families; in addition to the enormous emotional energy you expended in bearing and raising your children and trying to make a living from your dressmaking trade. I was undone when I learned that your husband sold your sewing machines behind your back.

I am sure that you were among those family members who cared for Mr. Reid when he was finally admitted to the Kingston Public Hospital in the summer of 1944. The final trauma that you experienced surrounded the events that followed after your father's death and homelessness for you and your three children, caused by your legitimate sister's eviction from your matrimonial home in Toll Gate, right after his death. You had nowhere to go; you lost your mind and someone, no doubt your husband, Cyril John Shorter, committed you to the Mental hospital as he had done with his father earlier. You languished for nearly ten years in the Mental Asylum before you breathed your last breadth, alone.

I do not know if you will find it a very wicked irony, as I did, when it dawned upon me what Cyril did with your children after Muriel's eviction. He fled with Sonia and Trevor, the two remaining children after one of his sisters came and rescued me the baby. He took the expensive mahogany bedroom furniture from the matrimonial home that was no doubt your father's wedding gift. He moved into and furnished the wattle and daub, dirt-floored, thatch hut of the stonebreaker and small farmer Eutedra Williams. He later snatched me from his sister and brought me to join Trevor and Sonia to live in the hut and work on Eutedra's farm for a few years. He lived as a kept man with his children until she evicted him. It seems that part of whatever bargain he made with her, he also farmed out us children as child labourers. In the first edition of writing my memoir, I recounted the various episodes of suffering and displacement that befell us growing up without you or any support from the Goodwin or Reid sides of the family. In it I described the furnishings that I beheld as I entered the hut to which my father took me to join Trevor and Sonia. That was how low the oldest son of the boastful pedigree of the Shorter family fell. Muriel died alone in old age from what I can only describe as the ravages of unhygienic conditions of a frail old woman. I hope that you will be pleased to know that I grew up appreciating the hard work and ingenuity of higglers like my grandmother, Miss Minnie. Her spirit must have been with me because I wrote a special tribute to the market women in the first edition of my memoir. They were kind to me when I was sent to buy the weekly produce for each family that I lived with. The marketplace has always held a fascination for me. I have learned that at one time the peasant farmers fed the whole island and brought in the largest proportion of the colony's revenue.

I have written your story to get to know who you are and were. I will continue to miss you and to honour your life. I am very happy to learn that I have inherited your character and sense of pride. I am an accomplished dress designer, seamstress and tailor as you were. I became a teacher also. I have also continued in the intellectual tradition of your grandfather Joseph Henry Reid and your father Charles Archibald Reid. I have attained the highest qualification that an educator can attain. I have travelled and taught at all levels of the education system in Canada; I have trained teachers. I cannot help thinking that these would have been some of your ambitions as a young woman. I would like to think that you were with me in the spirit through my life challenges. Not having you in my life inspired me to be the mother to my children, which I wished I had. But more importantly, I strove to be the mother that I thought you would have been, and were never allowed to become. I cannot help but express to you my paradoxical feelings after finding out about the miseries that you suffered: as much I have grieved my loss, I do believe that you are in a better place.

Now I can pass your rich but troubled legacy on to your grandchildren and great-grandchildren. Your late son Trevor John Shorter left behind—Sandra, Trevor Jnr, Leopold, Nichola, Courtenay, Tricia, Lavana and others whom I have heard about but have not met in

Jamaica. He also had lived to see his first-born grandchild, before he departed this life. He has never got over losing you. In Canada, where I have lived and raised my three children—Andrea, Gail and Winston—I have told them your story as I found information throughout my writing journey to find you. You have four great grandchildren from me: Devante, Deja, Ty Marie, and Peyton.

At last! At last! I can tell the world: I found my mother, Lucy May Goodwin-Reid-Shorter, and her people from Christiana in the parish of Manchester, the Colony of Jamaica! My fervent wish in this life is to meet a Goodwin descendant of my mother's maternal family so I could make acquaintance with my mother's people in the flesh. Who knows, we might find that all of us have been mourning the loss of a significant daughter, sister, aunt, cousin, mother and friend. I dream of a reunion and a celebration of the short life of Lucy May Goodwin-Reid-Shorter.

Sources for the Coda

ARCHIVAL SOURCES

Jamaica Archives (JA) Parochial Board and Privy Council Minutes
Daily Gleaner https://gleaner.newspaperarchive.com 1920–1944
National Library of Jamaica (NLJ)
Annual Report of the Lands Department for the Year End 31st March, 1943
Census of Jamaica 1943
List of Persons Entitled to Vote Parish of Manchester, 1929–1930; 1931–32
Jamaica Hansard Proceedings of the Legislative Council of Jamaica:
    1930–1944
Jamaica Gazette 1930–1944
Addresses to His Excellency Edward John Eyre, Esquire, etc., 1865, 1866.
    Kingston: M. DeCordova & Co., Printers, 1866. Parish of Clarendon,
    p 13 Digital Library of the Caribbean (dloc)
Registrar General's Department (RGD) Jamaica, Birth, Marriage and
    Death Records and Wills

Bleby, Henry (1853) *Death Struggles: Being Narrative of Facts and Incidents which occurred in British Colony, During and Immediately Preceding Negro Emancipation.* London: Hamilton, Adams and Company, Paternoster-Row.

Bleby, Henry (1868) *Reign of Terror: A Narrative of Facts Concerning Ex-Governor Eyre.* London: 40 Horton Square.

Bolland, O. Nigel. (2001) *The Politics of Labour in the British Caribbean.* Kingston, Jamaica: Ian Randle Publishers.

Bryan, Patrick E. and Karl Watson, Eds. (2003). Not for Wages Alone: Eye Witness Summaries of the 1938 Labour Rebellion in Jamaica. Social History Project, Department of History, Mona, Jamaica: University of the West Indies.

Gordon, Rev. R. et al., (1888) *Jamaica's Jubilee: Or Whut We Are and What We Hope to Be.* London: S. W. Partridge and Co.

Hickling. Frederick W. (2007) *Psychohistoriography A Post-Colonial Psychoanalytic and Psychotherapeutic Model.* London: Jessica Kingsley Publishers.

Holt, Thomas C. (1992) *The Problem of Freedom: Race, Labour, and Politics in Jamaica and Britain, 1832 – 1938.* Baltimore: Johns Hopkins University Press.

Jemmott Jenny M. (2015) *Ties That Bind: The Black Family in Post-Slavery Jamaica, 1834 –1882.* Kingston, Jamaica: University of the West Indies Press.

Moore, Brian L. and Michele Johnson, Eds. (2000) *The Land We Live in: Jamaica in 1890.* Social History Project, Department of History, Mona, Jamaica: University of the West Indies.

—— (2000) "Squalid Kingston" 1890–1920: How the Poor Lived Moved and Had Their Being. Social History Project, Department of History, Mona, Jamaica: University of the West Indies.

Moore, Brian L. and B. W. Higman ét al. (Eds) (2001) *Slavery, Freedom and Gender: The Dynamics of Caribbean Society.* Mona, Jaaica: University of the West Indies Press.

Reid, J. H. (1888) "The People of Jamaica Described" in *Jamaica's Jubilee: Or What We Are and What We Hope to Be.* London: S. W. Partridge and Co.

Underhill, Edward, LLD (1865) *Dr. Underhill's Letter: A Letter Addressed to the Right Honourable E. Caldwell, with Illustrative Documents on the Condition of Jamaica and an Explanatory Statement*. London: Arthur Miall.
Sherlock, Philip & Hazel Bennett (1998) The Story of the Jamaican People. Kingston, Jamaica: Ian Randle Publishers.

BOOKS ON MOTHERING AND MOTHERHOOD

Boff, L. (1979) *The Maternal Face of God*. Translated from the German by Ralph Manheim. Princeton University Press.
Daly, M. (1973 & 1985). *Beyond God the Father: Toward A Philosophy of Women's Liberation*. Beacon Press.
Fiorenza, E. S. (1989). *In Memory of Her: A Feminist Theological Reconstruction of Christian Origins*. Crossroad Publishing.
Lazarre, J. (1976). *The Mother Knot*. Dell Publishing Inc.
Rabuzzi, K. A. (1988). *Motherself: A Mythic Analysis of Motherhood*. Indiana University Press.
Rich, A. *Of Woman Born: Motherhood as Experience and Institution* (1986) Tenth Anniversary Edition. W. W. Norton & Company.
Ruddick, S. (1989) *Maternal Thinking: Toward a Politics of Peace*. Ballantine Books.
Ruether, R. R. (1985) Women-Church: Theology and Practice. Harper and Row.
Trible, P. (1989). *God and the Rhetoric of Sexuality*. Fortress Press.

Author's Note on Jamaican Patois and English Language Usage

————

IN PREPARING the second edition to *Dead Woman Pickney*, I have sought to correct some factual errors and to update some of the language.

THE USE OF THE WORD "MULATTO." One of the terms that causes endless debates surrounds the proper naming of people of African descent in the Caribbean and the Americas whose identities were formed in the crucible of dehumanization and enslavement when their distinct ethnic identities were reduced to the colour of the skin. In the second edition, I have replace the word "mulatto" with "near-white." I think "near-white" is a better usage for the times and for my writerly purpose, so I use it here to approximate the micro-hierarchy within Barclays Bank in May Pen. It distinguishes the differences in status among the skin hues: there is unmixed white (English, Scottish, Irish, German etc.) and Black (African); then there are the skin tones of the miscegenated relationships. Within the Black and White mixings, the skin tones vary widely from brown, olive, honey etc. Those who could pass for white are sometimes referred to as near-white. They were higher in the pecking order, as evidenced in the Barclays Bank staff.

A *Gleaner* article written by Barbara Gloudon, "That ten-types beauty contest" (2002), reminds me of how politics of skin-colour had been so fiercely debated that the *Star* newspaper that sponsored the annual beauty contest attempted to counter the predominance of the association of white skin colour with beauty attempted to break down the contest by featuring one of their ten skin colours each year: Black, Cool Black, Brown, White, Half-White, Chinese Full and Half, Indian Full Blooded and Mixed, and Middle Eastern Types. I remember young women waited their turn to come with such titles as Miss Ebony, Miss Satinwood, Miss Golden Apple, Miss Apple Blossom, Miss Pomegranate, Miss Sandal Wood, Miss Lotus, Miss Jasmine, etc.

THE USE OF THE WORD "PICKNEY." The description in the original edition of the book is accurate and explains the title very well:

> The author's question to understand the absence of her mother and her mother's people from her life is at the heart of this narrative. The title, *Dead Woman Pickney*, is in Jamaican patois, and its meaning unfolds throughout the narrative. It begins with the author's childhood question of what a mother is, followed by the realization of her own vulnerability as a child without its mother's protection.

In preparing the second edition, I was asked to clarify whether the term "Pickney" in the title was offensive, and in any way carried the same negative connotation as the American term with related root. I will say categorically that within the context of Jamaican culture as it evolved from the mixing and usage of various African languages mixed with Scottish, English, Irish, Portuguese, Chinese, and "East Indians," the word simply means a child. To be a "dead woman pickney" is to be a motherless child. With that status went certain vulnerabilities, as I capture in my story of growing up without the love and care of my mother. I put East Indian in quotes to flag that this was part of Western European conquest, mapping, naming and dispersal of people from what is now spoken of as South Asia, to the "West Indies."

Concern about language use is especially valid at this time of racial reckoning in which the Black Lives Matter Movement, which began in the United States around police killing of Black men, women, and children, has been the face and the voice of a worldwide project to address the historical and contemporary oppression and brutalization of Black bodies. Of course, I understand some of the difficulties posed for both the general and academic readers, who are unfamiliar with the historical period and location from which I write, and from which the Black Lives Matter Movement originates. I will quote from my doctoral dissertation, *Bodies, Memories and Empire: Real Life Stories about Growing up in Jamaica, 1943–1965,* which I hope in part will explain the significance of Patois in my identity and way of being.

When I grew up, we were discouraged from speaking Patois because it was said to be a mark of illiteracy and low class. During the period of which I write, the majority of the population spoke mostly patois. People judged quality of schooling by the ability to utilize the words and grammar of Standard English. Hardly anything in Jamaica provides such an endless source of ridicule and comedy as does the inability to maintain Standard English without consequent lapse into Patois. We would often describe someone whose normal speech is Patois, trying to sustain Standard English as doing "speaky-spokey." Yet it is not unusual to find Standard English mixed with Patois in the same sentence, by schooled and unschooled alike.

The ability to mix both speeches or to switch from one to the other is both psychological and functional. In the psychological dimension, patois speakers are self-conscious, aware of being looked down upon and judged by their inability to command the English Language. Functionally, fluent speakers of both languages act like chameleons in conversations and arguments. They code-switch to be impressive or to gain advantage in an argument, or to ridicule and put down. Equally, only the Patois can produce the biting retorts which superbly skewer the antics of middle- and upper-class pretension.

I love the Patois as much as I love being among the market people. It was the language of the government school yards that I attended and in most rural communities in which I lived. I draw upon it throughout my writing because, in my opinion, the wisdom required to survive displacement and dispossession is encoded in the oratory of Patois as forcefully as it might otherwise be presented in English language literature. I wish that I could have written the whole dissertation/book in the patois. This would not, however, be a form suitable for passive study, but would call for performance and recitation, in the style of late Louise Bennett, Jamaican poet, who wrote and spoke and performed her work in the Patois. The Patois cannot remain inert on the page, but lives in the speech of Jamaica.

I recommend going to YouTube to search for and listen to the Honourable Louise Bennett's performance of just two of her poems which will give readers of *Dead Woman Pickney* the definition of the Jamaica Patois and its significance: 1) "Jamaica Language" and 2) "Colonization in Reverse." The lyrics to the most beloved Reggae songs by Jimmy Cliff, Bob and Rita Marley and many other Jamaican artists and playwrights use the Patois combined with the related African rhythms to evoke the joys, suffering, and strength from and within the heart and soul of Jamaicans and all oppressed peoples. The University of West Indies has a whole department dedicated to the study of Patois, now regarded as National Language. I have gone one step further and provided a glossary of Patois terms used in each chapter. I hope the reader will enrich their enjoyment of reading by consulting this glossary.

Glossary of Patois Speech Used in *Dead Woman Pickney*

CHAPTER I

Me wa' fe sleep, me tyad.	*I want to sleep.*
You too young fe tyad. Put on yuh clothes and go outside to tek in de fresh morning air.	*You are too young to be tired. Put on your clothes and go outside to take in the fresh morning air.*
Drink yuh cerasee tea. It good fe clean out yu blood.	*Drink your cerasse tea. It is good to clean out your blood.*
Oats porridge good fe you. It mek you bones strong.	*Oats porridge is good for you. It makes your bone strong.*
Yu going to sit dere til yu drink dat tea and dat porridge.	*You are going to sit there until you drink that tea and that porridge.*
Harold yuh breakfast ready.	*H. your breakfast is ready.*
Harold, chew with your mout shut. You sound like a striking hog. Yuh mek me stomach sick.	*H. chew with your mouth shut. You sound like a striking hog. You make my stomach sick.*
You red kin bitch! You tink yuh betta ah me.	*You red skin bitch! You think you are better than me.*
See you laata	*See you later.*
Eat up. If yuh don't eat now yuh nat getting anyting to eat for the rest of de day.	*Eat up. If you do not eat now you will not get anything to eat for the rest of the day.*
Yuh stubborn like a mule, yuh are de bebil pickney!	*You are stubborn like a mule. You are the devil's child!*
Leave de chile alone wid me. Yu cyant look after har.	*Leave the child alone. You can't look after her.*
Yu comin wid daddy.	*You are coming with Daddy.*

People don't have dem pickney and give dem whey like chickens.	*People do not have children and give them away like chickens.*
If yuh want pickney, yuh have yuh big pussy, go have yuh own pickney.	*If you want a child, you have your big pussy, go and have your own child.*
de likkle girl	*the little girl*
Faader Chrismus	*Father Christmas*
Praise de lawd Jesus me deliva de byaby ahright. Me hab a bununus byaby bwoy.	*Praise the Lord Jesus I delivered a the baby alright. I have the healthiest and most handsome baby boy*
Him look like parson.	*He looks like parson.*
De pickney too ripe.	*The child is too grown up for her age.*
Oonu free papa soon bun.	*Your free paper will soon burn.*
Yuh gwan wid you mishavin, teacha a go fix yuh.	*You can carry on your misbehaving now because the teacher will punish you when school starts.*
You wah fe drowned pickney?	*Do you want to drown the child?*

CHAPTER 2

One day, de obeah man ah go tun yu mout back a yu.	*One day the obeah man is going to turn your mouth behind you*
Rain a come.	*The rain is coming in*
Set out de drum dem.	*Set out the drums*
Put out de wash pan	*Put out the washpan*
Lawd! tek up de close dem ahfa de line. Quick! Quick! befo rain wet dem up.	*Lord! Take up the clothes off the line. Quick! Quick! Before the rain wets them.*
Shet de winda dem, ar else de rain a go blow een.	*Shut the windows or the rain will blow in.*

Missa Shaata gaan mad!	*Mr Shorter has gone mad!*
Him a tek disadvantage a de poor dead ooman pickney dem.	*He is abusing the poor dead woman's children.*
dem kinda cigaret	*those kinds of cigarettes*
Go wash yuh stinkin so' foot.	*Go and wash your stinking sore foot.*
Clear aaf wid yu syphilis!	*Clear off with your syphilis!*
Yu too stink feh anybady feh want yu	*You stink too much for anybody to want you.*
Hap aan.	*Hop on.*
wooligans	*hooligans*
dem wutliss mumma	*their worthless mothers*
no-good black naygas	*no good black negroes*
de lickle thief dem	*the little thieves*
pap dem neck if dem couda catch dem. But dem gaan like de bloody rat dem.	*They would break their necks if they could catch them. But they have escaped like bloody cane rats.*
tief de game	*who stole the game (or who cheated)*
Me win de mos steelies mon.	*I won the most steelies, man*
Me nah go no whey. If anybody tink dem bad, dem cyaan come tek me out.	*I'm not going, if anyone thinks they are strong enough they can come and take me out.*
Lawd gad Hartense baggie drop offa har!	*Lord God, Hortense's baggy undergarment have fallen off!*
Do teacha no lick me! Me na do it again.	*Please teacher, I beg you, do not hit me! I won't do it again.*
fe tek bad tings mek laff.	*to make comedy out of a tragic incident.*
How Big Boy late de teacha man!	*How Big Boy made a fool of the head teacher!*

Yes mon, de bwoy dem late teacha, good good.	*Yes man, the boy made a fool of the teacher(very cleverly)!*
Teacha tek disadvantage of de likkle bway.	*Teacher mistreated the little defenseless boy.*
Teacher so bex im beat de bwoy til im neckstring naly bus.	*Teacher was so vexed that he beat the boy until his neck vein nearly burst*
Ah how come de teacha man so wicked?	*Why is teacher so wicked?*
If ah coulda, ah woulda jump up an grab teacha by im seed and drag im aafa de platfaam.	*If I could have, I would have jumped up and grabbed teacher by his balls and drag him off the platform*
Me woulda jump back ah im an lick im in ah im neck back.	*I would have jumped up and hit him in the back of his neck.*
Ah woulda give 'im a tump ina 'im sola plexus.	*I would have given him a thump in his solar plexus.*
Ah would ah trow a rock stone in ah im winda.	*I would have thrown a rock stone in his window*
What no cost life no cost nuttin.	*What does not cost life, does not cost anything.*

CHAPTER 3

Feesh, fresh feesh. dacta fish. Buy yuh daccta feesh, parat feesh an goat feesh. Buy yuh feesh, me wih scale it feh yuh.	*Fish, fresh fish, doctor fish. Buy your doctor fish, parrotfish, and goatfish. Buy your fish; I will scale it for you*
bakra tek de meat an doh pay far it.	*White men take the meat and don't pay for it.*
De meat married to de bone.	*(You have to take the bone with the flesh.)*
yuh smellin high	*you are smelling bad*

yuh smell like seven-day cabbage wata	*You smell like seven-day cabbage water*
Come mek we go tek de tes.	*Come, let's go and take the test.*

CHAPTER 4

Ah who de hell yuh tink a go do de housewuk and help in a de shap? Meh na pay one red cent fe yuh ga a dat school.	*Who the hell do you think is going to do the housework and help in the shop? I won't pay one red cent for you to go to that school*
You just like yuh black mooma. She did tink seh she betta am me. An ah it mek me get me bredda feh box har dung. Ah hav a mine fe box yuh dung, jus like how yu faader box yu mooma dung.	*You are just like your black mother. She thought that she was better than me. And that's why I had to get my brother to box her down. I have a good mind to box you down just like how your father boxed your mother down*
Yuh draw me blood!	*You've drawn my blood!*
Put yuh name pon it.	*Put your name on it.*
See yah, yuh put yuh name pon it far when me ded and gaane me no have nobady fe inherit de fruits af me laaba.	*See here, you put your name on it, for when I am dead and gone I won't have any one to inherit the fruits of my labour.)*
Poor me dead woman pickney.	*Pity me, I am the child of a dead woman. or Pity me, I am suffering because my mother is dead and cannot protect me.*

CHAPTER 5

Lawd missis me no wah feh married nobady. Me no wa feh mash up like Mistress (So and So). Me no wah no husban feh tun crassses pan me yah.	*Lord, my friend, I do not want to marry anybody. I do not want to look emaciated like Mistress (So and So). I do not want to have a husband to become a cross on my back.*

Missa Shaata nat home. You fambilly?	*Mr Shorter is not at home. Are you family?*
Just like yuh black mumma who thought she was better than me.	*Just like your black mother who thought she was better than me*
On a pint of aada. Mr President, a pint of aada.	*On a point of order, Mr President, a point of order*
On a pint of privilege Mr President, a pint of privilege.	*On a point of privilege Mr President, a point of privilege.*
Ah jus so im baan. Yuh cyant do nuttin bout it.	*That's the way the child is. You can't do anything about it (the character trait).*
Im have brain fe tek book learning.	*He has the brain for book learning. (The child is bright enough to study).*
Lawd Gad, teacha so sumall dat dem no see har!	Lawd Gad, teacha so sumall dat dem no see har!

Bibliography

Brathwaite, E. 1971. The Development of Creole Society in Jamaica
1770–1820. Oxford: Clarendon Press.

Brown, A. 1979. "From Canefield to Classroom: Schooling and Colonial
Consolidation." In D. Lowenthal and D. Comitas, eds., *Cosequences of
Class and Color: West Indian Perspectives*, 77–92. New York: Anchor Press.

——. 1979. *Colour, Class, and Politics in Jamaica.* New Brunswick, NJ:
Transaction Books.

Bryan, P. 1991. "Childhood, Youth and Education." In *The Jamaican People
1880–1902*, 110–30. London: Macmillan.

——. 2000. The Jamaican People 1880–1902: Race, Class and Social
Control. Kingston: University of the West Indies Press.

Campbell, C. 1993. "Social and Economic Obstacles to the Development
of Popular Education in Post-Emancipation Jamaica 1834–1865." In H.
Beckles and V. Shepherd, *Caribbean Freedom: Economy and Society from
Emancipation to the Present,* 262–68. Kingston: Ian Randle Publishers.

Cassidy, F.G., and R.B. Le Page, eds. 1985. *Dictionary of Jamaican English,*
2nd edition. Cambridge: Cambridge University Press.

"Charles Archibald Reid, OBE. Appointment as Member of Privy Council
of the Island of Jamaica." *London Gazette.* 17 February 1942, 776.

"Charles Archibald Reid, OBE, Biography." *Who's Who and Why in Jamaica,
1939–40.* Kingston, Jamaica.

"Charles Reid." *Daily Gleaner* [Jamaica] 2 October 1944, 6.

Curtin, P. 1958. *Two Jamaicas: The Role of Ideas in a Tropical Colony
1830–1865.* New York: Greenwood Press.

Dunn, R. 1972. *Sugar and Slaves: The Rise of the Planter Class in the
English West Indies, 1624–1713.* Williamsburg, VA: University of
North Carolina Press.

"Education: Training College Examination Results 1965." *Jamaica Gazette*, July–August 1965, 1245–48.

"Funeral of Hon Chas A. Reid." *Daily Gleaner* [Jamaica], 2 October 1944, 1.

Higman, B.W. 1988. *Jamaica Surveyed*. Kingston, Jamaica: Institution of Jamaica Publications.

——. 1995. *Slave Population and Economy in Jamaica 1807–1834*. Kingston, Jamaica: University Press of the West Indies.

——. 1998. Montpelier Jamaica: A Plantation Community in Slavery and Freedom, 1739–1912. Kingston, Jamaica: University of the West Indies Press.

King, R. 1979. "The Jamaica Schools Commission and the Development of Secondary Schooling." In V. D'Oyley and R. Murray, *Development and Disillusion in Third World Education*, 41–570. Toronto: Ontario Institute for Studies in Education.

Mathurin-Mair, L. 1998. "Women Field Workers in Jamaica during Slavery." In Shobhita Jain and Rhoda Reddock, eds., *Women Plantation Workers: International Experiences*, 17–28. New York: Oxford.

Moore, B.L., and M.A. Johnson. 2004. *Neither Led Nor Driven: Contesting British Cultural Imperialism in Jamaica, 1865–1920*. Mona, Jamaica: University of the West Indies Press.

Schwartz-Bart, S. 1982. *The Bridge of Beyond*. Portsmouth, NH: Heinemann.

Secretary of State for the Colonies to Parliament by Command of His Majesty. 1945. *West India Royal Commission Report: Education*. London: His Majesty's Stationary Office.

Senior, O. 1983. *A–Z of Jamaican Heritage*. Kingston, Jamaica: Heinemann Educational Books.

——. 1991. *Working Miracles: Women's Lives in the English-Speaking Caribbean.* London: James Curry and Bloomingdale and Indiana: Indiana University Press.

——. 2003. *Encyclopedia of Jamaican Heritage*. St. Andrew, Jamaica: Twin Guinep Publishers.

UN Educational, Scientific and Cultural Organization. 1963. *Source Book for Science Teaching*. Paris: UN Educational, Scientific and Cultural Organization.

Walvin, J. 2001. *Black Ivory: Slavery in the British Empire*. Oxford: Blackwell.

West India Royal Commission 1938–39. 1945. Presented by the Secretary of State for the Colonies to Parliament by Command of His Majesty. London: His Majesty's Stationary Office. (Also referred to as the *Moyne Report*).

West Indies Year Book including also the Bermudas, The Bahamas. British Guiana and British Honduras. 1941–1947. Montreal: Thomas Skinner of Canada.

Books in the Life Writing Series
Published by Wilfrid Laurier University Press

Haven't Any News: Ruby's Letters from the Fifties edited by Edna Staebler with an
    Afterword by Marlene Kadar • 1995 / x + 172 pp. / ISBN 978-0-88920-248-1

"I Want to Join Your Club": Letters from Rural Children, 1900–1920 edited by
    Norah L. Lewis with a Preface by Neil Sutherland • 1996 / xii + 250 pp.
    (30 b&w photos) / ISBN 978-0-88920-260-3

And Peace Never Came by Elisabeth M. Raab with Historical Notes by Marlene
    Kadar • 1996 / x + 196 pp. (12 b&w photos, map) / ISBN 978-0-88920-292-4

Dear Editor and Friends: Letters from Rural Women of the North-West, 1900–1920
    edited by Norah L. Lewis • 1998 / xvi + 166 pp. (20 b&w photos) / ISBN 978-0-
    88920-287-0

The Surprise of My Life: An Autobiography by Claire Drainie Taylor with a
    Foreword by Marlene Kadar • 1998 / xii + 268 pp. (8 colour photos and
    92 b&w photos) / ISBN 978-0-88920-302-0

Memoirs from Away: A New Found Land Girlhood by Helen M. Buss / Margaret
    Clarke • 1998 / xvi + 154 pp. / ISBN 978-0-88920-350-1

The Life and Letters of Annie Leake Tuttle: Working for the Best by Marilyn Färdig
    Whiteley • 1999 / xviii + 150 pp. / ISBN 978-0-88920-330-3

Marian Engel's Notebooks: "Ah, mon cahier, écoute" edited by Christl Verduyn •
    1999 / viii + 576 pp. / ISBN 978-0-88920-333-4 cloth / ISBN 978-0-88920-349-5
    paper

Be Good, Sweet Maid: The Trials of Dorothy Joudrie by Audrey Andrews • 1999 /
    vi + 276 pp. / ISBN 978-0-88920-334-1

*Working in Women's Archives: Researching Women's Private Literature and Archival
    Documents* edited by Helen M. Buss and Marlene Kadar • 2001 / vi + 120 pp. /
    ISBN 978-0-88920-341-9

Repossessing the World: Reading Memoirs by Contemporary Women by Helen M.
    Buss • 2002 / xxvi + 206 pp. / ISBN 978-0-88920-408-9 cloth / ISBN 978-0-
    88920-409-6 paper

Chasing the Comet: A Scottish-Canadian Life by Patricia Koretchuk • 2002 /
    xx + 244 pp. / ISBN 978-0-88920-407-2

The Queen of Peace Room by Magie Dominic • 2002 / xiv + 114 pp. /
    ISBN 978-0-88920-417-1

China Diary: The Life of Mary Austin Endicott by Shirley Jane Endicott • 2002 /
    xvi + 254 pp. / ISBN 978-0-88920-412-6

The Curtain: Witness and Memory in Wartime Holland by Henry G. Schogt • 2003 / xii + 132 pp. / ISBN 978-0-88920-396-9

Teaching Places by Audrey J. Whitson • 2003 / xiv + 182 pp. (9 colour photos) / ISBN 978-0-88920-425-6

Through the Hitler Line by Laurence F. Wilmot, M.C. • 2003 / xvi + 152 pp. / ISBN 978-0-88920-426-3 cloth / ISBN 978-0-88920-448-5 paper

Where I Come From by Vijay Agnew • 2003 / xiv + 298 pp. / ISBN 978-0-88920-414-0

The Water Lily Pond by Han Z. Li • 2004 / x + 254 pp. / ISBN 978-0-88920-431-7

The Life Writings of Mary Baker McQuesten: Victorian Matriarch edited by Mary J. Anderson • 2004 / xxii + 338 pp. / ISBN 978-0-88920-437-9

Seven Eggs Today: The Diaries of Mary Armstrong, 1859 and 1869 edited by Jackson W. Armstrong • 2004 / xvi + 228 pp. / ISBN 978-0-88920-440-9 cloth / ISBN 978-0-55458-439-0 paper

Love and War in London: A Woman's Diary 1939–1942 by Olivia Cockett; edited by Robert W. Malcolmson • 2005 / xvi + 208 pp. / ISBN 978-0-88920-458-4

Incorrigible by Velma Demerson • 2004 / vi + 178 pp. / ISBN 978-0-88920-444-7

Auto/biography in Canada: Critical Directions edited by Julie Rak • 2005 / viii + 264 pp. / ISBN 978-0-88920-478-2

Tracing the Autobiographical edited by Marlene Kadar, Linda Warley, Jeanne Perreault, and Susanna Egan • 2005 / viii + 280 pp. / ISBN 978-0-88920-476-8

Must Write: Edna Staebler's Diaries edited by Christl Verduyn • 2005 / viii + 304 pp. / ISBN 978-0-88920-481-2

Pursuing Giraffe: A 1950s Adventure by Anne Innis Dagg • 2006 / xvi + 284 pp. (46 b&w photos, 2 maps) / ISBN 978-0-88920-463-8

Food That Really Schmecks by Edna Staebler • 2007 / xxiv + 334 pp. / ISBN 978-0-88920-521-5

163256: A Memoir of Resistance by Michael Englishman • 2007 / xvi + 112 pp. (14 b&w photos) / ISBN 978-1-55458-009-5

The Wartime Letters of Leslie and Cecil Frost, 1915–1919 edited by R.B. Fleming • 2007 / xxxvi + 384 pp. (49 b&w photos, 5 maps) / ISBN 978-1-55458-000-2 cloth / ISBN 978-1-55458-470-3 paper

Johanna Krause Twice Persecuted: Surviving in Nazi Germany and Communist East Germany by Carolyn Gammon and Christiane Hemker • 2007 / x + 170 pp. (58 b&w photos, 2 maps) / ISBN 978-1-55458-006-4

Watermelon Syrup: A Novel by Annie Jacobsen with Jane Finlay-Young and Di Brandt • 2007 / x + 268 pp. / ISBN 978-1-55458-005-7

Broad Is the Way: Stories from Mayerthorpe by Margaret Norquay • 2008 / x + 106 pp. (6 b&w photos) / ISBN 978-1-55458-020-0

Becoming My Mother's Daughter: A Story of Survival and Renewal by Erika Gottlieb • 2008 / x + 178 pp. (36 b&w illus., 17 colour) / ISBN 978-1-55458-030-9

Leaving Fundamentalism: Personal Stories edited by G. Elijah Dann • 2008 / xii + 234 pp. / ISBN 978-1-55458-026-2

Bearing Witness: Living with Ovarian Cancer edited by Kathryn Carter and Lauri Èlit • 2009 / viii + 94 pp. / ISBN 978-1-55458-055-2

Dead Woman Pickney: A Memoir of Childhood in Jamaica by Yvonne Shorter Brown • 2010 / viii + 202 pp. / ISBN 978-1-55458-189-4

I Have a Story to Tell You by Seemah C. Berson • 2010 / xx + 288 pp. (24 b&w photos) / ISBN 978-1-55458-219-8

We All Giggled: A Bourgeois Family Memoir by Thomas O. Hueglin • 2010 / xiv + 232 pp. (20 b&w photos) / ISBN 978-1-55458-262-4

Just a Larger Family: Letters of Marie Williamson from the Canadian Home Front, 1940–1944 edited by Mary F. Williamson and Tom Sharp • 2011 / xxiv + 378 pp. (16 b&w photos) / ISBN 978-1-55458-323-2

Burdens of Proof: Faith, Doubt, and Identity in Autobiography by Susanna Egan • 2011 / x + 200 pp. / ISBN 978-1-55458-333-1

Accident of Fate: A Personal Account 1938–1945 by Imre Rochlitz with Joseph Rochlitz • 2011 / xiv + 226 pp. (50 b&w photos, 5 maps) / ISBN 978-1-55458-267-9

The Green Sofa by Natascha Würzbach, translated by Raleigh Whitinger • 2012 / xiv + 240 pp. (5 b&w photos) / ISBN 978-1-55458-334-8

Unheard Of: Memoirs of a Canadian Composer by John Beckwith • 2012 / x + 393 pp. (74 illus., 8 musical examples) / ISBN 978-1-55458-358-4

Borrowed Tongues: Life Writing, Migration, and Translation by Eva C. Karpinski • 2012 / viii + 274 pp. / ISBN 978-1-55458-357-7

Basements and Attics, Closets and Cyberspace: Explorations in Canadian Women's Archives edited by Linda M. Morra and Jessica Schagerl • 2012 / x + 338 pp. / ISBN 978-1-55458-632-5

The Memory of Water by Allen Smutylo • 2013 / x + 262 pp. (65 colour illus.) / ISBN 978-1-55458-842-8

The Unwritten Diary of Israel Unger, Revised Edition by Carolyn Gammon and Israel Unger • 2013 / x + 230 pp. (90 b&w illus.) / ISBN 978-1-77112-011-1

Boom! Manufacturing Memoir for the Popular Market by Julie Rak • 2013 / viii + 250 pp. (7 b&w illus.) / ISBN 978-1-55458-939-5

Motherlode: A Mosaic of Dutch Wartime Experience by Carolyne Van Der Meer • 2014 / xiv + 132 pp. (6 b&w illus.) / ISBN 978-1-77112-005-0

Not the Whole Story: Challenging the Single Mother Narrative edited by Lea Caragata and Judit Alcalde • 2014 / x + 222 pp. / ISBN 978-1-55458-624-0

Street Angel by Magie Dominic • 2014 / vii + 154 pp. / ISBN 978-1-77112-026-5

In the Unlikeliest of Places: How Nachman Libeskind Survived the Nazis, Gulags, and Soviet Communism by Annette Libeskind Berkovits • 2014 / xiv + 282 pp. (6 colour illus.) / ISBN 978-1-77112-066-1

Kinds of Winter: Four Solo Journeys by Dogteam in Canada's Northwest Territories
by Dave Olesen • 2014 / xii + 256 pp. (17 b&w illus., 6 maps) / ISBN 978-1-77112-118-7

Working Memory: Women and Work in World War II edited by Marlene Kadar and
Jeanne Perreault • 2015 / viii + 246 pp. (46 b&w and colour illus.) /
ISBN 978-1-77112-035-7

Wait Time: A Memoir of Cancer by Kenneth Sherman • 2016 / xiv + 138 pp. /
ISBN 978-1-77112-188-0

Canadian Graphic: Picturing Life Narratives edited by Candida Rifkind and Linda
Warley • 2016 / viii + 310 pp. (59 colour and b&w illus.) / ISBN 978-1-77112-179-8

Travels and Identities: Elizabeth and Adam Shortt in Europe, 1911
edited by Peter E. Paul Dembski • 2017 / xxii + 272 pp. (9 b&w illus.) /
ISBN 978-1-77112-225-2

Bird-Bent Grass: A Memoir, in Pieces by Kathleen Venema • 2018 • viii + 346 pp. /
ISBN 978-1-77112-290-0

My Basilian Priesthood, 1961–1967 by Michael Quealey • 2019 • viii + 222 pp. /
ISBN 978-1-77112-242-9

What the Oceans Remember: Searching for Belonging and Home by Sonja Boon •
2019 • xvi + 320 pp. (8 b&w illus.) / ISBN 978-1-77112-423-2

Rough and Plenty: A Memorial by Raymond A. Rogers • 2020 • x + 316 pp.
(9 b&w photos) / ISBN 978-1-77112-436-2

Limelight: Canadian Women and the Rise of Celebrity Autobiography by
Katja Lee • 2020 • viii + 360 pp. (6 colour images) / ISBN 978-1-77112-429-4

Prison Life Writing: Conversion and the Literary Roots of the U.S. Prison System
by Simon Rolston • 2021 • x + 316 pp. / ISBN 1-77112-517-8

Scratching River by Michelle Porter • 2022 • xiv + 168 pp. / ISBN 978-1-77112-544-4

Dead Woman Pickney: A Memoir of Childhood in Jamaica, Second Edition
by Yvonne Shorter Brown • 2022 • xxvi + 318 pp. (9 b&w images) /
ISBN 978-1-77112-547-5